Praise for *The Wonder Paradox*

"A journey into *The Wonder Paradox* will i............ imagination and search for timeless truths about existence but also your very capacity for that most human of tendencies: wondering about the meaning of life. Reading Jennifer Michael Hecht's tour of wonder will stir your soul."

—Dacher Keltner, author of *Awe: The New Science of Everyday Wonder and How It Can Transform Your Life*

"[*The Wonder Paradox*] delights . . . Warmth and enthusiasm suffuse Hecht's enchanting prose, which make this book a moving, hopeful read." —Zachariah Motts, *Library Journal* (starred review)

"*The Wonder Paradox* takes the reader by the hand and patiently, gently, and with great care introduces us to the delights, joys, and wisdom of poetry. If Jennifer Michael Hecht is starting a movement—sign me up! Finally, here is a party worth joining."

—Ilya Kaminsky, author of *Deaf Republic* and *Dancing in Odessa*

"Hecht writes about how those who haven't found a home in religion can still find magic in the world, seeking meaning in culture and in literature."

—Michael Schaub, *The Orange County Register*

"[A book of] insightful sweeping grandeur."

—George Yatchisin, *California Review of Books*

"I was immediately trapped by and then happily and gratefully in the thrall of a writer who shares my world and makes it brighter. *The Wonder Paradox* makes us better and smarter by assuming we already are. This is a rare heart." —Roger Rosenblatt, author of *Making Toast*

"*The Wonder Paradox* is such a brilliant, generous, funny, helpful book. Jennifer Michael Hecht knows just what to say to guide us through our modern confusions. I've never read anything like it, and I want to give it to every friend I know."

—Matthew Zapruder, author of *Story of a Poem*

Max Hecht-Chaneski

JENNIFER MICHAEL HECHT

THE WONDER PARADOX

Jennifer Michael Hecht, a historian and poet, is the award-winning and bestselling author of the histories *Doubt*, *Stay*, *The Happiness Myth*, and *The End of the Soul*. Her poetry books include *Who Said*, *The Next Ancient World*, and *Funny*. She earned her PhD in history from Columbia University and teaches in New York City.

Also by Jennifer Michael Hecht

NONFICTION

Stay
The Happiness Myth
Doubt
The End of the Soul

POETRY

Who Said
Funny
The Next Ancient World

THE WONDER PARADOX

THE WONDER PARADOX

Awe, Poetry,
and the
Meaningful
Life

JENNIFER MICHAEL HECHT

Picador

Farrar, Straus and Giroux | New York

Picador
120 Broadway, New York 10271

Originally published in 2023 by Farrar, Straus and Giroux
First paperback edition, 2024

Owing to limitations of space, all acknowledgments for permission
to reprint previously published material can be found on pages 351–352.

The Library of Congress has cataloged the Farrar, Straus and Giroux
hardcover edition as follows:
Names: Hecht, Jennifer Michael, 1965– author.
Title: The wonder paradox : embracing the weirdness of existence and the poetry of our
    lives / Jennifer Michael Hecht.
Description: First edition. | New York : Farrar, Straus and Giroux, 2023. | Includes
    bibliographical references and index.
Identifiers: LCCN 2022049726 | ISBN 9780374292744 (hardcover)
Subjects: LCSH: Poetry—Appreciation. | Poetry—Therapeutic use. | Conduct of life in
    literature.
Classification: LCC PN1075 .H43 2023 | DDC 808.1—dc23/eng/20221024
LC record available at https://lccn.loc.gov/2022049726

Paperback ISBN: 978-1-250-32185-5

Designed by Gretchen Achilles

Our books may be purchased in bulk for promotional, educational,
or business use. Please contact your local bookseller or the Macmillan
Corporate and Premium Sales Department at 1-800-221-7945, extension 5442,
or by email at MacmillanSpecialMarkets@macmillan.com.

Picador® is a U.S. registered trademark and is used by Macmillan Publishing Group,
LLC, under license from Pan Books Limited.

For book club information, please email marketing@picadorusa.com.

picadorusa.com • Follow us on social media at @picador or @picadorusa

P1

For John, for Jessie, and for Max

Contents

Preface

I didn't mean to write this book. I meant to write this book's introduction, a gentle manifesto about how art can bring us meaning and sanity. Many of us who are happy to live outside religion still suffer from a lack of things religion gives its members. It seems to me the remedy to this suffering is a shift in the way we think about ritual and the poetry of our lives.

The thing is, a lot of nonreligious philosophy in the past has been too shocked by the loss of religious meaning to notice that there is meaning all around us, and too angry at religion to want to retain any of its behaviors. But surely religion is a human creation to organize human needs for celebration, gathering, meditation, inspiration, and comfort. Many nonbelievers see this and participate in some religious behaviors, for love and fun, even without the light of the believers. That disconnect can feel unnecessarily stressful. The mistake we are making is that the light was always a combination of poetry and ritual.

Even though the supernatural isn't real, the feelings of connection are. Within human experience, which is where I spend all my time, there is a lot of poetic connection. Ocean-deep and dazzling as daybreak on white-capped waves.

We see poetry fulfill the same role as prayer at weddings and funerals, and we can get much more out of this idea. We can extend it to other parts of life where we might need a sweet taste of ceremony and inspiration. Many cultures set people up for life with a preset set of poems (often in religion, education, or song) and instructions on when to (re)read them. But when we think of poetry outside of these venues, we tend to find it by the bookful, or reading full, poem after poem, without an explanation of how a particular poem can help us live.

Poetry can help us make up for the loss of the supernatural, can connect us to one another and to meaning in our lives.

That's all I meant to write, or would have dared, but fascinating and brilliant people I met along the way insisted I try setting out what that might actually look like. Thinking this through and writing this book took forever, longer than any other book I've written, and writing these essays changed my life. As I chose poems and began to discuss how they fit each need or moment, I felt unexpected insights pop into my mind about how we live now.

I want to tempt you to compile a clutch of poems for holidays, events, practices, and emergencies. I'll show you how to gather and get to know them, how to take them into your daily life and your heart. Happily, some of us might pull our favorite poems from the well of well-known world poetry, which means we'll end up with poems in common. That could help bring us together.

So maybe some of us don't believe in the spirits that once seemed to be the electricity that lit up all the traditional rituals. Poetry though, available to all, is a sufficient source of power to light up ritual and guide us toward meaning. It's as if we have lamps but won't plug them in because our ancestors believed electricity was spirit-made. Having lost belief in spirits, we sit in the dark. There's no need. We have holidays and rituals, crafted like tungsten and glass for glowing. We have poems that buzz with electric charge. Let's plug them in.

THE WONDER PARADOX

Introduction

I was raised as an "atreeist," in a New York–based antiarboreal coven.

I'm kidding.

Sort of.

It's true that my Jewish identity felt bound up in not being allowed to have a Christmas tree. I didn't desperately want one, but most people seemed to have them, and treasure them. Along with the evident fun, it pained me to feel different. I also adored the colored lights on the neighborhood houses, but my glee was icily received by my parents until I, too, came to believe that if we strung lights, it would "betray" our people. Doesn't the fact of the Holocaust demand that we keep being visibly Jewish? Wouldn't it be too tragic if they all died for an identity no one cares about anymore?

My whole family knew that Hanukah was invented as a family party holiday so that Jews could join in with the consumerist gala that Christmas had become within the century. For that reason, like other Jews I met, we told non-Jews that Hanukah wasn't *actually* a big day on the Jewish calendar whenever the subject came up. But who doesn't like presents and special food? Putting the menorah in the window was a way to join in with the seasonal celebration of lights. We loved it, but it was complicated.

I had an uncle who got red-faced, spitting mad when asked about Jews who have Christmas trees. He showed up one year in a vintage

London cab, shining black, and took us out driving to look at the Christmas lights. Lovely, but confusing. Feeling tiny in the cab's cavernous back seat, I was happy that an adult wanted to enjoy the spectacle, and while staring, cheek to the cold window, at the fantasy—here a house all blue, there a tree in rainbow—I worried the contradictions like a triple-knot shoelace. People have both ecstatic and intensely painful feelings linked to rituals, and even in one family you're tiptoeing through a minefield. These are dark subjects for a child.

All over the world, many millions of people don't believe in any kind of supernaturalism, and a lot of us don't much mind its absence. Many have told me they don't miss the fantastical aspect of religion, whether they're talking about God and heaven, karma and rebirth, or bodhisattvas and Pure Lands. But let's notice what *else* we lose when religion fades away, such as community and the feeling of a year as a round of celebrations, meditations, and readings.

Religions provide detailed stage directions for welcoming newborns into the protection of the group and give parents a way to think about the support available, at a moment when it's hard to think. Hinduism celebrates milestones in samskaras, including a baby's first haircut. Religions have mandates to apologize and forgive, as on Yom Kippur, one of the *actual* big days of the Jewish calendar.

If you join in the religion of your community, a lot of psychological and social work gets done for you, whether or not you believe. But repeating religious ways and words, when we don't believe, can make us feel hypocritical and disappointed. Lonely. Even if we'd never trade away today's pluralism and freedom, we might still ask ourselves if there wasn't something deeply reassuring about such popularly held beliefs. What if we had a set of texts of wonder and insight in which we do actually believe? Wouldn't that be life-changing?

When the words of religion ring hollow, how can we make up for that loss? For poetry readers, the answer may be obvious. In the mid-twentieth century, the American poet Wallace Stevens wrote, "After one has abandoned a belief in God, poetry is that essence which takes its place as life's redemption." Stevens often clarified that when he praised "poetry" in this way he was speaking of all the arts, but especially lyric poems, those short-lined bursts of words, famously dedicated to truth and beauty above clarity or ease.

Poetry takes in our whole outrageous situation as ambitious mortals, hanging curtains in a sandcastle nursery in the shade of a rising wave (kiss the baby, glance at the wave). Art pushes us away from the everyday, the worldly, and toward transcendence. By "transcendence" I mean the feeling of being at one with the universe in vivid bliss that is, by wide report, available to humans—though hard to find, keep, or handle.

Art welcomes contradictory truths and invites input from feeling and imagination. A poem can do this by juxtaposing evocative words and ideas to create a field of thinking; or, say, by describing an ongoing inner argument. Poetry can offer cosmic perspective, or specific advice.

Poems remind us of the inner lives of others, and thereby stoke empathy—much needed in times of strife. They can reach into our deepest solitude and greet us. There are poems on failure that see an unwinnable quest as heroic—for some the only life story worth living. A decision poem can help you at your crossroad. A mourner's poem can be ready to engage with the pain of the unknowable when you are not.

There are many stories of people finding nonreligious salvation in a piece of poetic writing. Mine starts in a town on the South Shore of Long Island.

Live the Questions

My physicist father didn't believe in God but kept quiet about it when we kids were young. I believed from the time my mother told me God was there until one day when I was twelve, standing in my parents' living room, when I had an uncanny mental shift. I suddenly knew I might be anybody, anywhere, but instead I happened to be here, being me.

The proximate cause was ordinary loveliness: a steep slant of late-afternoon light serrated in the folds of a diaphanous blue curtain; nylon maybe. Yellow sunlight in a glowing fabric curlicue. I saw that we are just one species among great nature, and as the trees very slowly rot, so do our pampered haunches. That's it. There is no reason to imagine a guy in the sky bowling to make thunder and brooding over how we fail him. Then the sounds of the world returned to my hearing. I never lost interest in such perspective shifts and I never again believed.

For a while I missed God and was in turmoil. Life without that framework was disorienting, and sometimes terrifying, like being caught by an ocean wave and pummeled under, unable to tell which way is up, a rag doll in blank horror. I had questions about the meaning of life, the purpose of the universe, what all this human effort is for, and it seemed there would be no answers.

Adults were sorely split on God, and for me that started at home. According to Mom, God hints at answers as we live, and after death he'll likely spill big secrets. For Dad there was no God, the universe is an accident, and there's no meaning to life beyond what we make ourselves. Both Mom and Dad seemed proud of their philosophies, but both also suffered consequences. My dad hated the fact of death and often groaned that "life is a fucking circus." He wanted to leave his mark, be remembered, and sighed that everyone is forgotten. Meanwhile, Mom worried about angering God by falling short in piety or goodness. She wished he wouldn't curse so much. My mother had lost her father to a heart attack when she was only seven and didn't hide her magical thinking about it: that if she was good it would keep the people she loved alive.

Beyond my Hempstead home, the God question was even more riotously divided. There were schools of thought against every school of thought. I wasn't fine in this rough surf and when things went wrong I'd slide under. I wanted answers and solace and I kept getting hit with pointlessness. As with waves that crash-roll your body toward shore, you just hope the tumult lets go of you before you need air.

Then one day, standing at a shelf in the middle of my middle-school library, I took down a slim paperback with a photo cover, truly called something like: *Poetry Anthology for Depressed Teenagers*, a title that both attracted and repulsed me. Teen-sure that the adult world would talk down to me, but hungry, I read a few poems. Standing there, I was smugly unmoved. Then I must have riffled the pages, because out flew a small glossy square of paper, floating up fast then feather-slow to the floor. Retrieving it, I saw that it had been cut out of another source by the vigorous use of a blue ballpoint pen. It read:

> Be patient toward all that is unsolved in your heart and try to love the questions themselves, like locked rooms and like books that are now written in a very foreign tongue. Do not now seek the answers, which cannot be given you because you would not be able to live them. And the point is, to live everything. Live the questions now. Perhaps you will then gradually, without noticing it, live along some distant day into the answer.
>
> —Rainer Maria Rilke

The insight that we solve life's questions by living, solved me; as did the new awareness that this Rilke, whoever she was, felt the way I did. As I stood reading that swatch of paper, the effect was immediate. *You can love the questions.* You can live your way into new knowledge, but you have to give it time. I carried that scrap in my wallet for years. It retained the buzz of having actually fluttered into my life, exactly when I needed it, having been cherished by someone before me.

The passage turned out to be from Rilke's *Letters to a Young Poet* (1929). Of course, she also turned out to be a man—a bummer for a bookish girl—but I got over it, and his poetry and prose have since been on my life's desks and desktops.

Other People's Questions

Later I became a poet and an academic. I wrote a book called *Doubt: A History*, a study of religious doubt and disbelief all over the world throughout history. I was invited to give talks about the book, and whereas the presentations were focused on scholarship—if at times passionately delivered—many of the audience questions were surprisingly personal and emotional. A bestiary of especially urgent questions kept appearing and began to roar. This is how I accidentally became a sort of priest of unbelief.

It started right from the beginning. At Caltech, I was signing books after my first large-hall *Doubt* lecture when a terrifically pregnant couple handed me the book to sign and asked permission to pose a quick question. "Sure," I said, expecting a query on Galileo or Darwin.

No. They explained that they were atheists within families of believing Jews, and their awaited baby was a boy. They asked me what I thought of them having a bris. They worried that it would be disloyal to their rationalist beliefs, and that a faithless rite would be an insult to the family's faith. She caught my eyes and with two words gave me quite a startle: "Can we?"

In the moment, I proceeded as if I had been asked the question in my capacity as a historian. I had spent years of research on the history of Judaism, along with other religions, and knew that there are many ways to be Jewish. I told them about the ancient world's Hellenistic Jews who believed in God but didn't circumcise their sons, and modern "cultural Jews" who don't believe in God but *do* follow the rite. The couple clearly wanted to have a bris, so I told them to go right ahead. *Mazel tov.* To help the ritual feel uplifting, I suggested they include some poetry. "Maybe some Whitman?" I told them where, in *Leaves of Grass*, Walt Whitman has questioned the point of life, in despair, and responds with the word "Answer," and these two lines:

> *That you are here—that life exists and identity,*
> *That the powerful play goes on, and you may contribute a verse.*

"You may contribute a verse," I repeated. Take part but be creative. Why shouldn't your honest encounter with the Abrahamic tradition be as valid as any made by interpreters of the past? They were delighted. My husband, John, sitting nearby, was as charmed as I was. Later as we strolled Caltech's fragrant lane of orange trees, he kidded that all that was missing to make sense of the scene was the honorific *Rebbe*.

It happened again and again. People heard in my talks that I was both pro-reason and pro-ritual and it gave them a chance to ask about conflicts in their families and in their own minds. Others told me about their own beloved revised rituals. For instance, in Islamic custom, on the day a baby is born, the close family has a ceremony called *tahnīk*. Baby's first taste is to be a smidge of mashed date and a loved one is given the honor of this feeding—it used to be honey but that's no longer recommended for newborns. Today this tradition has morphed into bringing candy to the maternity ward, and even many nonreligious Muslims keep the custom.

In my travels, I also heard some anguish that was not about ritual. Instead, it was about the loss of religious meaning, consolation, and guidance.

For these moments, too, I led with history . . . at first. If you think the world is divided between people who believe in heaven and are happy, and those who are facing an abyss and are at best resigned, the rationalist life is going to look like the booby prize. But if you get to know the many religions that offer *no* afterlife and that direct attention elsewhere, suddenly the abyss feels more clearly an illusion, an afterimage from having had heaven in your eyes for so long.

Because I was there to speak about history and philosophy, I'd automatically approach my answers through these disciplines. But when face-to-face with a troubled person, I found myself reaching for something more immediate and personal to offer. I'm a poetry reader and favorite poems feel like secret sources of power in my life, in their ability to lift me up and shift my point of view.

I'd find myself answering the question by offering the person a poem. These worked like the charms they are. For instance, I remember an older man who took the mic at a Q&A to say that he didn't believe in God and that I was wrong to be a nonsupernaturalist who believed in meaning. He sadly said, "Without religion we are islands." He was referring to the centuries-old idea, mulled over by people in corners who'd lost their religion, that God was what held us together and without him we are each alone. Luckily, I immediately thought of Muriel Rukeyser's poem "Islands," so we all looked it up and read it together. The pertinent stanza is the first, and I read it aloud.

O for God's sake
they are connected
underneath

He laughed, then the whole audience laughed, and the mood in the room was exhilarating. Of course the magic doesn't always work, and sadness is real, but also, we are connected, and when we try to show it, it shows. A provocative, positive thought or even the smallest kindness can gather the lost to the fold. Surprisingly, one's own pain about meaning or belonging is lightened by helping someone else with theirs.

The Marriage of Rituals and Readings

I started to think about the way rituals and readings work together.

They are a powerful combination inside religion, but outside, too. Presidential inaugurations have come to include poetry, bringing a moment of reflection, an opportunity for collective focus and quiet. In the United States, the Pledge of Allegiance has been recited every day at school, for decades, to reinforce the idea of a purposeful and unified community. The pledge is an embodied creed: we stand for it, hand on heart. Then over the popping loudspeaker comes the national anthem and, as with so many rituals, our intentions are sealed with a song.

We may think of rituals as performed to appease an otherworldly rule, but *rituals are always performed in the service of humans.* They are a way of learning: they show us what time of year it is, what time of life. They direct us to enact our emotions, with dates in the calendar set up to hear music, fast, feast, swim, travel, and rest. You can take part in all the rituals you want. Rituals from your childhood can be the most comforting and potent, whatever you believed then or now. You have the right to practice them for the poetry of the experience. Ditto rituals that came into your life through close family or other ties.

Regarding rituals that don't belong to you, try the ones expressly open to outsiders. Accept invitations to rituals from friends. Keep your eyes open for advertisements for gatherings that are expressly public and open to all.

For instance, the Hindu festival of spring, Holi—where all involved toss colored powder on one another—is fundamentally public and welcoming. In India everyone who is out and about is part of the party; the streets and parks are a Holi party. Tourism invites the world to India to take part. It's also celebrated in parks and open spaces around the world and posters call it an open celebration of friendship and fun.

In New York City, advertisements for celebrations of Holi regularly include the phrase "All are welcome!" My little family has been three or four times and there has always been live music and dancing. They sell the organic colored powder there and no longer let you bring your own, so the celebration is environmentally safe. Some have an entrance fee, some don't, all sell snacks. You dress in all white so the colors show. You have encounters, see a person with only yellow on their white T-shirt and brighten them with blue; they may flinch, but then your eyes meet and you smile. We first attended because it seemed wonderful, but after a while I had two Nepali nieces and that sweet family connection made Holi that much more meaningful.

In the United States Holi is sometimes combined with Kite Day and the music is often billed as Bollywood. One ad for a 2022 party says to bring the family and "fly handmade paper kites and splash vibrant organic colors on each other to spread love, peace and unity."

If you want to begin fresh, try this starter ritual: Choose a date, a poem, and a place—out in the world, or a spot at home. Keep that appointment. While there, read your poem and jot down what you do, see, and hear, eat, drink, and feel, both choices and surprises. When you do the ritual the next time, repeat the features, and take notes again. On the third occasion you'll plan your ritual from both sets of notes, weighing what felt good or useful, and then settle on the features. That's your ritual for that purpose. Over time, you can keep adjusting it.

What if you had a ritual and a poem for many moments, something that was yours and carried personal meaning, that stitched a consistent element across your life?

Your Book of Poetry

Imagine a personal anthology of perhaps a dozen poems, just for you, each marked for a particular celebration, daily practice, life event, or crisis. A unique anthology.

The chapters of the book I've written, the one you're reading, are themselves possible categories for such a book. Some of the poems here might be a nice fit for you. You can also use old favorites. My advice is to choose poems with attention, but without long deliberation. Trust your subconscious to have reasons for attraction. If you want, gather five poems that seem right for your subject, wait a bit, and make a choice from those. This poem has something for you and now belongs to you in a unique way.

Choose a poem from a movie. People seem to think that's cheating. It's not. When you fall for a poem in a movie, tremendous talent and wealth has charged up that poem for you. Why waste it? In the same way, don't be abashed to "steal" a poem from a friend—it arrives precharged with that friend's interest.

Sharing a canon, in a flexible way, binds us all together, but with elbow room. Poems that help us "live the questions" cannot be counted on always to flutter into the air when needed. Even when that happened for me, we'll have to admit: I was in a library, in the poetry section. A few judicious arrangements can set favorable conditions for the uncanny and the uncommon.

Poetry may well be the best art to organize our hearts in the absence of religion because of its shared traits with prayer and meditation. It slots right into established habits. It's the right kiss for awakening our sleeping beauty because poetry is:

- Language, so it can relate a message or story.
- Free, to break rules and not make clear sense.
- Short, so we can have a moment's encounter with it, over and over.
- Metrical, a trance-inducing percussion instrument.
- Deep, made with creative intensity, expected to reward rereading.

- Intimate, a whispered secret.
- Common at celebrations.
- Memorable, due to rhyme, meter, and form.
- Sublime. We call any work of art "a poem" to say it is perfect, balanced, true.

This book is meant to help you feel around for the poetry and ritual that can help support the life you want to live, and light up the year. We can excavate rituals that do work from doctrines that no longer do.

A Brief Lexicon

My terminology should be clear in context, but it may be useful to have a few definitions at the outset. *Cultural liturgy* means nonreligious words and acts that are established methods to invoke reflection. This means the works of literature and music that become staples of weddings, funerals, and other events. "Liturgy" means a set of ritual acts and readings. The word itself reminds us that responsibility for human services toggles between religion and politics: early Christians borrowed the word "liturgy" from the ancient Greeks, for whom it meant state-mandated feasts and parades hosted by local landowners. We already have poems popularly accepted as benediction. Cultural liturgy includes nonreligious sacred words, such as "I do solemnly swear," and gestures, like kneeling, bowing, rocking, or finger tipped to thumb.

I invented the term *Interfaithless* to refer to the nonreligious who feel positively connected to others through that identity. We have faith in the "inter." We have community among our present-day unbelievers, and also with all those in history who shared a sense that the real excitement is in art, nature, and love. Interfaithless might be seen as a fresh variety of the old moniker *humanist*, which can sound species-centric today and can be caught up in old European arguments.

I also call myself a *poetic realist*. It means I'm a science-and-reason person, and I use art and its ideals to understand experience and speak beyond what can be known.

I use *poetic sacred* to express sacred feelings that are not religious. Anthropology and sociology often use "the sacred" to explore what people "hold sacred." Etymology supports nonreligious usage, tracing all the way back to the Proto-Indo-European *seh k-*, meaning "to sanctify, to make a treaty." Words and acts invoked at sacred times become enchanted with memory and can carry the sacred elsewhere, to hallow new ground.

* * *

Nonbelievers of every major religion have told me they take part in rituals without belief—often to please parents or a spouse—and some of them say they get a lot out of it. Religions offer scripts and actions for when we are scared witless, a place to take your body when you are gutted by grief or stunned with relief. Some of us have strong feelings against certain words or gestures, but can sense a lack in the loss of them, and could use a reframing or a replacement. What about you? Do you have a potent way to sustain your sense of meaning, courage, peace, and awe? Do you have a coherent way of thinking about your occasional encounters with elevated experiences?

These chapters respond to concerns of real people who spoke to me at my public talks, primarily on the history of religious doubt, and in my private life as well. I have made large adjustments to a few to ensure anonymity, but the core of each story is true. The questions people ask light up the sky for me, showing the shape and direction of yearning. I think if we want to know ourselves and the world we are floating in, we have to risk swimming out past the breaking waves. It's deep out there, but to switch metaphors, the task is not to solve anything, but to find out what happens when we try to live the questions.

I've been surprised by waves of ocean metaphors that kept arising as I write this introduction, and have kept them, and let them interact with other metaphors. Listen, as a historian of science I've come to respect and suspect metaphors for their capacity to control our thinking, and so in the present lyrical work, there's more accuracy than consistency in my similes. Mixed metaphors are the only ones I trust.

The chapters all follow the same headings, looking at how religions handle a human need, how that need can be met with art and science, and how a poem can help. It's amazing how keenly words can matter, a paradox that there can be so much mending in mere mention, so much action in the act of naming.

The wonder paradox is the miracle that we are blown away by the experiences of consciousness. Religion and art invite us to a world bigger than normal life, into contact with the weirdness of our human situation. We live within paradoxes. We feel permanent though well aware of death. The consciousness paradox is the startling fact that soft matter afloat in a bone bowl made Mozart's sonatas, Shakespeare's plays, and the whole astounding modern world.

My favorite paradox is the one about wonder, the sublimely curious fact that we evolved, materially, as beings equipped with the ability to feel awe. The meat thinks and is amazed by the white stripe in the night sky and figures out that it is our galaxy. We can be dumbstruck by the beauty of a face, or city, color, ocean, or song—we live with the turbulent wild fact of wonder. With our white coats on we might explain why we crave beauty, noting that facial symmetry signals a healthy partner, but explaining it doesn't explain it away. We still live these feelings. Part of the paradox of wonder—for me and by wide anecdotal report—is that thinking about it feels true, feels worth one's time. Considering our contradictions and embracing the weirdness of existence feels, when you are doing it, as if it is a valuable thing to do. Poetry can help us to do it.

PRACTICES

On Decisions

What Alice Lost

"How am I supposed to make a decision if I can't pray on it?"

I'd just met Alice when she asked me, with sparkling, teary eyes and a laugh, "How do you make decisions if you can't pray on it?" She was my host at a four-day college festival on "doubt" and we hit it off on the drive from the airport. It was no idle question. She was agonizing over staying with a man she loved, a sculptor, who didn't want children, though she really did. She had left the church, she said, and no longer believed the universe had an ear for words and wishes.

Coil curls, classic features, hearty sighs, and those bright, sad eyes. She was crazy in love, thrilled by the man and his work, and oddly sure of his future success. What to do? It may seem obvious that if your partner doesn't want babies, yet your heart throbs at the sight of swaddle and it's getting late in fertility's day, you'd best move on. But such logic ignores the awful, awesome specificity of love. She loved *him*.

Until she was in college Alice had "prayed on" every decision she made, laying out the puzzle of contrasting loyalties between feuding friends, or arguments for and against taking the last donut. In the car that first day she assured me her praying wasn't about obvious answers, which she illustrated, in a God voice, saying, "Change your major." I borrowed her baritone to add, "The future's in tech."

That's when she almost killed us, turning to give me a little push on the arm and swerving a tick into oncoming traffic. Correcting, and back to her usual octave, Alice said, "I miss getting told, 'Go pray on it.'" In the world of her childhood, "Go pray on it" was part of any advice given or received. She could hear that phrase echo in her mother's voice, her favorite teacher's, her baby brother's, or anyone close to her. Over the few days of the festival, I mulled over what Alice had lost. Whatever else, she had lost a dedicated time for introspection, empty-seeming time safeguarded from and by outside authority, by school, by chums, by mother.

When Alice drove me back to the airport, I asked if she had heard of the century-old Spanish poem "Traveler, There Is No Road," by Antonio Machado. "*Caminante, no hay camino.*" She said the title rang a bell. I suggested that when she had an impulse to pray on a decision, she might turn instead to the poem. Find a quiet space and sit with it awhile.

Perhaps that poem came to my mind because we were on the road, but it also seemed apt for the task of soothing worry. My idea was mostly a strategy to regain her time alone, to give a nonproductive moment an aura of legitimacy. But the poem came to mean much more.

Years after we first met, Alice came to say hello at an event. Looking at me with the same affecting eyes, she said, "*Caminante, no hay camino,*" and I knew who she was in an instant. The sculptor had warmed to the idea of babies; he's a doting father to their two girls. And she was right about his art. Stories of patience don't all end so sweetly, but I'd bet nearly all sweet stories require some patience. She said that the poem gave her a way to check in with herself. She added that knowing she had something to sit down with again, in another dedicated moment, helped keep her from stressing nonstop. Her religious tradition of a brief written prayer followed by a period of loosely focused thought made the poem ritual a good fit for her.

How Religion Helps

Not all religions offer "petitionary prayer," that is, an opportunity to ask a supernatural force for items, answers, or outcomes. Compared to most gods, the Jesus of much American Christianity stands out as available to listen to his followers anywhere, anytime, and like a friend.

Catholics ask Jesus or Mother Mary to speak to God on their behalf. Some branches of Christianity await direct answers from God, and may cite the Old Testament prophet Jeremiah, who reported God's words to him: "Call to me and I will answer you and tell you great and unsearchable things you do not know" (Jer. 33:3). Some Christians believe that such prayer can lead to obstacles divinely removed. Some speak of emptying oneself of thought so that the voice of God can be heard.

Religions that don't promote petitionary prayer still often supply a ritual for contemplation and may promise that the act of contemplation itself helps one's fortunes. Buddhism doesn't have official rituals, but in each country or area rituals have developed. One that has grown in popularity around the world is to tend a Zen garden, a mini sandbox with a tiny rake with which to drag lines and shapes, to make roadways and doze them under.

Hindu *puja* ceremonies can include placing fruit—perhaps an artful display of ripe mango, banana, and coconut—at the foot of a statue or framed image of a spiritual being. Puja rituals include walking circles around that icon, called *pradakshina*.

Even without the supernatural parts, such rites allow for contemplation. Those who perform them can feel that they gave their issue its proper space and time.

How Art and Science Help

Brain science speaks in terms of our negotiating the world using two distinct mental systems—one for quick problems and one for hard ones. For small decisions our limbic system wings it on vague associations and half-forgotten assumptions perceived as "gut feelings." We make these calls all day long, and though our guesses are not much better than chance, the stakes are low. For hard or important problems, we engage our ventromedial prefrontal cortex. It requires a lot of energy. People walk and talk all day, but to solve an equation we tend to veer over to a curb and stop walking—and we won't bother to work that hard unless it's pressing.

How do we get ourselves to pull over?

Decision theory in business breaks down the steps of a well-analyzed problem. Naming the obvious can help us get a good look at it, and to check that we aren't skimping on the hard parts. Decision models today are often versions of the following seven steps:

1. Are you sure you need to make a decision here?
2. What facts do you need? Is it even possible to act now?
3. Isolate and describe the best alternatives.
4. Time to do all the math, and start asking around.
5. Search for details on the risks. Ask advice.
6. Create a plan, get others on board.
7. Consider the process and outcome. What can be improved?

There is room for musing in these models, but when the risks are high, CEOs without an express aversion to prayer might well try that too.

For instance, in 2005 German researchers published a study of Sri Lankan business leaders including Buddhists, Christians, Hindus, and Muslims. When asked anonymously if and when they practiced religion at their secular workplaces, many said that they did, for decisions. Though they had been schooled in multiple management protocols for making choices, and some had even been assigned specific versions by their companies, participants with Buddhist backgrounds set up shrines and practiced reflection and stanza chanting; Hindus conducted puja ceremonies, recited mantras at work, and prayed for clarity; Christians worshipped with crosses and other symbols and celebrated mass at work. Business leaders with Muslim backgrounds spoke of aligning behavior to the principles of Islam.

The study used the term *the ultimate*, to include references to "God, transcendent reality, or truth." One participant "admitted" that he turned to the ultimate when faced with critical decisions and added, "Perhaps it is psychotic, but I have done this for the last 30–35 years. I feel it makes me a better man and it helps me to take the right decisions." Researchers found that results of the decision, good and bad, were often attributed to the quality of the ritual experience. The business leaders said the rituals provided "solace, guidance, and inspiration."

Your Ritual Draws on Both

Both checklist and shrine can help us take risks and assess the results, but they are each limited. We can do a better job than religion in guiding our attention through rational steps, and a better job than Business 101 at inviting in quiet thoughts and unclear feelings.

We can make a retreat for ourselves by bringing water to a plant and taking a few moments to sit in repose and read a poem.

It may seem like common sense to devote a few moments to thinking about a choice. Languages around the world have idioms for "Sleep on it," or "Decide in the morning," which shows we are aware that we require time, and various states of mind, to know what we think. In sports, when you get hurt, someone often says "walk it off." Also when you get mad. Perhaps we could add "walk it out" for a decision-making ritual where you take a stroll.

Find a way to walk without care, a perambulation around a clutch of trees, perhaps. Walking meditation is a staple of much Buddhism. The Vietnamese Buddhist monk Thich Nhat Hanh speaks of the practice, there called *kinh hành*, as a way to feel the present, mindfully connecting one's feet to the earth and moving with kindness through the world.

Religions often accompany ritual with mood-altering words to proclaim aloud, or savor in silence; to chant, sing, or mutter. For the Interfaithless, what can hit the sweet spot of gravitas and pleasure is poetry.

Our Poem

The poem I suggested to Alice, Machado's *"Caminante, no hay camino"* (1912), is one of the best-known Spanish poems across the globe.

Traveler, There Is No Road

Traveler, your footprints
are the only road and nothing else;
Traveler, there is no path,
the path is made by walking.
As you walk, you make the road,
and turning to look back
you see a path
that will never be traveled again.
Traveler, there is no path
only a foam trail on the sea.

The poem opens with praise for those who make their own way, by preference or need. The first five lines of the ten-line poem hint at lasting accomplishment in footprints and path forging. Things change when line six taps you on the shoulder to look back and see the record of your efforts. Nada, or not much.

The line "that will never be traveled again" sneaks into the poem the limits we usually hide from. All we leave behind is the froth of a ship's wake, full of energy, but so brief. The poem ends in that frothing erasure, but the order of claims can matter less in poetry than in prose, which is to say that the poem contains both truths, so we do and we don't leave footprints.

The word "traveler" appears only capitalized, so it always looks like a proper noun, Traveler. The poem invites us each to feel called by that name. There are travelers with stamped passports, travelers of the heart, travelers in time, and travelers of the mind. What kind of traveler are you? The poet was also perhaps talking to himself. When poets seem to be lecturing, handing down wisdom from on high, they often can be read as addressing themselves—cajoling, convincing, reminding. The poem exemplifies Machado's spare, moody style and sustained metaphors.

Poetry Lesson: Translation, Repetition

English translations of this poem can retain the hypnotic echo of *caminante* and *camino* of the original Spanish, but it's not always easy. "Wayfarer, There Is No Way," was once a popular version, but those twin words—"wayfarer" and "way"—are no longer commonly used that way. There is also a temptation to use "road" sometimes and "path" other times, but is it worth losing the hypnotic repetition? Three times the poet says, "Caminante, no hay camino," and it has a different weight each time. There's a walking beat to it. The poem calls the listener into being as a walker and doubts the walk until the listener is almost nothing but listening.

Spain has a rich walking culture, including the paseo, meaning a street or plaza designated for strolling, and also meaning the daily evening stroll. Machado was also influenced by French symbolists and by Buddhism. Because the Taoist *tao* has long been "way" in English—*camino* in Spanish—it feels poignant to say, "the way is not the way," though it could mean a range of things. That connection has been noted for some time, but the more recent use of the phrase "no way" to mean "I'm amazed," "that's impossible," and "I refuse" also can add texture—and humor—to a reading of the poem.

The road taker is real, though the road isn't. Roadster, there's no road. Walker, there is no walk. Path taker, there's no path. Goer, there's no going. Way follower, there's no way. Why does this move me? A lot of people hear an inner call to service that is out of sync with any outer call from the world so far. Not everything is available to everyone, all the time, so in one way or another, we all may be natural-born skiers in a land without snow. Born singers but there is no song. In such an O. Henry "Gift of the Magi" world, what does it mean to make your plans and decisions?

Machado's use of repetition here is powerful. In any human endeavor, repetition can be a form of investigation. To examine a case repeatedly, with controlled adjustments, is good science. At the same time, I can think of incantations like the name "Beetlejuice!" whose ignition turns only when you've said it three times. Repetition is also important to soothe and to hypnotize, it rocks us to-and-fro.

Machado's poem works wonders by doubting that our big choices are what they seem—they are not roads on a map, they are a gust of wind on which you ride with just more control than a driven leaf. Caught on the to-and-fro of its rhythm, we are able to loosen up and live with a calm heart while waiting and learning. Also: If there is no road, there is no other road—nothing to miss out on. "Traveler, There Is No Road" can help you escape from the lines on the map altogether and the limitations they place on you.

* * *

I fell more in love with this poem after it helped Alice; after she gave it back, so to speak. Machado called himself an atheist or an agnostic, and saw God's absence as a sorrowful or disappointing fact, for example: "My philosophy is fundamentally sad, but I'm not a sad man . . . My faith in the human race is stronger than my intellectual analysis of it; there lies the Fountain of Youth in which my heart is continually bathing." The loss of God saddens him, but he rejoices in love, art, and invention.

Once aware of Machado's beliefs, I came to see the poem's repeated "there is no" as a skeptic's refrain, and part of what I found so compelling from the start without realizing it. His skepticism had spoken to mine.

In college, on a break, I was traveling badly with a companion in Spain, had little money, and was often alone. At night, whole families emptied into the streets of Madrid, of Barcelona, to promenade and have random encounters. It was intoxicating. I'd never seen children playing in bars while their parents drank. I'd never seen butcher windows with suckling pigs hanging from a line of hooks, so freshly killed that drips of blood from their mouths were still bright red, even wet, reflecting light. I'd grown up visiting Chinatown in New York where beak-to-feet roast ducks hung in windows by their limp necks, sad as *Swan Lake*, yet almost unbearably delicious, but it was shocking to see lines of baby mammals suckling death. The crowd of walkers carried me along and as a young woman alone I'd follow near families to feel safe.

I didn't know then how I'd be changed by Spanish streets, by dark eyes and red dresses, by the temptations and threats of desire. At times, the best work we can do to create a life is to go where it's exciting and walk around there a while. In Alice's dilemma, she was in an exciting, scary place, and the poem helped her stay awhile, allowing time for change and the unknown.

Your Poem

To find your own poem to help with making decisions, look for one that mentions choices or roads.

We want to reach a field of contemplation, a state of mind near daydream, a mood of thought without the stress of a demanded answer, because when we're there we can hear more parts of ourselves.

Religions often remind people that we don't have control over our lives—God, gods, demons, or karma intervene. Art and the humanities also often remind us that individuals tend to be overpowered by chance and unseen systems. How many lives in history have been thrown into chaos by war, famine, contagious disease? There are many poems that remind us that while we have some control over our lives, we don't have much. Decisions matter and also don't. There are poems that suggest we accept despair but try anyway; the trying is the sacred, honoring this absurd and wonderful life by living it with honesty and experiment.

If you are looking for a gesture or poem, but nothing rustles your chimes, pick some anyway and they will grow on you. In that way, to read a particular poem sitting in quiet drinking jasmine green tea is to prep now for the chimes to ring out next time. You will still be surprised when they do. Life surprises. As a kid, I loved the roast duck in Chinatown, even the wince from the gruesome windows, and so I thought myself wise to the brutal, succulent world. But life has more to show, especially when we can bear to be mindful of that possibility.

The poem and ritual grow on you and you grow on them.

* * *

I recall Alice's big, teary eyes and wonder about all we can't know. She loved the sculptor enough to bear the anxiety of not knowing everything. Major decisions often require patience, supported by a method for checking in. It's hard to wait, as dream plans flicker in and out of our imagined future, but we can trust that there are many ways to end up slightly happy, which is all the happy one gets. There's no "end up" even, since change continues. I think it's okay to imagine another life—I was just doing it (one yet quieter)—but also good to drop that and engage in today in a way that feels like traveling, moving through with awareness and agency. Even when stuck in place we can be travelers at heart: people with well-used luggage, yes, but also people who dream of escaping home, and so many people far away from home—all the lost, hunting to be found.

If all there is, really, is you and the moment after, then you are a road. The whole world, as far as you know it, is made up of your passage through it. The road is the shape of you in space-time. The passage is you and vice versa.

Traditional ritual sets an occasion for decision theory's steps to be taken. Mesh the religious model with the rational one and deep thought comes to vibrant life. Maybe you trace Zen garden roads, and smooth them over, and get comfortable knowing the drifting paths of time. Maybe you take a peaceful walk and learn by listening to whatever your feet turn out to already know.

You may find, as many have, that when you carry out a ritual and read a poem, the experience acts on you. Each time you do the ritual and reread the poem you lead yourself to engage in this ineffable manner, this way without a way.

2

On Eating

Okakura's Tea, Lee's Peaches, and Emily's Worm

"Can't we have something good to say before a meal?"

I'm at a poetry conference and they ask a few of us each night to select and read a poem at what we're calling a banquet. Happy to. But which poem? You don't want to bring a poem everyone knows, which means you need one that people can enjoy in one go, listening while hungry, at tables in a crowded room.

I have an inspiring poem to read, the not-yet-too-famous "Wild Geese" by Mary Oliver. It can't miss. But when the night arrives things go askew. I skew. The altitude? Yes. The bright lights, too. Also, there are bowls of lollipops in the hall and I am looking out at people with candy bulges in one cheek. This includes most of the big-name authors in the front, older than their photos, and childlike with suckers.

The readers before me have gone on a bit, selling me on brevity's role in wit. I am tired, and I haven't eaten, and I am freaked out by the lopsided lollipop faces. It's been a long week and I've been annoyed by the lack of historical or world poetry. So I call an audible (a sports term for changing your mind about sleeping with someone while you are on the date). I can feel the servers with the salads patiently standing by.

I say that given the lateness of the hour, I've put aside the poem I'd planned to read—and oops, was approved—in favor of a poem by Li Bai. I let the audience know that the preeminent Chinese poet lived for much of the eighth century (701–762).

I take my wine jug out among the flowers
to drink alone, without friends.

I raise my cup to entice the moon.
That, and my shadow, makes us three.

It's the first two stanzas of one of his most famous poems. Pretty and inspiring, but sly. The prettiness comes from the flowers, and these being night flowers (this being night), we can smell their rich and delicate night-flower perfumes. The inspiration is toward finding friendship in oneself and in nature. We don't know if he is alone by choice, or rather, to what degree. When you are alone a lot, you don't care if it would look crazy from the outside, you learn to make friends with the woodwork.

The slyness is heightened because it praises wine and solitude, imaginary friendships with the moon, and with one's shadow. It is rebellious to praise this private rapture or even name it.

There is only one reader after me. To my surprise she announces she's also setting aside her poem—for a stanza of a Hafiz poem. She tells the audience Hafiz was born and died in Iran and lived for much of the fourteenth century (1315–1390).

If I've left the mosque for the tavern,
Don't complain: the ceremonies stretch on far too long
And time is short.

After dinner we find each other, and find ourselves around a table with others, talking about poetry, food, and benedictions. The conversation is vivacious and in all directions I'm taken aback by the passion the subject ignites. This matters to people. The way religion prays over food impacts the way poetry works as a benediction. We are what we eat with. Banquet poetry is a well-established way to create a mood of warmth and significance. Privately saying a few poetic words when one eats may or may not appeal, but there is a lot of overlap between public tropes and private ordeals, public hopes and private meals.

Our subject ever returns to poetry and I am repeatedly compli-
mented for the brevity of my reading. Over and over I admit that
this was all I could remember when I got up there. Someone says, "Funny
how unappetizing some of the poems were." Someone says, "Funny that
there is no settled poetic benediction over a feast." Someone says,
"Funny that there is no such benediction over a private meal." All dis-
agree on what it could possibly be. Few of us can imagine ourselves
muttering words over our regular, daily meals, but many of us believe
we would benefit from a pause between grabbing a snack and disap-
pearing it.

What is clear is that food is tricky. A lot of us could do with a bit
of help with it. We don't always know how we *should* eat, and we don't
always like how we *do* eat. Especially for we the overweight, the food
disordered, and the worried welterweight, food trouble takes up a lot of
our minds. But food isn't only trouble.

Food is pleasure. Many of us live for delicious food, spend time and
attention preparing it, and bask in our delight in it. Eating together
is fundamental to communion between friends, neighbors, strangers.
Eating is cheerful, and can return the exiled to life. Some of our ideas
about food separate us from the joy of it.

We already say things to ourselves about food. Don't we? Do you
have food concepts and food rules? These may play in our heads un-
asked for, or we may purposefully repeat them. Some of our private
food sayings are probably helpful. Many are based on information that
hasn't been reexamined scrupulously or recently. Surely some of our
private food mantras are bad—unhealthy and self-punishing. Overall,
there must be better things for us to be saying before our food.

How Religion Helps

Okakura Kakuzō wrote a treatise called *The Book of Tea* in 1906, in
English. He put the beauty of Taoism into poetic terms that Western-
ers could understand, and radically improved how the West viewed the

East. He was Japanese, educated in Chinese classics as well as English. Here's how the opening essay starts:

> Tea began as a medicine and grew into a beverage. In China, in the eighth century, it entered the realm of poetry as one of the polite amusements. The fifteenth century saw Japan ennoble it into a religion of aestheticism—Teaism. Teaism is a cult founded on the adoration of the beautiful among the sordid facts of everyday existence. It inculcates purity and harmony, the mystery of mutual charity, the romanticism of the social order. It is essentially a worship of the Imperfect, as it is a tender attempt to accomplish something possible in this impossible thing we know as life.

This friendliness and insight bounce along through the text. Allow me to set up how that same chapter concludes. It's odd. Okakura says, "The Taoists relate that at the great beginning of the No-Beginning, Spirit and Matter met in mortal combat." Matter lost and in agony slammed his head against the sky and "shivered the blue dome of jade into fragments." Who can fix the sky? "Out of the Eastern sea rose a queen, the divine Niuka, horn-crowned and dragon-tailed, resplendent in her armor of fire." He says she fixes it, with her rainbow cauldron, but misses two pieces, accounting for the dualism of love. "Everyone has to build anew his sky of hope and peace." Here's the finish:

> The heaven of modern humanity is indeed shattered in the Cyclopean struggle for wealth and power. The world is groping in the shadow of egotism and vulgarity . . . The East and West, like two dragons tossed in a sea of ferment, in vain strive to regain the jewel of life. We need a Niuka again to repair the grand devastation; we await the great Avatar. Meanwhile, let us have a sip of tea. The afternoon glow is brightening the bamboos, the fountains are bubbling with delight, the soughing of the pines is heard in our kettle. Let us dream of evanescence, and linger in the beautiful foolishness of things.

Well, Okakura, you've got me. I like to dream of evanescence and linger in the beautiful foolishness of things. Eating and drinking can have a poetry to them. Religion often gives an order to that poetry.

How Art and Science Help

When it comes to diets, the science is uncertain. Diets can work but most people gain the weight back and a biological mechanism bumps up our norm to a few pounds extra. As a consequence, these days, scientists suggest mindful eating, which means getting in the habit of thinking about what you are about to eat and how it will make you feel. The expert advice is to be wary of expert advice and to pay attention to our own bodies and feelings.

A banquet poem is supposed to create a moment of sweet solemnity. It functions in the way prayer does at religious occasions. The Oliver poem I'd planned to read has been read at countless group meals by now. It has no food in it, fowl on the wing notwithstanding. I've read it at banquets myself. The poet is speaking to a person, perhaps a part of herself, who seems hurt unto exile, but the action of the poem is calling that being back, telling them that they are part of "the family of things."

Friendship is especially important in this age of solitude and surfaces. Sharing food is a foundation of sharing the self. The Epicurean ideal friendship of the ancient world took place in a garden, eating simple good food together, talking about ideas. In ages of national division, the symbolism of communal bread-breaking is precious and should be raised in meaning and happiness anyway it can be.

Your Ritual Draws on Both

Do you already have food sayings and are they good for you? Do you have phrases that you repeat to yourself, regarding eating? We are creatures of habit. Anything that could get us to be more mindful of our choices can help.

The tea ceremony has information to teach us about eating. Slow down. Value the imperfect. When you follow precise rituals it can create a sense of peace. That peaceful precision gets all the attention, takes all the prep time, but it's just a theater for lightheartedness.

Do the nonreligious miss prayer over food? Not really, it seems. Yet there are hints that our feelings are more complicated. For instance, in mainstream movies and television our leading characters don't generally pray, but if prayer comes up it is often around a dinner table. There's a little formula to it, right? Our main characters are asked to join hands and their first response is to laugh with sneering derision, to ape confusion, or even to refuse as if in the throes of an allergic reaction. Once they hold hands though, the prayer tends to be one that any human would be moved by—and they are moved.

It is worth asking ourselves if we are attracted to such moments and what about them. What makes this modern fantasy scene keep reappearing?

If a person wanted to adopt a poetic expression for daily use, I would think it should be quite brief. The banquet benediction poem is expected to be of a normal poetry length. Such a poem isn't usually expected to be about eating, but I think it can be a nice way to go. At least make sure the poem is not directly in opposition to people's appetites.

If you are celebrating an institution, perhaps incorporate words and gestures from the tradition of the place. If you have children, it can feel good to repeat aspects of benedictions that you said over suppers with your own parents.

Our Poem

Li-Young Lee was born in Jakarta, Indonesia, to an illustrious Chinese parentage of difficult fortunes, and the family came to the United States when he was young. This is from his 1986 book, *Rose*:

From Blossoms

From blossoms comes
this brown paper bag of peaches
we bought from the boy
at the bend in the road where we turned toward
signs painted Peaches.

From laden boughs, from hands,
from sweet fellowship in the bins,
comes nectar at the roadside, succulent
peaches we devour, dusty skin and all,
comes the familiar dust of summer, dust we eat.

O, to take what we love inside,
to carry within us an orchard, to eat
not only the skin, but the shade,
not only the sugar, but the days, to hold
the fruit in our hands, adore it, then bite into
the round jubilance of peach.

There are days we live
as if death were nowhere
in the background; from joy
to joy to joy, from wing to wing,
from blossom to blossom to
impossible blossom, to sweet impossible blossom.

First let's take in the poem straight through, reading for grammatical sense and expecting story. Note that the stanzas are each one sentence.

On a country road they followed a sign for peaches down a bend in the way and now they have a brown paper bagful. As the poet and his companion feast on the peaches, the poet thinks of the story of the fruit, heavy on the tree branches, then the heavy work of harvest, and then the crowded basket. The poet thinks of the dirt on the peaches that makes him recall past summers as they eat. He calls the dirt "dust," echoing the biblical "dust to dust," and nicely making the dirt less reminiscent of filth or fertilizer, and so more edible.

The third stanza-sentence is an ecstatic repetition of the first two. It is a rush of pleasure to be able to admire the orb as a thing of beauty and then let it enter you, while standing in the place that produced the fruit, feeling each stage of the ripeness, the darkness too, and the time. You can feel the slow time of growth, moment on moment.

The final stanza-sentence starts in a universal voice, making a large claim. It claims that there are days when we don't worry about death, because we experience one joy after another, as if we are flying. The poem reminds us that at times we can suddenly taste the shocking improbability of all this life and eating, and the flowers leading to fruit, and all the rest of it. This life of eating and drinking.

If we go back and read it more slowly, we see more. The poem's first two lines are arresting, a poem in themselves. The theme is peach blossoms leading to peaches, but the poem is not wrong to include the brown paper bag as made "from blossoms." Gentle blossoms lead to everything. We can't help riding with the acceleration of the first stanza to the boy, down the bend in the road.

As an American poetry reader, the line "at the bend in the road where we turned toward / signs" recalls the first stanza of Robert Frost's "The Road Not Taken."

> *Two roads diverged in a yellow wood,*
> *And sorry I could not travel both*
> *And be one traveler, long I stood*
> *And looked down one as far as I could*
> *To where it bent in the undergrowth*

In that poem, the speaker can't see far enough, he can't even tell which road was more worn, and those are the poem's only facts, the rest is imagining and theorizing. Frost's poem is about a road not taken, the road we do not go down is that bending one.

Lee is taking us down the bending road. Following the bend, one sees successive signs painted with the word "Peaches," but they are just signs (*Ceci n'est pas une pêche*) until we arrive there. It's heaven to arrive there. The first two stanzas begin with the word "From." That helps to explain how they both feel like tumbling down a chute. They just race. Both come to an unexpected dead stop with "signs painted *Peaches*" and "dust we eat."

In the second stanza, there are three repetitions of "from," followed by "comes nectar" and "comes the familiar dust." Note the three iterations of "dust." Dust to dust to dust. In that middle one, we eat. Funny that the Bible leaves that one out, noting only the dry dust from which we come, and the dry dust we become, and not that inside time when we are the dust that gets to eat.

What do you make of "from sweet fellowship in the bins"? We can first enjoy the lively idea of peaches delighting in one another's company in the baskets, finally, all bunched together after a month of separate growing. "Sweet fellowship" is traditionally assigned to the farmhands at harvest, and is happening for the poet's people in this scene, so the words do triple duty. By assigning sweet fellowship to peaches in a bin, which isn't terribly realistic, the sweet fellowship is able to float around the poem.

How about the "O, to take what we love inside" stanza? We may feel like turning away when we see the poetic use of "Oh," as if witnessing something private. It is a poetic technique avoided in eras with a taste for irony, suspicious of sincerity. Writing "O" signals sincerity, which not only can make you look like a sap, but also is a hard lutz to land. When it works, as now, it's a wow. By the second line our little selves contain an orchard, a wide field of tree after tree, nature made orderly. Paradox is this rant's business. It offers two *not only this, but that* lines, and in each case, the rules of that rhetorical game are cleverly broken. The *this* and *that* should be similar and make sense as *that* being an advance on *this*. We are going to eat "not only the skin, but the shade." The reader's brain provides the missing sensible options *not only the skin, but the fruit* and *not only the sun, but the shade*. See how "fruit" and "sun" were hidden words?

You do the next line. Try "not only the sugar, but the days." Fill in words that seem expected or reasonable here: Not only the sugar, but the _____; and not only the days, but the _____. What kind of words are hidden?

Especially because of Lee's unsettled childhood we can see an exile's longing in "O, to take what we love inside, / to carry within us an orchard, to eat." Eating is such simple pleasure, and yet it is also a longing to hold what we have lost, to take in, to not let the peaches pass by. There is, too, the obvious voluptuousness of a peach, in taste, but almost blushingly so in form. Poetry readers are reminded of T. S. Eliot's only half-ironic worry for his age of anxiety, "Do I dare to eat a peach?" Notice in stanza three there are two little phrases hanging off commas, ", to eat" and then ", to hold." Where can you eat a peach and still hold it? In bed. That's the tone of the whole stanza. Even beyond the bedroom suggestions, the poem has been giving us a euphoric, carnal peach party. The smell of peach and the dirt on the peach skin and the bite into warm, round peach juice and flesh. They seem hungry. They "devour." They "adore." The peaches have "jubilance."

We are lost in the sensuality of eating, so it is surprising when stanza four comes in like a narrator, summing up, interpreting. The stanza reminds us about death, disguised in talking about forgetting about death. Now death is "in the background" and we see more clearly, with more insight, what all this bliss is about. It's life itself. Life catches the fire of the peaches, and the moment burns bright.

In an interview in the year 2000, in Santa Fe, Lee spoke about the meaning of his work and his devotion to poetry.

> I believe that aesthetic presence, aesthetic consciousness, is the wholest or highest form of presence we can achieve. It sacralizes what we observe, or what we attend to. It makes sacred, I shouldn't say "makes sacred," it uncovers the sacred nature of our lives. Uncovers the sacred, because you don't project it, you don't make it sacred, it is sacred.

I love everything about that: its primacy of presence, observation, and attention, and the stakes of the aesthetic. For me, too, the (poetic) sacred was there before you got there to admire the peach. Great nature and the consciousnesses of all human beings before and around you, it's all quite enough to hold the sacredness of the peach steady with or without your help. This beauty you stumble upon and learn to see is everything.

Poetry Lesson: Alliteration and Assonance

How does the poem catch so much excitement about fruit? If they're just pieces of produce, how did the poem put the whole world in them and into adoration of their form and nectar?

Poetic technique makes peaches glow with peach light and we also do so when we bite in. One well-known poetic technique is *alliteration*, use of words with the same first letter. Look at all the words that start with "b" in the first stanza. It's a bona fide bonanza. The clauses keep rolling dependently down the line, as does the action, and those "b"s bounce us along, making us feel airborne when they stop short after "bend," and catch us again with "boughs" and "bins." It's language but it's love and drenching sweetness and long waiting, short having, stopped into memory.

There are all sorts of sound repetitions in the poem, which add to its hypnotic singsong. *Assonance* refers to matching sounds such as the vowels of "dusty," "succulent," "devour." They repeat "uh" and "ee." When we get to "dust we eat," our ear was expecting it. Like a loved one's awaited wheels in the gravel driveway, that crunch is sweet to the ear. A sound that is the fulfillment of a pattern can be a pleasure to hear.

Focusing on the poem's alliteration and assonance, we can hear how it runs like a herd of antelope, leaping from like sound to sound, with a neat clatter of hooves on the dry ground. Patterns and their fulfillment can feed, they can be fulfilling. The habits of eating can be as important as the food.

The word "death" here is the only word with that vowel sound. It gives it more heft. Like the dark of the den sets off red eyes in the depth, all these other-vowelled words set off "death" in the poem. From

the ground, the poem leaps to flight. Maybe repetition is necessary for
liftoff. There's not much new information in the last four lines of the
poem—instead there's repetition of joy, of wing, of blossom. Then
leaps the leap of that lovely last line, "impossible blossom, to sweet
impossible blossom." That the commonplace is impossible is a paradox
of wonder.

* * *

What could I use for a private prayer over food? What comes to mind
is "and ate the fellow, raw." With review of the Emily Dickinson poem
from which this line was plucked, I can't see why I shouldn't adopt the
two stanzas of it I can easily memorize.

> *A Bird, came down the Walk—*
> *He did not know I saw—*
> *He bit an Angle Worm in halves*
> *And ate the fellow, raw,*
>
> *And then, he drank a Dew*
> *From a convenient Grass—*
> *And then hopped sidewise to the Wall*
> *To let a Beetle pass—*

Granted, it doesn't make much sense as a prayer replacement, but
it came to me. Honestly, I have my eye out for something better. Yet it
does make me laugh and the eating and the drinking here is elemental.

Assonance and alliteration make this charm work. It is mostly "W,"
and "D," with a bit of "B," and a lot of "aw" vowels. A BirD came
Down, DiD not know, then Bit, and Drank a Dew, and hoppeD siDeways.
The vowel fugue of "aw" seesaws along in "walk," "saw," "raw," and
"wall." Note, too, the pattern of how the lines begin. There's a neatness,
a decorum and concision. How much do sound patterns matter in poetry? I'd say about as much as the lyrics matter in song.

Your Poem

For a banquet poem you need to think about what other people will understand and appreciate. You might want to have a *special occasion meal poem* for large gatherings or even eventful days at the family table. As we have noted, the convention does not ask such poems to be about food or eating. Any poem that leaves one feeling alive and good is a fine candidate. Here is the now classic poem by Mary Oliver that I had planned to read at that long ago conference meal.

Wild Geese

You do not have to be good.
You do not have to walk on your knees
for a hundred miles through the desert, repenting.
You only have to let the soft animal of your body
    love what it loves.
Tell me about despair, yours, and I will tell you mine.
Meanwhile the world goes on.
Meanwhile the sun and the clear pebbles of the rain
are moving across the landscapes,
over the prairies and the deep trees,
the mountains and the rivers.
Meanwhile the wild geese, high in the clean blue air,
are heading home again.
Whoever you are, no matter how lonely,
the world offers itself to your imagination,
calls to you like the wild geese, harsh and exciting—
over and over announcing your place
in the family of things.

It is a banquet of words. We are pulled out of ourselves three times by "meanwhile": "Meanwhile the world," "Meanwhile the sun," "Meanwhile the wild geese." Raindrops as "clear pebbles" show that the element of time subverts much perception. The poem calls to the lost within all of us, especially we who feel misfit or broken, saying that you are still family. "Wild Geese" distinctly rejects the religious worldview of penance, with you as the penitent, and life as a long crawl. Inside the poem you are not bound to religion nor to pretending life is better than it is, but you are also not in control. Stop thrashing. The lone human action in the poem is sharing despair, a part of the natural sacred. The geese take us up high, where we can see a little more. Reading the poem has you say "wild" three times.

Let the communal-meal poem be warm, let it call to a better life that is right here beneath our normal noticing. Poetry can invoke the public poetic sacred. Even when everything feels impossible.

For a personal blessing think brevity. Privately, we can say *Thanks* to our food. If it is meat we are eating, we can say *Thanks* to the animal, and every human down the line who—let's face it—killed and slashed to bring the meat to you. Whatever we eat, I think we can reasonably say the word, *Thanks*, and pause for a moment in the name of all that happened in order to feed us. It might be better than some of the crazy food things we say to ourselves.

Along with *Thanks*, what if you had a poetic phrase or stanza to help slow yourself down? It might sound like an active thing to do, and a wacky one, but what if you are already in a trance and a bad one? Billions are being spent to keep us in purchasing and munching and dieting trances, so it seems a small effort to try to pepper our days with wakeful pauses. I say "try" because it's not super doable. Luckily, the attempt itself can be meaningful.

* * *

Without a prayer, meals can still have a ritual of appreciation and thanks. For eventful meals a poem can cast a spell of sanctity and fellowship. A poem can take us all someplace together; to peaches, down the bend in the road, to the boy selling the peaches, to the paper bag, from blossoms. Death and forgetting death. I think of the major authors with lollipops bulging their cheeks, and the bird who bit a worm in halves "And ate the fellow, raw." I hear people and their food anxiety and food identities and am at times inspired, but more often unsettled.

The ceremony of tea creates a careful frame for a lapse into glorious repose and relaxed friendship. We take the whole world and its foolishness inside us, hoping not to be further exiled, to never again be lost. Like a ritual you once did with your parents and now your children do with you. Poems in which feasting is attentively observed can help us take in the time of taking in, in which we yet linger.

3

On Gratitude

Tasty Lists

"Okay, sure, I'm full of gratitude, but to whom am I grateful?"

I'm writing to you from inside the pandemic. It's been an emotional whiplash of a situation, sorrow and fury at the loss, profound gratitude for ordinary good. Daily trying to make right-enough decisions. At the beginning of the pandemic, here in New York City, there were ambulance sirens all the time. You'd be reading about it and also hearing it, all day and night. You'd see the pictures of the makeshift morgues on the old docks.

Someone on my feed said something like, "When I hear the siren, I know the person in the ambulance is gasping for breath and I breathe deep in honor of them. I give my hope to them and am grateful to be only miserable about this lockdown that is driving me out of my mind." Empathy followed a sound, a tone, to an image of a speeding white van, and then saw into that vehicle to an older man maybe, young for a grandfather, with much life to live, gasping, soon to be intubated, and avoided, by mandate, like the plague. *I'm so sorry for you*, one says on the outside. *I'm so grateful it isn't me or mine*, one adds on the inside.

Maybe it's not the nicest, but it is a real human feeling. Bedrock real. It may come up a lot in a single afternoon of strolling and scrolling. When does that inside feeling have a chance to get out? When do you get to breathe out and say, *Hooray it wasn't me, it wasn't us, today*?

Across years of listening to people talk about irreligion, gratitude has been one of the central themes. I meet people who tell me that they don't believe in God but they choose to live as if they do. Sometimes they say they make this leap because they need his help with the sadness. Sometimes it's the opposite. They are in an embarrassment of riches, and they know it. Suffering an agony of abundance, they've been spared the worst and are aware of that, and they say, "I believe because I need a way to say *Thank You*."

I remember a conversation with a particularly wide-awake person of this sort, who said, straight out, "The part of me that wants to say *Thank You* doesn't give a hoot about reason."

I'm hearing birds and sirens as I write this, but there are long patches of only songbirds. I fill birdfeeders with songbird seed and throngs of colorful songbirds have crowded the trees behind our place. Sunflower seeds bring a pair of cardinals, fast. How do they get the wire? This consistently brings me outsize delight.

In the pandemic, the gratitude issue has a different matter. We are dumbstruck by the ruckus of ongoing abnormality. Part of the time we are angry and sad, part of the time we are grateful for what we have, in that brand new way you get grateful for quiet safety when a new threat looms.

How Religion Helps

Religion is full of ways to say *Thank You*; it is one of the major categories of prayer. Meister Eckhart, the Catholic mystic of the fourteenth century, wrote, "If the only prayer you ever said in your whole life was 'Thank You,' that would suffice." Consider too the title of a book by the insightful spiritual writer Anne Lamott, *Help, Thanks, Wow*, which she calls the three essential prayers.

Gratitude itself is praiseworthy in Islam. In the Quran, Allah is said to favor those who feel gratitude. "And Allah will certainly reward the grateful" (Quran 3:145).

You know how common wisdom advises forgiveness to others for the sake of your own heart? The Quran suggests the same is true for gratitude. "Be grateful to Allah. And whoever is grateful is grateful for [the benefit of] himself" (Quran 31:12). The depth of the idea is that the experience of being grateful, which can be humbling at times, at times exalting, is good for you.

There is also a Muslim teaching that gratitude has three levels.

It is good to feel grateful in your heart.
It is better to put it into words.
Best of all is to spend your gratitude helping others.

In Hinduism, Buddhism, Jainism, and Sikhism, the practice of cultivating generosity is *dāna*. Gratitude and helping others are linked. The *Tirukkuṟaḷ*, a Tamil philosophical work beloved across various religions, includes such ideas as "Great, indeed, is the power to endure hunger. Greater still is the power to relieve others' hunger," for anyone who thinks fasting is the fast way to express gratitude. The Mahabharata describes how to be grateful through generosity to strangers, secretly, including planting public orchards so that weary travelers can benefit from the succulent fruit and the cooling shade. What a grand way to give a gift and be well away before the day it gives sweet succor to some stranger who will never know your name.

In Leviticus in the Hebrew Bible, similar terms are set for the welfare of those in need:

And when you reap the harvest in your land, you shall not reap the corners of your field; neither shall you gather the gleaning of your harvest. And you shall not glean your vineyard, nor shall you gather the single grapes of your vineyard. You shall leave them for the poor and the stranger.

It seems excellent to join the expression of gratitude to the idea that we do not have to wring every drop of value out of what we have, especially when our taking the easy way means someone else eats, or is treated to an unexpected find.

Powerful too is the Jain idea of *aparigraha*, that owning things is an impediment to inner freedom. Jain monks have few possessions, and lay Jains are encouraged to own only what they need. *Aparigraha* can include not hoarding one's time and talent, and instead participating in the community and supporting others, including animals.

Perhaps religionists have an advantage over the Interfaithless in having a god, or a saintlike being to whom to say *Thank You*. We can thank the chef, instead of a god, for lunch, but often there is no human contender for our gratitude, such as in the realm of health and weather.

How Art and Science Help

On the art and science side, sometimes some of us feel that lack of direction acutely. We want to send a *Thank You* and have nowhere to address it. But art and science have their own advantages, such as being true and aimed at awakening our jaded eyes to the wonder of the real world.

Even just trying to think of something "to be grateful for is apparently good for your brain and mood. Studies support keeping a gratitude journal and trying to log an item in it every night. Coming up with something to write every night is such a pain in the neck that people report finding themselves more alert to moments of gratitude, all day, to have a note for the journal. Research shows you get more of a lift from thinking about your gratitude *to people* than when thinking about how grateful you are for objects or events.

We can learn to notice the wonder of the ordinary. The English Romantic poet Percy Bysshe Shelley wrote, "Life and the world, or whatever we call that which we are and feel, is an astonishing thing. The mist of familiarity obscures from us the wonder of our being. We are struck with admiration at some of its transient modifications, but it is itself the great miracle." Evaporating the mist of familiarity is the artist's job. Shelley wrote the above line in his book *The Necessity of Atheism*, which got him kicked out of Oxford in 1811. The primary unlikely gift is the astonishing fact of life and the world, the wonder of our being here.

Dying in 43 BCE the Roman statesman and scholar Cicero lived before the birth of the leaders of the two largest religions on Earth, Jesus and Muhammad, and he could see that "A thankful heart is not only the greatest virtue, but the parent of all the other virtues." If this is so, then when I wish I were better, I don't have to start with any of the active virtues, but will profit the world later, by profiting now from a quiet exercise in thankfulness. Cicero says gratitude will help me see all the rest more clearly.

Your Ritual Draws on Both

We can start with simple gratitude for our family and friends, our health, and good work, or good times, if we have them. Gratitude for things is nearly always complicated in our world of surplus wealth and bitter poverty. Note that in Japan and the United States today there is a refreshing anticlutter cult. Presumably in Japan the problem is a lack of space and in the United States the problem is that we all overpacked for life. So whether you live on a tiny island with millions of people or have room to spread out but have had too much fun filling your cart over the years—it can be rewarding to toss things out. Giving things away can inspire gratitude for what you keep. It can feel wrong to give away items that have value. Try thinking of it this way. If you aren't in love with late-capitalism, why are you letting it store all its stuff at your place? So passing on what you do not need is a crowning way to celebrate and rekindle one's gratitude. The best is when you use your gratitude to help someone.

Say the words *Thank You*. You don't need a direction for those words. Too awkward? Then find a gratitude poem with the words *Thank You*. Many poems can inspire gratitude. So the ritual is to be kind, give away what you don't need, value what you keep, and read your poem.

Our Poem

This one is by Denmark's most honored poet, Inger Christensen. I chose it because I feel that list poems are excellent gratitude poems. This one is deep. I'm giving you the first passages of her book-length poem, *alphabet*.

alphabet

1

apricot trees exist, apricot trees exist

2

bracken exists; and blackberries, blackberries;
bromine exists; and hydrogen, hydrogen

3

cicadas exist; chicory, chromium,
citrus trees; cicadas exist;
cicadas, cedars, cypresses, the cerebellum

4

doves exist, dreamers, and dolls;
killers exist, and doves, and doves;
haze, dioxin, and days; days
exist, days and death; and poems
exist; poems, days, death

5

early fall exists; aftertaste, afterthought;
seclusion and angels exist;
widows and elk exist; every
detail exists; memory, memory's light;
afterglow exists; oaks, elms,
junipers, sameness, loneliness exist;
eider ducks, spiders, and vinegar
exist, and the future, the future

6

fisherbird herons exist, with their grey-blue arching
backs, with their black-feathered crests and their
bright-feathered tails they exist; in colonies

they exist, in the so-called Old World;
fish, too, exist, and ospreys, ptarmigans,
falcons, sweetgrass, and the fleeces of sheep;
fig trees and the products of fission exist;
errors exist, instrumental, systemic,
random; remote control exists, and birds;
and fruit trees exist, fruit there in the orchard where
apricot trees exist, apricot trees exist
in countries whose warmth will call forth the exact
colour of apricots in the flesh

Christensen wrote *alphabet* according to two rules. The first was to do with the alphabet, as is easy to spot. The second is mathematical, and less obvious. The number of lines in the poem follow the Fibonacci sequence, where every number is the sum of the two previous numbers. Fibonacci numbers appear often in mathematics, as well as in biology, where they describe the branching of trees, the patterns of leaves, the growth of a pineapple, an artichoke, a pinecone, and a fern uncurling. Take a look at the packed-in double-spiral pattern of sunflower seeds as they grow and you see a phenomenon of the same numbers. The Fibonacci numbers also describe ocean waves, as they are curling.

Poetry readers enjoy the longer numbers as distinct poems, or anthologists use a chunk of the beginning, as I have done here. About the alphabetical constraint, Christensen told all the book's translators that she preferred them to choose meaning over matching the first letter, if both could not be managed.

"A" is for "apricot." Apricot trees exist. The doubled statement brings apricots to mind with their deep-orange flesh, tartly sweet, and just resistant to the teeth. They are small for a stone fruit; it would take two or three to add up to the flesh of a peach. What else? Oh yes, the pit is a poison parcel; when eaten, cyanide is created. It can be fatal. The twin statement also includes the apricot trees, and with them all the activity, all the bees and blossoms. What happens for you when we add or remove the word "exist"? For me the word calls up the improbability of everything; it makes me feel lucky. Grateful.

Bracken exists. It's a lovely fern and hardy. Ferns unfurl starting as fiddleheads. Also bracken is poisonous to humans and livestock, and is carcinogenic. Blackberries are pure delight, just the fruit, repeated. Bromine can be used like chlorine, to sanitize. Bromine also can be reduced to bromide, at one time prescribed and sold as a daily sedative. That is why people might say, "Don't give me your bromides about everything happening for a reason." Bromine itself, though, is highly toxic. We arrive at "hydrogen, hydrogen."

Cicadas are a pest, but also a fascination, sleeping for years underground and then emerging, en masse, shedding their monster skins and flying away on iridescent, architectural wings. Citrus trees mean oranges, lemons, pink grapefruit—bite into a sweet-tart segment. Cicadas swarm on every line.

Doves perch on two lines. After the innocence of "doves exist, dreamers, and dolls," it is like a thief in the night that "killers exist" and later the poison, dioxin. Reading the fourth stanza aloud it unfurls a genius of a little poem on its own, rhythmic and rewinding.

Early fall is a season of mellow fruitfulness and melancholy as we move toward the frigid months of winter. Everything is included in "every / detail exists." It's elegant how solid entries like junipers, ducks, and vinegar are entwined with such ethereal entries as "sameness, loneliness," and "the future, the future."

Fisherbird herons exist and suddenly Christensen takes her time describing her entry, detailing the fisherbird's colors and places. The sound of the poem has a biblical swing to it now. There are fish and birds. There is sweetgrass. When the poet says "the fleeces of sheep" she includes sheep, their fleece, and it is also an allusion to the sheep fleece that helps Odysseus escape in Homer's *Odyssey*.

Fig trees exist and lull, but we find we are misled and instead "the products of fission exist; / errors exist." What kind of errors? Well, "instrumental, systemic, / random." Then we turn aside from error and it is fruit for the rest of the stanza. It is orchards and apricots, but the apricot flesh is also human and it is all so warm and wonderful and also all so vulnerable.

Fibonacci didn't invent the numbers; he brought the Indian numerical system, which was based on the sequence, to the attention of Europeans. One feature of the Fibonacci sequence is that if you let it get big (instead of repeating its early numbers to make petals on a flower, say), once it gets big, it gets immense, fast. Any student of humanity and its habitat will see the comparison in that. We've gone exponential.

By the letter "N" the poem changes plan, unable to go on, stopped for that reason of multiplying scale, but also a poetic reason, as the poem can't get past nuclear war without a change of program. Christensen's poem cherishes the world as it names its keen dangers.

Poetry Lesson: Japanese Lists, West African Griot, European Cosmic List Poems

TASTY LIST STORY I

The sublime diary of Japanese court lady Sei Shōnagon, *The Pillow Book* (1002), was written at a time when people regularly exchanged original poetry, in a sort of dialogue. It was a major part of the lives of elite men and women in the Heian period (794–1185), an artistic golden age. Exchanged poems could be shared with others, and the ability to recite them became a rich aspect of life at court.

There is a list-like aspect to many works of the period because each contribution was often short, but *The Pillow Book*, which Shōnagon kept under her pillow, has true lists created just for the pleasure of them. To my ear there is gratitude in these careful acts of naming, sorting, and preserving.

Elegant Things

A white coat worn over a violet vest.
Duck eggs.
Shaved ice mixed with liana syrup put in a new silver bowl.
A string of rock crystals.
Wisteria blossoms. Plum blossoms covered with snow.
A pretty child eating strawberries.

Things That Give a Clean Feeling

An earthen cup. A new metal bowl.
A rush mat.
The play of light on water as one pours it into a vessel.
A new wooden chest.

Note that the lists are full of action; the coat and vest aren't just together, they are *worn* together. The ice is first *mixed* and then *put* in a bowl. You'll see that there are other verbs. The stillness we feel in "Things That Give a Clean Feeling" comes happily alive with the play of light on water as one pours it. It's like that sparkling action had to be handed to us in oven mitts of stillness, the earthen cup and the wooden chest.

TASTY LIST STORY II

Griots, or *jeli*, are West African poet-singer-historians. The UN recognizes sixteen countries in West Africa, economically led these days by Ivory Coast, Ghana, Nigeria, and Senegal. Old empires of immense might, gilded and poetic, have reigned for centuries and fallen out of name in this area.

The age of the Mali Empire was circa 1235–1670; the Manding languages were spoken here and their culture spread wide and far. We know about it partly because of a few key visitors from North Africa who wrote accounts of the world, and because of the oral histories of the Mandinka tradition, recorded and remembered by griots. Griots give astonishing performances, in terms of both musicality and memory (promising baby griots start training early). The griot's other major role is as an advisor and diplomat for kings and other rulers.

"Griot" is a European-derived word. The local, traditional names include "jali" or "jeli," but the word "griot" is now naturalized and more or less standard. It's a superb role for poetry in a society. Griots are often men, but the profession is open to women and there have been many storied storytellers among them. This is a hereditary job, open only to the griot families. Griots mostly marry other griots, and if you will allow me to get fancy, that makes them an endogamous caste.

Each village had a griot and he or she knew your family story way back and knew about you. Imagine: what you did became part of the wise person's song.

Griots have their own instrument, the kora, a gourd-bodied, long-necked, lute-like instrument with twenty-one strings. In the hands of an extraordinary player like Sibo Bangoura, or Sona Jobarteh and her band, the kora is exquisite. Griots sing praise poems and poems of gratitude.

In the rise of modern states, the griots lost their key advisory role, and with the rise of writing and books, the griots lost the need for lists of rote memory of people and events. The beneficiary of all their historical dedication has been their role as entertainers. Youssou N'Dour, one of Africa's most famous musicians, was born into the musical environment of a griot family in Senegal and started his craft young. He has sung traditional griot songs at Carnegie Hall. Griot musicians influenced rap and are a major force in world music.

TASTY LIST STORY III

There are long passages of lists in the Bible. The King James Version especially influenced many poetic lists in the Romance languages. The list poem is an ebullient form; its canter tends to break into gallop and go wild.

Large swaths of James Joyce's *Ulysses* have been called list poems. A tiny pinch of one shows their characteristic dynamism of wording and banality of content: "Flaskets of cauliflowers, floats of spinach, pineapple chunks, Rangoon beans, strikes of tomatoes, drums of figs, drills of Swedes, spherical potatoes and tallies of iridescent kale." This dynamic banality suggests gratitude for all that is normal and amazing.

For gratitude, let's look at what I call *cosmic list poems*—poems that give a sense of the whole of everything. One technique to create a sense of totality is to list unlike things so your list evokes all that's between them. Lewis Carroll did it when the Walrus spoke "of many things: / Of shoes—and ships—and sealing-wax— / Of cabbages—and kings—."

Another technique to invoke totality is to mention the world itself. List poems can be explicitly gratitude poems. Here's the end of a Mark Strand poem that spends many lines before this finale lost in the night with the rest of the world dark and asleep.

For whatever reason, people are waking.
Someone is cooking, someone
is bringing The Times *to the door.*
Streets are filling with light.
My friends are rubbing the sleep from their eyes.
Jules is rubbing the sleep from her eyes,
and I sit at the table
drinking my morning coffee.
All that we lost at night is back.

Thank you, faithful things!
Thank you, world!
To know that the city is still there,
that the woods are still there,
and the houses, and the humming of traffic
and the slow cows grazing in the field;
that the earth continues to turn
and time hasn't stopped,
that we come back whole
to suck the sweet marrow of day,
thank you, bright morning,
thank you, thank you!

It's a good one, right? There are more out there, in many flavors. In the Wisława Szymborska poem "Birthday," the world's wonders are declaimed in complaint, praising, but tired. "So much world all at once— how it rustles and bustles! / Moraines and morays and morasses and mussels," for the poet, in this moment, it is all too much, an "excess of kindness." She adds that "while trying to plumb what the void's inner sense is," you are likely to miss "all these poppies and pansies." This poet thinks about all we miss or forget. (If an entity made the world, for us, didn't he overdo it?) So much intricate beauty lives and vanishes unadmired.

* * *

What I'm grateful for is that when I put out birdseed the birds come, especially the cardinals, him and her, who must hover nearby, so fast do they appear for sunflower seeds. Or have they a telegraph system in the branches? I'm writing this in winter and the snow has painted every last thing in New York City white. What a careful brush! So imagine Mr. and Mrs. Red against that white.

I go out in my coat-like, bright-orange puffy slippers and I broadcast a sunflower-seed-heavy wild-bird mix, and here they are, and that's what I'm grateful for. I sit so still thinking at my desk that they come right near me to eat, until I get an idea and lean in to write it, and they scatter to the sky.

I'm grateful for red flocks of house finches, the blue jays, dark-eyed juncos, and all the LBJs, to drop bird-watching lingo (Little Brown Jobs).

My stomach has not been right lately, so the happiness of food is not my place for gratitude at the moment, but if you can eat ice cream, be grateful, and do. No, but even now food is my love and, braised right, even some iridescent kale can make me say, "Yes, yes, yes."

I've been writing this book for years, and it's not the first time this chapter has come up in the rotation in autumn. I come upon my description of dapple. Out the window, the swaying dapple of sunlight on the concrete is so beautiful I can hardly look away to write this. It shivers and ripples in the puddles. I guess dapple happens in the fall because there are mature leaves, with spaces left by losses. It is happening again.

I'm grateful we're not underwater yet. All our other problems are going to get wet. It's not always time to think about that.

I ask myself, beyond the obvious great gifts of my life, for what am I right now grateful? Friends, I'm grateful that I get to write to you. I feel thankful for the music I'm listening to, which is kora accompanied by guitar and drum. Friends, I'm grateful that when I feed the birds, the birds come.

Your Poem

There are many praise poems and exciting list poems. In the United States, two of the most famous list poems are Walt Whitman's *Leaves of Grass* and Allen Ginsberg's *Howl*. You can pick a gratitude poem from either, and find passages rated either PG or MA.

There is a poem by Billy Collins in which he pours himself a drink and is grateful as he sips that the forces of the universe made everything just so.

> *for not making the earth too hot or cold*
> *not making it spin too fast or slow*
>
> *so that the grove of orange trees*
> *and the owl become possible,*
> *not to mention the rolling wave*

The poem ends with him growing ever more "cockeyed with gratitude." Find a poem whose sense of what is sublime is similar to yours. Rolling waves. Orange groves. Owls. There are poems out there that are perfect for you, many. Pick one and put it in your poetry collection. Get to know it. You can let it inspire you to write lists of your own, too, if you want. Include your people.

The griots remind us that we are part of the lists of life too. The taxonomies, and the systems, and mathematics, and also you. Your name here. Maybe the kids don't long for fame in a bad way, maybe they just need to know the wise person has written down their name in the safety of a rhythm and refrain, and is watching, and can see them. What fault to us if it turns out we need to be seen?

* * *

What has appeared on multiple gratitude list poems in my personal research? Berries—strawberries maybe especially. Why? Shape of the heart? Red flesh against the white of teeth? Blueberries and blackberries when people find them growing in the wild, a gift. The Earth turning, that's a big one, the sun continuing to burn. Citrus trees. Cicadas exist. Dapple in the autumn; redbirds in the snow. Giving away, paring down. Sweetgrass. Rolling ocean waves.

The griots remind us that we are part of the lists of life. Coffee appears on gratitude lists, and tea, and light playing on water. The Fibonacci sequence exists. Getting through a pandemic exists.

> *junipers, sameness, loneliness exist;*
> *eider ducks, spiders, and vinegar*
> *exist, and the future, the future*

The mad seesaw of rage and joy, rebellion against the horror and gratitude for the rain. Plum blossoms in the snow. Water and time. Owls. Thanks for the interconnection of everything and for my inclination to feel part of it. Forever and ever, through love and attention, so may it be true, and also for you.

4

On Sleep

Looking Over Your Shoulder

"Everyone used to pray at bedtime. Now what do we do?"

One night Mary and I are at the bar in the entryway of the Blue Angel Theater. It's a narrow space and people are standing right behind us waiting to be let in. I look over my shoulder for a quick survey and turn back around, eyebrows up. I say to Mary, "Mary, Dolly Parton is standing right behind us."

Mary looks over her shoulder and back and is equally starstruck, but also looks at me with pity and says, "Jennifer, that's Fran Lebowitz." These are two exceptionally different-looking famous women. Dolly is a yellow-haired beauty with a famously feminine silhouette. Her dress tends to the princessian. Fran is all masculine gravity. Short black hair, black sport coat, no makeup. Fran is such a New Yorker that she's almost a symbol for the city, and Dolly is the face of Tennessee.

I look over my shoulder again. "Mary, that's Dolly Parton!" I'm too warm, I'm wearing the perfume I for a long time used exclusively, Obsession; it's a sweet citrus but with a musk that made me feel high.

Mary checks and retorts, "Jennifer, it is Fran Lebowitz." Reality takes a record scratch. We both swig our drinks. We look at each other. I purse my lips with the problem, she creases her eyes at me. How I remember it is that Mary thought this impasse was due to me being wrong, while I thought time and space were collapsing.

* * *

Mary's theory wasn't unfair, I made mistakes. I came out of a child-hood where television was more limited than most and was then in grad school in a program that didn't allow time to let in much pop culture. Strange girl in a strange land. But Mary can see that I am sure, and is shaken. I am shaken, for sure. She did not have ditches where such knowledge should be, so I was thinking that the sci-fi movie part of life had begun. So we turn full around. Together. We are facing Dolly Parton and Fran Lebowitz. The two are out together for a night of the-ater. Both have beautiful hazel eyes.

Sure, the universe was back together, but only later did we find out that the writer and the singer were theater buddies. That night, the pairing kept our mood dreamlike, even after the primary puzzle was solved. Night is the time of doubles, obscured faces, trying to say some-thing urgent and not being heard or concurred. The dream is a theater of the absurd. I was always more or less crazy about Mary back then; we were often dressed to the tens in boots and skirts largely for our own amusement but always a little out of our minds. The night is longing, and not for the lark. We were a blond and brown duo, too, her eyes sky blue, mine dark.

I haven't thought of that night in a while, which is funny, because the way Lebowitz writes about sleep helps me loosen up my own nerves about it and also makes me laugh.

> I love sleep because it is both pleasant and safe to use. Pleasant because one is in the best possible company and safe because sleep is the consummate protection against the unseemliness that is the invariable consequence of being awake. What you don't know won't hurt you. Sleep is death without the responsibility.

She's good, isn't she? There are sleep lovers and sleep avoiders. Maybe sleep lovers are not life's biggest fans. By contrast, sleep avoiders do not like the loss of action for one-third of a lifetime. For instance, in 2020, a headline proclaimed that at seventy-four, Dolly Parton says that she sleeps only a maximum of five hours, and that her philosophy is, once you are awake, get to work.

I don't know who is fooling whom. Well, to some degree it is Lebowitz who is fooling me. I found the above quote out of context and read it as if it were an answer to an interviewer's question; perhaps, *So I've read that you sleep a lot?* It is only my training as a historian that saves me, after taking a week to kick in, from a mistake. Research! It's my own rule to never use a quote without reading the book or at least—at least!—the page it came from.

When I remember to find the context I go to my bookshelf and take down her book, and right in the table of contents, I see, "Why I Love Sleep." It is a two-page comic piece defending sleep as if it were a troubling new trend, and with ironic dramatic flair outing herself as a user. The essay reminds me of the common characteristics of comedy and poetry: concision, daring, and surprise. But yes, I'd read the above quote quite seriously at first and found it insightful and personally useful in taking pressure off the way I'd been feeling about sleep. I also like praising what is not usually praised, that life is a batch of itch and sleep is a way out "without positively having to go," as the British poet Stevie Smith put it, speaking of work. ("There I go again. Smile, smile, and get some work to do / Then you will be practically unconscious without positively having to go.") So I suppose I've come full circle and found sleep and work are more the same than I'd thought.

* * *

Is sleep a problem for you? On bad nights everything bores me and nothing puts me to sleep. Aspects of sleep are fraught for a lot of us. A lot of us love being up late at night and then sleep with a passion into the day at the expense of the morning. Some people are scared of the borderland between wakefulness and sleep; they don't like what they think there. I'm scared of the borderland between wakefulness and sleep.

I'm talking to some students at a picnic table under a tree and when this book comes up a British one with big eyes asks, "It's meant to replace prayer with poetry?"

I say, "Sort of, yes. The way you put it assumes prayer came first, and I don't think it did, but you're also not wrong. I'm thinking about how religious people use prayer, and when, in order to learn about what people need and like, what feels natural, what makes us feel supported."

A bespectacled youth, adorable and energetic, stops dead his jittering leg and says, "Oh, what about sleep. We used to pray before sleep. Now what do we do?"

I say, "You tell me," and we all looked around at one another with general mirth. Sleep is private.

A lot of people find relief with sleep-specific words to say and some ritual. If you want that support too, it takes thinking about what sort of problems you tend to be wrestling, and finding words that feel right to you for those concerns. The rest is time and repetition and eventually you will have something steady to say against the phantoms of the night. The stakes are high. The issues are worth naming, interrogating.

How Religion Helps

Religions help people with sleep in a variety of ways. In many Christian homes children are taught to say this prayer before bed:

> Now I lay me down to sleep
> I pray the Lord my soul to keep
> And if I die before I wake
> I pray the Lord my soul to take.

It's catchy, has a nice beat and good rhymes. It's a frightened prayer though, no? The running theme is that I might die, and even *then* I might be in trouble. Religious help with night isn't always, or even usually, offering a cuddly prayer about a snuggly world. This one doesn't even assure us safe passage through danger to morning. But you're not just lying there. You've got something to recite, and it at least seems to know how scared you are.

Religion can also paint night and sleep as especially safe, informative, or fascinating. Bedtime prayers may knit us into the real when they remind us to check in on the suffering of others, wishing them well. Thinking of other peoples' struggles can stop our indulging in self-important imaginings. A Jain prayer before sleep is brief, cheerful, and focused on others. It also subtly yet powerfully broadens one's sphere of interest.

May all be happy.
May all be healthy.
May all achieve perfection.
May all be blessed.

Some religions specifically help with dreams. Native American and First Nations dream catchers catch nightmares in their netting. The Spider Woman, an important supernatural figure, is particularly concerned with protecting children, and these rings of netting began as protections for sleeping children. Also in these cultures, dreams can be understood as bearing information or even as freestanding events of their own, with consequences in waking life.

Religions also tend to regulate some of the entrancing parts of night that can get overwhelming if they go unregulated. Whether you are dreaming or you are awake when the world is asleep, nights can be confusing. Night is the time of labyrinths and doubles. Night is the time of romance and sex, the time of music and dancing. Not to mention drink and drugs. Dreams are a source of creativity and contemplation, nearly an art form, nightly a mystery, whether half or well remembered.

How Art and Science Help

Which of these ring bells for you?

1. Death hovers around sleep avoidance because death and sleep are cousins and not just because death and sleep both lie down. It's the sense of wasted days, the squandering of limited time. Yet we may question the slander of squandering itself, in a universe as odd as this one, given the limitations of choice while alive, and of life span, such that squandering time is a nearly

meaningless notion with only the smallest arguments to the contrary, such as protecting the natural world, helping others, and being wide-awake for your one true and glorious life on beautiful planet Now.

2. Nightmares.
3. Wakeful worry before sleep, shame, self-scrutiny, rabbit holes of memory, and wonderlands of rage.
4. Refusal to go to sleep. Perhaps due to an advanced delight in the otherworldliness of night. Night living can be an art. Secrets are secreted here. Pleasure, yes, erotic and exotic and intoxicant. But if we live too much in the night, we can become divorced from day. The problem with that is, except for artwork and early romance, night isn't known for progress.

Many Americans used to fall asleep to Ed Sullivan and Johnny Carson on television and many still tune in to the comfort of late-night shows. These are rituals with repetitive words and music. They all assure us, as Sullivan used to assure audiences every night, that life, even our life, is a really big show. "Shoe," actually, is how he pronounced it. *We've got a really big shoe for you folks.* You couldn't be here on a better night.

"Man is a genius when he is dreaming," wrote the illustrious Japanese filmmaker Akira Kurosawa. I think it means that what we seek in art is common in dreams. The early twentieth-century author Aldous Huxley wrote, "Every man's memory is his private literature," and we can add, perhaps, that every person's dreams are their experimental literature. Film terms apply to dreams, terms like "montage," "dissolve," and "close-up," but no one is monitoring for continuity. Our dreams forgo concern with such details. The dream is the model for surrealism. Is all modernity a shadow of mere nightly loss of consciousness? It's not just dreams that refuse the bounds of reason but also night thoughts that may spin us out on conjecture way too wild to worry us in the good sense of daylight.

Every night some of us fall asleep or midsleep awaken to thoughts we may not want. It's the way a lot of minds work. We scroll through our pet stash of agonies. We see only half of the world at best. Mary, that's Dolly Parton. Dolly Parton, that's Mary. It's a really big shoe. I fall asleep or midsleep I awaken to thoughts I do not want.

Sigmund Freud gave us a new game to play with our dreams, and a new way to cope with our nightmares. Reading dreams for information can make them less frightening, as is true when religion does it. It's also true that facing what is really bothering you will be frightening too, at least at first. The truth will set us free, yes, and more to the present issue, the truth shall let us sleep.

Your Ritual Draws on Both

I guess it matters a lot what kind of hole you are stuck in, because these tools are pretty specific. It does seem, though, that a lot of us are all in this alone, together. We could, at least, remember that fellowship of the sleepless. And that there are dramatically different ways to think about recurring thoughts, memories, and images.

Life is a great novel with a terrible pacing problem. In the twilight between wakefulness and sleep there is time for other edits on the footage of our lives.

If you ever liked a moment before sleep to tally up your hopes, *Sankofa*, as the Africans say. Left something behind in life? "Go back and get it." *Sankofa* means "to retrieve" in the Akan Twi and Fante languages of Ghana. The image that represents Sankofa is a long-necked bird whose head is turned backward; it is getting its beak around an egg that rests on its own back. One version of the saying that goes with the symbol is, "It is not wrong to go back for that which you have forgotten." I love the rhythm of "go back and get it." There is so much that we might not have left behind. In our culture and in our lives. It can seem easier to keep going forward, but it isn't always easier. How do you know when to go back? Maybe the word or phrase will come to mind as it does for me. Sankofa. *Go back and get it.*

Some people sit at a shrine before sleep. Some kneel at the side of their beds. Some make a gesture with their hands or bow their heads.

Some lie beneath covers and wait to settle deeply before they begin. Often they repeat the same words, night after night, with or without a freestyle portion. These are all ideas to consider, to help one's body know the day is done.

It would be good to have a quite short poem, or a piece of a poem or other poetic text, for nightly use. Also you may want to choose a poem about sleep, of any length, to reread on each repetition of some celestial event; it could be the full moon, whenever you happen to notice one. Whatever is right for you.

Remember how when you were awake at night in childhood threats seemed to loom? Car headlights would cast frenetic, film-noir shadow-shapes across the ceiling and walls. Maybe your sister is awake too and you play *what color car is coming next out the window* or *doll child-birth*. Alone awake at night in childhood, threats are visible in the room. The catastrophe of an empty dress—in truth some of our clothes will outlast us—is suddenly visible, as a ghost, to the child's eye. The dress on a hanger, hooked to the back of a door, and its shadow.

I ask Mary if she remembers what we were seeing at the Blue Angel Theater that night with Dolly Parton and Fran Lebowitz, and Mary remembers. It was called *Pageant: The Musical*, and it was billed as a drag extravaganza. The year was 1991. It all came back to me the way a dream does.

Our Poem

Fernando Pessoa was a poet who would rather I didn't describe him. I'll say he was born and died in Lisbon, Portugal, 1888–1935. He died relatively unknown and is now considered one of the key figures of modern literature. We'll read a poem before saying any more.

The Sleep That Comes Over Me

The sleep that comes over me,
The mental sleep that physically hits me,

The universal sleep that personally overcomes me—
To others
Such a sleep must seem a sleep to fall asleep in,
The sleep of someone wanting to go to sleep,
The very sleep that is sleep.

But it's more, it goes deeper, higher than that:
It's the sleep encompassing every disappointment.
It's the sleep that synthesizes all despair,
It's the sleep of feeling there's a world within me
Without my having said yes or no to it.

Yet the sleep that comes over me
Is just like ordinary sleep.
Being tired at least softens you
Being run-down at least quiets you,
Giving up at least puts an end to trying,
And the end at least is giving up trying to hope.

There's a sound of a window opening.
Indifferent, I turn my head to the left,
Looking over the shoulder that felt it,
And see through the half-opened window
The girl on the third floor across the street
Leaning out, her blue eyes searching for someone.
Who?
My indifference asks.
And all this is sleep.

My God, so much sleep! . . .

Okay, where to begin? At each first reading the poem starts out putting me to sleep. It puts me to sleep until the very end, with the little girl. Then I realize I've been drifting off into a deep space, drift, drift, drift . . . only to have an uncanny encounter with this girl.

Is it an encounter with myself? With the poet? With you, reader, sharing the experience?

If we decide not to let the poem lull us like a lullaby, we can read it for content. The first stanza is punctuated as one sentence, but it needs the next stanza to finish the grammar. Here are the bones of it: "The sleep that comes over me, / To others / . . . must seem . . . / The very sleep that is sleep. / But it's more, it goes deeper, higher than that:." The deeper, higher explanation begins in a poignant cry of disappointment and despair, graduating into a stirring observation that there is a world inside us to which we never gave consent.

While the reader is still responding to that revelation, Pessoa flips his first claim and says that his sleep is ordinary sleep. It's peculiar. Then things get somber again, ordinary miserable thoughts, how weakness and fatigue at least ease sleep, and the wretchedness and relief of giving up hope.

That's when we find the poem's half-open window and see the blue eyes of the girl. The poem's "I" hears the window at first. Not caring, he turns his head. Specifics are useful for inducing a hypnotic trance and Pessoa is a master at invoking them without our half noticing. The specific "to the left" reminds us that at times in life which way we turn our head makes all the difference.

He says that he is "Looking over the shoulder that felt it," that *felt the sound*, and then he sees, though still with the barriers of the merely half-opened window, and of being all the way across the street, not a court-yard, say. Streets can be narrow in old towns, but we can also understand this as a normally impossible sight. Then, wonderfully, the girl herself is also trying for connection, leaning out the window, searching for someone. The question raised, "Who?" is the poem's only one-word line. The poet claims that it is his very indifference that poses the question, a condensation of the usual begging for answers while claiming indifference. Then the poem sums up rather briskly, as if caught in a secret act.

The penultimate line, "And all this is sleep," seems scholastic, outside the drama of life, but in a heartbeat the final line remembers the actual, the urgency, "My God, so much sleep!"

Poetry Lesson: Fernando Pessoa

What if we didn't want to be a person? Pessoa didn't. One way to solve the problem is to disappear as a public person. If "being yourself" never made any sense to you, another way to go beyond that advice and not be a self is to be several people. True, the culture at large regards having an integrated personality as maturity, but it's not the only way to think about the self.

When Pessoa died, a trunkful of writing was found at the foot of his bed. Writing by a few authors. Full lifetimes' worth of achievement collections. Except Pessoa had written all of them. Why shouldn't he be all of them? He did try to make it as a writer but if that wasn't going to happen, why should he be only one of the authors that it felt right for him to spend his life being?

Why do we think of ourselves as one and the same with our feelings and thoughts? We don't always. Sometimes we know we are hungry or tired and therefore don't trust our reactions. We doubt at the edges, but mostly speak of ourselves as a unified feeling and thinking thing, though this notion can freeze us as a narrow identity, and makes us blame ourselves for our anxiety over being pulled in many directions. It has no real basis in reality that I can think of. Pessoa rejects the whole thing. His best known work is *The Book of Disquiet*, which is a marvel, and the intimacy of its disquiet is a great solace.

I think of myself as an I, a unified feeling and thinking thing. It's both my default setting and (big surprise) seems like good common sense. But I am persuaded to the contrary when I give it thought. If I give the idea of a singular self any thought, I can't keep it up in good faith. I find myself working too hard to make the data fit.

There's the person you would have been if you'd had big luck, and the person you are when you have the least of what you need. There's the part of you that is loving and kind and a barking under-wraps dog that only wants. What if you identified more strongly with a usually dimin-ished aspect of your story? With a slight variation to a story it can be a drama or comedy and depending how we tell your tale there might be a true-crime, romance, sci-fi, and literary version of you.

Pessoa isn't the first writer to scintillate others by popping corks on sparkling wines that we hadn't realized were under such pressure. But wow.

Perhaps all modern art was invented first by sleep. Perhaps all modern artists look over their shoulder and see a pillow.

* * *

Those fast film-noir shadows when we lived near a busy corner. I'd do a lot for sleep, to stop overthinking my life. I used to drink but stopped. Lately I get by on overthinking other people's lives, listening to memoirs and fiction instead of drinking. Stories, stories, like bottles, clanging around. There are odd consequences to any bingeing.

I don't know what's back there, but I know if we take turns looking over our shoulders, we won't see the same thing, and it's not because it's not the same thing back there. (Checks over her shoulder.) It's the same thing back there. I stopped using Obsession, by Calvin Klein, because someone let me know how *over* it was. I hadn't known that scents had fashions. I did know that for a while Obsession was everywhere; until I bought my own I'd practically float-follow girls like a cartoon bear on a whiff of pie. At twilight the streetlights go on. When the sun gets itself over the buildings in the morning, the streetlights go off again. I've always had to stalk sleep. I have so many sleep-hunter skills, but no luck. Or bad habits. I'm up nights.

Your Poem

For nightly use, consider an excerpt or fragment. For most purposes, it seems best to choose a whole poem, because if we are to meditate on a text, it's nice to know it was carefully made to be the subject of meditation. If, however, you want to use the words on a frequent basis, brevity is crucial. There are tons of tiny poems. Or you can grab a swatch of poetry or poetic prose. If you do, though, it's best if you know a bit about the larger text before you commit to the fragment, and try, over time, to learn more, when the occasion arises.

You'll find comments about sleep in much great writing. Look for any few lines that feel worthy of regular regard. In *Macbeth*, Shakespeare calls sleep every good thing but sneaks in more:

> *Sleep that knits up the raveled sleeve of care,*
> *The death of each day's life, sore labor's bath,*
> *Balm of hurt minds, great nature's second course,*
> *Chief nourisher in life's feast.*

Sleep is a knitter knitting back to rights a sleeve that has come unraveled in the day's work. Sleep is a hot tub when you are sore, sleep soothes our hurt feelings and pained thoughts. He even says sleep is life's chief nourisher. Yet, note the scary one in there, at least for people who bristle at the idea of death.

It is popular to pray right before bed. To some degree, prayers become common because they are poetic, because they rhyme or have a compelling strangeness. Rationalists too should lean into the poetic if they desire words to finish the day and ease them into dreamland. Dreamland is a strange land and deep, so we know the staircase down to it might spiral out of the norm. Also if the grammar of our day were never garbled it would cut our capacity to notice when the truth is at odds with the known. Put pieces of poems or inscrutable prose into your poetry collection and if you feel like saying some poetic words before bed, you do.

Pick a poem with dream, sleep, or dozing in the title, for their power of suggestion, or insomnia (for company), if it applies.

* * *

On bad nights everything bores me and nothing puts me to sleep. Now I lay me. It's better with lines to say. It's better with poetic ideas and company. It's all behind us and right here for us to find, perhaps just over your shoulder. May all be happy, all healthy. We see only half of the world at best. Mary, that's Dolly Parton. Dolly Parton, that's Mary. Fran Lebowitz, this is Jennifer Michael Hecht. It's a really big shoe.

"It's the sleep of feeling there's a world within me / Without my having said yes or no to it." Film clips of memories, imaginary triumphs, imaginary tragedies. Asleep we've a thousand eyes, and awake but one, but the wakefulness of one good eye is like the sun. "Jennifer, that's Fran Lebowitz." The night has its hazel eyes. The little girl has blue eyes, leaning out of a window, looking for someone. Who?

Night is the time of doubles, obscured faces, fun-house mirrors, trying to say something urgent and not being heard. The dream is a theater of restoration, of the cruel, of longing, of the absurd. "Sleep is death without the responsibility." Maybe we need some rest? Or should we all stay up and make something? Research! Go back and get it.

Why do I sleep? To find out what I don't think.

Night is the turning of this Earth's face from the light. If we are looking over our shoulders, we won't see everything. The empty dress. Those darting film-noir shadows when we lived on a busy street. Then later, I stop using Obsession, the streetlights go on, and sleep knits up the raveled sleeve of care. "And all this is sleep." Dolly and Fran and *Pageant* at the Blue Angel Theater, which is no longer there. If day is prose, night is poetry. And so we sleep on, our backs to the darkness, our eyes shut to the violet moon, curling in our beds into the shape of our spiral galaxy. And what a galaxy, to be producing dreams like these.

5

On Meditation

Contemplating a Poem

"Meditation saved my life twice, but I can't get myself to do it."

Off the stage, post–book signing, I'm sitting with a dozen people still discussing. At talk of meditation a muscular older man, gray at his temples, shakes his head *No* in long, slow swings. "I love meditation," he adds, "but I can't get myself to do it—even though it saved me. Twice. Years ago."

It all began with a sports injury. He'd been leading his team to victory when he heard his body crack. It seemed career-ending. In the hospital he was emotionally shattered too, to the extent that it had been hard to keep thoughts of ending his life out of his mind. But the team's trainer also led a Hindu meditation group, and when he joined, it eventually brought him back to the field and to glory. Years later, a new injury forced him to retire, and depression hit hard, until he went back to that meditation group. It worked again and he was soon happily coaching.

Now he needed it again, but it felt too hard. His old master was long gone. He tried meditation centers and temples, learned many techniques—mostly sitting-still, empty-mind meditations—and practiced each for a while, but nothing caught. Many who try meditation and sing its praises find they can't keep at it. It's a riddle. The graying athlete had once practiced regularly and with impressive results. Why couldn't he do it anymore? What was missing?

He guessed habit, adding that he'd rarely felt like doing his group's meditation chants, even in his most active period. He'd had a love-hate relationship with particular chants; when he discussed the Guru Gita he described it as more like boredom-ecstasy. You can't really hate something that sometimes shoots you into the stratosphere.

In the moment, in the circle, I agreed that habit was a wondrous-strange human feature, both bountiful and cruel. I, too, had gained much from meditation, of various kinds, and I, too, could lapse fla-grantly, unable to start up and be steady at will. Maybe you rock at it, but statistically, it's likely you have been more of a rolling stone.

Our ex-athlete allowed that in service to his theory, that habit was the crux of the cure, he should go back to the same meditation his coach practiced, or close. That sounded right to me. I was figuring that, beyond mere habit, community and purpose were important to his past success, and I hoped he'd reconnect with people from his old group.

I later learned more, about Hindu, Buddhist, and Jain meditation, becoming entranced with a world of poetic chants and came to under-stand more about habit, purpose, and connection. It's funny to look back and see these themes in the context of sports. When our athlete's meditation worked, he'd had his team's zeal and a teacher-coach—and they all had games to win. In the religious setting for meditation, it is commonly associated with forcefully ingrained habit, and grand pur-poses, often communal. Those of us who practice nonreligious medita-tion tend to forget that.

Another factor that now seems key is the significance of the chants themselves, as meditative ideas in words. Words matter. If our ancestors trained us to speak words while we wonder, why not give some thought to what we're saying?

How Religion Helps

Meditation practice, or dhyana, began in ancient India and became a feature of many of humanity's major and minor religions. Earliest men-tions of dhyana are in the Vedas, the oldest religious texts on Earth. Meditation was born with poetry—the Sanskrit root of "dhyana" is *Dhi*, relating to the goddess of wisdom and poetry. Later in the Vedas, in the Upanishads, dhyana is contemplation of three worlds: human poetry, nature, and unseen forces—all mutually influenced. As such, spending time with poetry was a potent act. What happens in the poetic imagination translates into matter. Matters.

Early Hinduism and Jainism developed meditation as an inner search for one's true self, in harmonious peace amid the tumult of nature and desire. Practices for pursuing this state of mind grew up over centuries to include fasting, standing still, keeping silent, and chanting verses. In religions around the world an array of trance behavior is on offer, often practiced with a paradoxical idea or poetic writing. Jains chant mantras while focusing on "subtle facts" like "life and nonlife," or the vastness of the universe. Our athlete's chant tradition includes the belief that with more voices come stronger results; when you join the chant, you are always helping.

The Buddha lived as much as a millennium after the origins of the Vedas. He used many enlightenment techniques and awakened to know that there is no self. What we think of as the self is in fact a flow of sensations and matter. We are not separate from one another, nor from the world.

The Buddha explained that poetic, philosophical insight could be the royal road to enlightenment, for those with minds suited to it. Poetic texts have been central to many threads of meditation.

These poetic texts include Zen koans, short, enigmatic provocations such as, "What is the sound of one hand clapping?" Sit with this and roll through any responses. I pause first on the idea that clapping isn't a thing one hand does: the problem seems bogus, semantic. But that's not a stopping point, because knowing this invites a luminous correlate: living isn't a thing a person does alone. Our noise, our existence, comes in relation to one another. We believe one another into being. It's just one possible interpretation. Let's try another koan:

What is your original face before your parents were born?

I first respond to "*What is your original face?*" and think of my child-hood features. Next, "*What was your face before you were born?*" conjures the self in utero. And then, with "*before your parents were born?*" my "I" goes blank. How tender and strange to imagine your parents, the first keepers of the courthouse of your heart, still curled, blameless, not yet even understood as in the room they're in. A single koan can startle forever. Often, acolytes are assigned just one koan for life.

Koans developed from Chinese meditation and poetry. After the heyday of a Chinese literary game that produced short cryptic poems, these became the focus of a meditation called "Chan," in China's Song dynasty (960–1297). Here's a beauty by twentieth-century Chan master Hsu Yun.

> *One hour and then another.*
> *Inevitable trek, step by step.*
> *Whenever I meet you, we each smile.*
> *But who is it who drags your corpse around?*

It begins by invoking the inexorable forward motion of time. Many changes flow back and forth but not time; time won't budge backward, ever, no matter the stakes. We're invited on the trek and told to go step-by-step. The poem speaks to the pretense of social smiles in the words "we each smile. / But," and these lines also prompt memories of true friends. Like friends, koans aren't to be resolved; you stay with them and notice how they act on you. The stunning final line rattles my sense of self whenever I read it. Even as a child, my little will was dragging this body around. And into the future.

How Art and Science Help

The term "mindfulness" is ubiquitous today because psychologists in the 1970s borrowed techniques from Buddhist mindfulness practice to help their patients. The Buddha said that not everyone could devote time to meditation alone, but one could still practice mindfulness for periods of time while working. He described staying in the moment, noticing exterior sensations and interior thoughts and feelings, as they pass through.

One technique common in modern mindfulness is called a "body scan," wherein you bring awareness to successive areas of the body. Studies have shown that staying in the moment in this way can be a keen relief for the anxious and the traumatized. In general, scientific studies of meditation have shown marked benefit for those who suffer from stress and depression. Meditation can help control pain and aid in addiction recovery.

Recent studies have shown that meditation can help control "rumination"—repetitive thinking about negative emotional experiences—which is key because rumination is a partial cause of a range of mental illnesses, such that reducing rumination reduces the later appearance of diseases quite resistant to treatment once they arrive. Study of depression led the way, and for decades now, robust and careful studies show that posttreatment degrees of rumination predict the likelihood of relapse of major depressive disorder. More surprisingly, controlling rumination also appears to significantly diminish the symptoms and relapse rates of schizophrenia.

A primary feature of meditation is repeatedly bringing the mind back to focus on something singular or simple. Poetry has patterns of sounds. It often presents an image and wanders away from it in returning waves. Reading poetry itself can be a meditation; it awakens us, and bores us, and reawakens us.

Your Ritual Draws on Both

Any mindfulness can be a respite from screens and social media, from world-scale distress, and from the quest for success.

If you join a meditation group, you can join in their rituals. See how it feels. Burn their incense, drink the tea they offer, adopt the group's greetings and farewells. If you meditate alone, perhaps include a few of the cultural pleasures that are their own kind of meditation, such as drinking tea, arranging flowers, or considering an enigmatic poem.

We need a middle way. On one hand the most science-friendly

versions of meditation are missing out on more than we acknowledge in losing the religious and traditional aspects of meditation. Individuals, clumps of monks around the world, and whole cultures have devoted themselves to meditation for the inner experience, yes, but they also kept at it because they had delightful or majestic gods to visit, and a sense of world-shaking group purpose. Whether they meant karma and getting the world into balance, or saving souls from hell, religions have encouraged followers to meditate for other people, for group salvation. On the other hand, the more religious versions feel rich but offend reason. In between all the hands is the heart. We can frame meditation more in terms of imaginative adventure, or concentration on a generative idea. Poetic meditation can be as simple as rereading a poem and sitting with it with meditative purpose, remembering that others like you are doing the same.

Poetry offers positive perceptions of what humanity is and what we mean to one another. Ideas matter, words matter. What we do on Earth together matters. Aren't you and I doing something that matters right now? Here I am writing this and you are reading it and it feels intense to me, talking to you about this. I'll never forget it. I recall the graying athlete at the head of this chapter saying that he was able to remember the meaning of small pieces of the chants, especially in the Guru Gita, because they made him happy.

We could read a poem. You can read over the whole poem each time or choose a few lines for special focus. Anything that beckons your attention will mushroom with meaning over time.

Our Poem

The title, "Wannabe Hoochie Mama Gallery of Realities' Red Dress Code," has a lot going on—even the individual words in it prime us to longing and hidden pleasure, science and philosophy. The word "code" alone recalls a hospital crisis, a cipher, a credo, and the combination to a lock. With such a title, thank goodness the first line is easy and about meditation. Then buckle your seat belt, because without betraying its

stillness the poem expands to take in the whole world. The poet is Thylias Moss.

Wannabe Hoochie Mama Gallery of Realities' Red Dress Code

I have learned to be still
I have learned that I don't have to go anywhere
to find the center of the universe
Anything can be that center
From any point, any speck, any dust mite
I can widen
what that speck includes
what that speck is willing
to embrace
what that speck can be the center of
until everything that is possible to get to
is included in the circle
so I have learned to be still
to let everything pass through me
as sieve
as net
that manages to catch
awareness of what passes through
me as I pass through them
in an exchange of tiny ropes of essences
(so I can wear necklaces everywhere, protein loops)
There is a claiming of me by what passes through
and the part of me passed through
are claimed by parts of what passes through
that touch it
so these point by point embraces
together make up realities
and can be put together in any order
to form one big remarkable thing
as what passes through me

passes through what passes through
everything else
in every form of reality
that is possible to make
from any locations possible
in any reality that is possible
including realities
made in imagination
for so much passes through
the mind
—O see, O hear, O touch how things connect—
Because of what's possible
Because of all the hands
all the specks—which can be any shape
made of any substance
which can be any form—
Because of all the hands
all the specks touching in the exchanges
and groping their way
Because of all the hands involved
in shuffling pieces of maybe unlimited numbers
of flexible realities
& because of how easy it is to connect dots
one day red might arrive
some planes and geometries might meet
an event of red dress might happen
for dress is not always red
red happens to dress
red dress is an event
red might slip by dress
when they are on paths that do not cross
somewhere for some length of time
I do not put on a red dress
It is something outside of wardrobes
acceptable for me

some of what I do
some of what I believe and practice
could be questioned
if I put on a red dress
but if I am still
an event of red dress might happen
if I do not move from this spot
so that specks of both red
and dress
can find me
then there will be
—while they pass through—
realities I can feel
specks of red
and specks of dress
outfit and configure different parts of me
at different speeds
for different lengths of time
during which hoochie mama gets in
at least one of all possible equations
and I will walk out of here
where I have stood as if hard at work
on display in a gallery
no worse for the where I've been
apparently unchanged
but the red dress
was put on under my skin
and it fits me
Oh it's so amazing
that everything that passes through
fits.

The poem begins with "I have learned to be still" and ends with a premonition of the speaker moving. She's been trapped but she's growing, and she's certain that in due time she'll saunter out the door.

For me the poem has a story in it, as well as four smashing ideas. The first idea is based on the fact that cosmologists today say there is no center of the universe; space doesn't work that way, any place can be the center. The poet digests the loss and revises: Okay, then I am the center of the universe. Anyone can be that center, all it requires is awareness.

The story starts here too, because we glimpse that this ode to the glorious center is aspirational, a concoction of philosophical balm for the pain of life on the margins. The poet's persona is sidelined but has moxie.

The next big idea in the poem is based in the microscopic, the sub-atomic. It, too, is an insight that seems intended to refute evidence of her distress. She says that on a micro level, you get everything the world has to offer, because everything passes through. You change and you change the world because occasionally, in all the transit, something "manages to catch," influencing both sides of the encounter. It brings new meaning to Milton's line "They also serve who only stand and wait" because there is no such thing as only standing or only waiting. Her witness is more than witness; it alters the world it meets, has wit. If you are being, you are interacting, and if you are interacting, you are learning and influencing.

The personal story, it seems to me, is that our speaker has to stay still and someone else gets to be the center of the universe. The phrase "center of the universe" means egotism, and is also used to describe a hotbed of activity, or an object of devotion. Our speaker doesn't seem to experience or to be any of these centers. Instead, she has the insight that awareness is all. Holding that insight isn't simple. The poem's use of a "speck" as a main actor will carry its opposite, the universe, with it, but we are out of the macro and into the small for the rest of the poem.

The third idea is also a consolation. Here it is fine to make no definite designs, because once you include everything in the universe in your art, it can be left to its own order, "one big remarkable thing." This whole truth must include realities made in the imagination because the specific way our minds process things determines a lot. We cannot know reality without using some imaginative play, if only to get beyond the kinds of order our brains tend to see. The poet closes what I think of as the first part of the poem with an exaltation, "—*O see, O hear, O touch how things connect*—," celebrating how we are already interrelated.

The center of the poem is a chunk of "Because of" lines that offer a reason to hope when it seems like you'd have to be a dope. It's because of all the hands. That is, the answer to all the unbelievable things that humans have done, from the pyramids to the boot-prints on the moon, is that there were so many hands on the job, over generations.

The "Because of" section codes in how that might work with lapidary care. Ask it this desperate question and find here a quite logical answer. Why should I have hope? Why should speck-like me even try? "Because of what's possible / Because of all the hands involved." Because people groping toward knowledge or change does actually slowly add up to knowledge and change. These "Because of" lines are also a fine answer to the "How?" of thought and free will. What can't be expected emerges from all the constant exchanging.

The final part of the poem takes all the above and applies it to a hot red dress. There's a fifth "because of" that starts us off with the idea of a red dress at random: "some planes and geometries might meet" such that the red dress happens. It's a delectable notion, that "red dress is an event." Seen with a squint of time's eye, all things are events. All things come into being, are changed and create change, and then melt out of being. There are no things, there are only events.

The poet desires the red dress but avows that it could send the wrong message, could make people question some of what she believes and practices. Probably a lot of us want to be in a red dress too, and there are a lot of reasons we're not. It's an internal war for many of us, at times, the question of whether our red-dress quotient is the right way to spend our lives. It is a paradox of the human experience that travel and adventure seem best, and so does staying put and creating (a family, a contribution, roots). That's just the deal. You can be ripped apart by it, or not be—by practicing gratitude that you got any life at all, that you got one in.

That's the fourth idea. Moss reminds us how peculiar the odds were against any of us existing at all when she says, "hoochie mama gets in / at least one of all possible equations." The "hoochie mama" of the title is suddenly here and inseparable from the speaker. The red dress is also "redress"—compensation for wrongs. She tells us she expects to walk away with the redress under her skin.

We are kept at enough of a distance that we have room to come toward the poem ourselves. We are what fills in the gaps. You will fill in the gaps differently than I do. A reader may fill them in differently on different days. This can be true with any poem, but with free verse poems, like this one, freedom of interpretation is part of the point.

Poetry Lesson: Free Verse

What is free about "free verse"? Often poetry is defined as emotion contained in rules of form, so the simple answer is that free verse breaks the old rules of form while still serving profound expression. The earliest mention of "free verse" was in France in 1909, as *vers libre*, but this new style really caught on after the barbarism of World War I discredited the civility of civilization. Why obey the strictures of a society that razes its splendid ancient cities and grinds up its gorgeous young men?

Social rules had been breaking down in the last decades of the nineteenth century, one could say because of the rise of big cities (all that served them and came with them). Yet it seems that it was the war that removed a sense of obedience in matters of culture. The dead and the demented and the grotesque of it all.

It is also understood that the joy of free verse was linked to the joy of free sex. Both were in radical bloom at the beginning of the twentieth century. Free sex and free verse both pounce and riff instead of playing the notes of set ceremony.

Also, free verse mimics the meandering of thought and conversation. Taking readers into the roaming of your thought flow conjures up intimacy. Free verse feels improvisational, has room for the unplanned, the not quite right. In confusion is the possibility of new insight.

While not sticking to the rules of philosophy, free verse escapes a knotty philosophical problem, which is that we can't know what we don't know, except somehow we do learn, imagine, make progress, and invent the internet. The poet zones out and listens to what arises, and that material is still shaped in free verse, but now around meaning, feeling, or sound, without fealty to preset forms.

Free verse can include the voice of madness. We want to include the voice of madness because modernity tends to the mechanical cookie-cutter bureaucratic. Sometimes chaos feels true.

* * *

When I was young my family—parents, sister, brother, and I—attended a school of the Maharishi Mahesh Yogi, the Beatles' guru. It was on a series of Saturdays. I know it was 1978 because one day I worried throughout the session about being late to *Superman*, with Christopher Reeve, at the mall, with a friend I was meeting there. I was a weirdo to be on my way over from meditation, but I was already a known weirdo, so it was fine.

There was rage in my childhood home. My parents were hippie-ish, but mostly at a distance, into the fashion, ideas, and music that you can enjoy when you can't drop out because you are married and have spent your twenties having three babies and getting a physics professorship. They'd married young to get out of brutal childhoods. When we asked how they fell in love they both said, "We got married to get out of our parents' houses." It was on brand that we went to the meditation classes—it seemed cool, good, and advanced. We were a mess though, on the secret side. Someone leaving the table crying midway through dinner, capping some table-wide competitive battle, was not unusual.

The meditation we learned was calming and also exciting, as the deeply interior experience changes both slowly and suddenly. Adults were to do it for twenty minutes, children for the number of minutes of their age. I was preteen. In one-on-one sessions, we were each given a mantra, a Sanskrit word, and told it was a secret. When the young woman initiating me started saying my mantra, bobbing her long, blond ponytail and waiting for me to echo her, I didn't get it and she laughed and motioned for me to join in. Even here, without the element of embarrassment I'd never have remembered the scene.

For years my family would each separately meditate in the morning, and before dinner my parents would call out, "Meditation time," and we'd retreat to our corners. I'd sit on a giant black floor pillow my mother had sewn. We'd all drowsily head to the table after. It helped a bit with the crying, but it definitely helped me somehow, then and later, still. I've practiced different kinds of meditation, not that much, but various, and yet when I'm troubled, it's my childhood mantra that comes to me.

It's also true that the hallway leading to the classroom was lined with large photographs of people cross-legged and supposedly "flying." The claims of flying were bizarrely central to that branch of meditation, which otherwise offered more reasonable goals. Dad laughed at them every time we passed. "They're on trampolines and have bounced," he'd say, and we'd chime with his "Look at their hair!," which was indeed caught midbounce.

Isn't it enough that a florid and disgruntled little house in Hempstead was taught to take a break twice a day and repeat our Sanskrit words? Do we also have to pretend it makes you fly? To me, the nutty idea more worth cultivating is that hope is lighter than air, and launchable from most any willing runway.

Your Poem

Look for a poem that talks about the porousness of things, about interaction and exchange. It's a significant theme in poetry, as it is in meditation, so it will be easy to find one. Stillness is another poetic subject that suits meditation and is a rib cage of poetry, so if you look around, you'll find those bones.

Or take an inspired jump from the Moss poem and look for a red dress. Whatever catches your eye. Some image or notion in a poem that slots into this subject for you like a lucky nickel at the great carnival in the sky. Pick that one. Place it in your poetry collection, in its designated section.

If the idea of often rereading your poem straight through is not enticing, start smaller. Choose a line or any snippet you can remember, at least for a few moments at a time. You can meditate by reading or reciting these words. You will likely find they lose and gain meaning over time.

When you go back to the poem as a whole, you will likely find it fascinating to see how your snippet fits into the larger frame.

* * *

Rumination is a problem of holding on and not letting go. The iconic modern person is sketched with a short attention span, but a long capacity for worry. A sprint of an attention span for books, say, and other countries' disasters; and long-distance legs for personal anxiety. We can meditate by reading poetry if we give it that intention. We get hit with so much life to manage and yet can feel that the struggle is making us miss out on life. Poetry shows us porous, continuous with the world, gaining through mere being. Gaining through loss. Poetry can be a way to be free, alive, transcendent.

I hope the graying athlete found his way to some practice. Or maybe he continued to show up for cultural events and stay late in deep talk with people. Spiritual awakening and poetic epiphany are related experiences. I love many meditations, but for me meditation on poetry has been my steady practice. Stillness, yes, giggles the poem, and proceeds to use stillness to encompass the entirety of space-time, psychology, and religion.

It is in poetry that we learn that nouns are really verbs, caught in a moment as a dancer in a strobe light. Atoms are just being your chair for now. In our roiling world a red dress is a happening. Red might randomly happen to dress. All the hunger and multiplicity concludes that it is glorious and sufficient to have one life. And whatever passes through, fits. Because of all the hands. Because it is not always our turn to win. Because sometimes it is our turn to win, and we have to get back up and do it. Because in many flamboyantly troubled families, there were also a lot of sweet stories. Because the redress we need is under the skin.

HOLIDAYS

6

On Happier Holidays
Stocking Your Cabinets of Culture

"It's a pagan holiday! Right?"

Many nonreligious people celebrate religious holidays along with family, friends, and country—to one degree or another. They enjoy it, or put up with it, but a lot of them find that playing reindeer games of a faith not your own can be stressful, too. Psychology calls it "cognitive dissonance" when pressure causes us to trust a belief against solid evidence. It's psychologically costly, an unseen drain on your battery charge.

When ex-Christians tell me they celebrate an aspect of Christmas, they often add, "It's a pagan holiday!"—delivered with a laugh, as if eating a caramel apple and proclaiming, "It's fruit!" They are saying, *These behaviors can belong to people who are not believing Christians, because they were enjoyed before Christianity began.* They use it to resolve a conflict about taking part in these pine-wreathed festivities. More serious tones are reserved for the practical reasons they celebrate Christmas, such as to make their kids happy, or to stay in grandpa's good graces, or just for the social enjoyment of it.

Some of us have heard holiday bells chime and breathed feast-day aromatics all our lives. Maybe that's you. Maybe even solo on a space station you'd at least gesture in the holiday's direction. Perhaps as Mecca rolls by below, the tan desert amid a blare of ocean blue.

The truth is that holidays can't help but have features that predate them. So not only are ex-Christians right to chirp that Christmas is a pagan holiday; we all should be chirping something like it about all holidays. Today's religious symbols and gestures have stood for other beliefs, religious or cultural. A spruce sprig has symbolized ideas that jibe with many a worldview, such as spring renewal or evergreen love. When there is a gesture you feel hypocritical or melancholy about doing, because you don't believe, you are free to have your own meaning for it. That water ritual might actually be as much yours—some ancient rite of poignant hope nothing to do with the religion in which you were raised—as anyone's.

Imagine this anthropological thought experiment: How would life feel for a Jan Doe if all the sacred-sounding talk they heard rang false to them? How does Jan feel if the wisdom offered at annual sacred times is known by them to be untrue? How does it feel for Jan Doe if the texts are explicitly against them? Many people, in many societies, have had their beliefs and life stories supported by the message of their holidays and the words spoken there. A lot of us don't get that. Do you?

People can thrive when their actual beliefs are incorporated in their holidays. We make our holidays, and then our holidays make us.

A disjuncture between actual belief and public action can make life feel empty, sometimes, whether you see the metaphysical chasm you're in, in all its gory glory, or you're mystified and don't know why you are crying. It is weird to live in a moment wherein so many celebrate in words we don't believe. We can turn this around and have fun doing it. Let's think about how to tailor the fit.

How Religion Helps

Are your holidays happy? People often show up for religious celebrations for beliefs they don't share, and with a few tweaks these special days will better suit our needs. Traditional ceremonies often have religious explanations, but there are also human reasons for such rites. At the very least, annual celebrations help us feel the progress of each year, and bond those who take part, nurturing a community.

Specific traditions address specific issues: this holiday easing fear of death, this one lifting shame and regret, another for rest, yet another coaxing hope for the future of the planet.

How do your religious holidays work? Let's start with a quick self-assessment about the major religious holidays in your life. Note down at least one or two answers to these, if you can—it will help to have some answers inked in already when you come to the next part.

- What holidays would you feel uncomfortable missing entirely?
- What holidays do you personally work hardest on, in whatever way?
- Are there holidays you dread?
- Which holiday most delights you?
- Are there holidays outside your tradition that you find attractive?
- Which holidays do people in your life care about most?

Now consider that each holiday has distinct traits, which I'm calling their *cabinet of culture*, containing all a holiday's traditional doings, and none of the doctrines.

Everyone has noticed that a cache of treats and traits appear on major holidays, in brief abundance, and then vanish for a year. I believe charting this in more detail brings lasting insight. To that end, I've worked out a template to organize the holiday features onto shelves.

Specific Holiday

A singular drink, type of meal, kind of sweet,
particular music, special plant, featured beast,
decoration and light, way to greet,
style of dress, featured hue or two,
an outdoor crowd event,
a signature live show, a film, an avatar,
and a quick rebellion where the usually tame
are allowed to be hellions,
or the rich serve food to the poor.

Not all religions have something for each cabinet compartment as I've just sketched them. Ancient holidays have had time to accrue traits, so the cabinet of such a holiday can be overflowing. Newer ones can be comparatively spare.

Here's a cabinet limited to one example for each feature, based on my local experience.

Christmas Cabinet

Eggnog, baked ham, sugar cookies,
"White Christmas," potted poinsettia, reindeer,
window candles, "Merry Christmas!"
dressy casual, green and red,
town-square tree lighting,
The Nutcracker, It's a Wonderful Life,
Santa, kids ripping open presents,
Donations to nonprofits soar.

Note that the items here aren't religious doctrine, but are linked with the holiday. Once you've jotted down a few cabinets for the holidays you listed above, take a look and see if the holidays you love have full cabinets, or mostly empty ones. What patterns do you see? Here are some questions you might ask yourself:

- Does decoration and light tend to mean a lot in the holidays you like?
- Do you love or dread the holidays for which you work the hardest?
- What do your favorite holidays have in common?
- Do you show up for your favorite holiday features, or often miss out on them?
- Do you create the holiday features?

A map helps us see the land, and a graph helps us see ourselves. A holiday cabinet is a bit of both, but all yours, so you can reach in and add things, or take things away.

Wouldn't it be kind of amazing to have even one more click of clarity and power over how your year takes care of you? Think about the people you love and whether they have this clarity and power. Do they? Do you? I don't have all the clarity I want and even less power, but when I work on this I get a bit more insight now and again, and it's worth it.

How Art and Science Help

Secular holidays can fill the same template, especially if they have been around awhile. In my world the older common nonreligious holidays are Thanksgiving, Halloween, New Year's Eve, and Independence Day. These have special foods and drinks—I think of turkey, candy corn, champagne, burgers on the grill. Costuming is mild for Thanksgiving, wild for Halloween, and ritzy for New Year's Eve.

Halloween has a role as a countercultural holiday, a goth prom, a day to dress scary, witty, or sexy. It is also a rare chance for disguising masks, for many people. To be out in the world with a foreign face can be a kind of bliss, a new glimpse of yourself. Ditto hitting the streets with face paint that says you're one of a group today, not quite a person. If you look at the holidays that made your list above, how much does the costuming have to do with your attraction or avoidance? Perhaps try out what you usually dodge. Is there a way to double up on what you love, say, a masked ball for New Year's Eve?

Independence Day puts us outside and has us cook there, like we did every night for a few hundred thousand years. How could it not matter that at least one night a year our culture hustles us outside again to char our chow under the stars? Independence Day also arranges a spectacle of fireworks, as do many nations' day of violent break from king or colonizer. It's not random. Fireworks, in person, are warlike in noise, sulfuric smell, and shock of flash.

Beyond the battle-feel of an up-close display, fireworks are also a sweet example of *Homo sapiens* at play, improving on stars with action scenes and color. As familiar as such displays are for days of military and political victory, fireworks also tend to be elaborate on New Year's Eve, surprising us into feeling we have arrived at a fresh start.

New Year's Eve has two avatars: a baby, naked but for a sash telling the new year, and a robed white-haired man, for the year ending. The modern New Year's Eve spectacular is the live broadcast of successive world capitals as they count down and erupt in jubilation. It's the past rolling hourly into the future, around the globe—the ultimate bleacher-style human wave, in sparkled light. We are reminded of the whole Earth that night, as time rolls over it in spangles.

You may choose to consider each of the holidays you noted above as important to you and fill in the template of its cabinet. Circle the cabinet items you do every year, or nearly. Put stars on items you like but often miss, for one reason or another. Are your holidays overstuffed? Empty? If the holidays that move you are modern, like Pride, or Martin Luther King Jr. Day, or Yom HaShoah, which is Holocaust Remembrance Day you may find the cupboards are bare. They haven't had time to accrue a full pack of features. Why not take steps to fill them in?

Japanese tradition celebrates the first of many things done in the new year. Some of these significant firsts are *kakizome* (first writing), *hatsuyume* (first dream), *hakizome* (first housecleaning), and *hatsuburo* (first bath). Children are often left out of the celebration of the turn of midnight. If you have kids around, would they too like to refresh the page?

Your Ritual Draws on Both

Secular holidays tend to be newer and about something that someone today cares about. Religious holidays tend to be old and about amorphous ideas and historic battles. But the cabinets of secular holidays tend to be nearly empty, while the religious ones are overflowing. We can create a better balance by adding fresh meaning to the old religious ones and adding a few more engaging features to the newer ones.

Within religion the sensory stimulation of a bountiful holiday cabinet often does dedicated psychological work. If the Interfaithless want the same, we can think about the holidays we take part in, find a core idea we like in each of them, notice what we savor in its cabinet of culture, and create a link between the adored ideal and the cherished holiday feature. Such connections exist, but we can enhance what we like if we are intentional about it. The first and perhaps largest step is noticing.

We could assign items to holidays, and see if they stick. Invent a beverage and serve it with a poem. The poetic sacred doesn't always happen on its own, so it's good to create a designated moment to feel what there is to feel. Maybe you have already felt that such a designated moment was missing for, say, Memorial Day.

For believers, some features of holidays are also urgent business, opportunities to secure luck, forgive and be forgiven, accrue good karma, or prepay for an afterlife worth after-living. Believers in the poetic sacred can also have important relationships with holidays. We can look for opportunities to reflect.

Ask yourself what a given holiday means. Many holidays mean family. Others take on romance, hope and rebirth, shame and forgiveness. Some are public grief over common loss. Many holidays are for the harvest and can be recast as days for the Earth. Some holidays mean let's all start again because I really need to. A lot of people do.

Our Poem

Big happy holidays may already have poems associated with them, and these are likely to mention the classic features of the day either in a story or a list. They are not likely to be any poetry reader's favorite poem—almost by definition they are a bit simple.

Consider two examples. Diwali, "the festival of lights," is a Hindu holiday that has a big presence around the world, and every year people share poems listing its features: sweets, fireworks, firecrackers, hung lights, and temple visits. And in the United States, the poem "A Visit from St. Nicholas" by Clement Clarke Moore is key to Christmas, also a world-famous holiday; it provides images, names the reindeer, and invents the nonstirring mouse. What great poetry does is more secret and sideways than that. What if we saw encountering such holiday verse as a prompt to read a better poem, one that can take some existential weight?

The great poems about holidays tend to be more ambivalent than the marquee holiday poems. Our poem is by one of the greats of haiku, Kobayashi Issa (1763–1828).

New Year's Day—
everything is in blossom!
I feel about average.

There is so much inside this tiny poem; the punch and economy astound. The rules of haiku ask for a temporal marker, some way to know the time of year, and the marker is usually natural. "New Year's Day" works with "blossom" because before the Japanese switched to the Gregorian calendar in 1873, New Year's coincided with the sudden pink cherry tree blossoms of spring.

With many haiku, having indicated the fact of New Year's, the point would be to zero in on a less obvious feature of the moment, perhaps dusty steps since New Year's housecleaning is common; or perhaps a dusting of snow, showing that the warmth of summer sun is late in coming this year and we all know how that feels. So it is a lighthearted surprise to read a straight report on the ideal event, which has come on time. Then we come to find out it's still just *okay*.

On big, happy holidays the tone of the event is so joyous that our inner experience is bound to compare badly at times. So the happier the holiday, the more likely it is that the poem will slip into the minor key, the sadder sounds of music.

T. S. Eliot's line about this is "April is the cruellest month, breeding / Lilacs out of the dead land." April is the start of spring, and like the happy holidays, it can be a rude wake-up for the full-time melancholic among us when the seasonally melancholic suddenly get joyous in the sun.

Maybe the haiku works on you right away, maybe it takes longer, but I've read it and recited it over a lot, for a long time now, and can confirm that it is a tricky piece of magic, a magic piece of trick. You have to admit the words are simple. You have to admit the lines are clear in meaning. None of these phrases are at all unusual. So why do I feel I have been so cheekily nudged from across three centuries?

The poem suggests that even when it all comes true, it's still you, or me, it's still our raggedy-old self that shows up for it. That is a warning about that day when it comes, yes. But it is also a word to the wisdom-wanting who are still yearning for that New Year's Day when all is in blossom. Even if/when that faultless day comes, you might still "feel about average." Therefore, it could be crucial to learn to feel the good of whatever day you are in.

Poetry Lesson: Haiku

Annual holidays are time markers, markers of the seasons. Haiku are a season-oriented form of poetry. So they go together well.

What we know of as haiku started seven centuries ago as part of *renga*, a patterned conversation poem, written communally by individuals sending lines back and forth. Renga alternate three- and two-line stanzas, and go on in long columns. The renga's first stanza was the *hokku*, seventeen syllables, in three lines, that set a scene and tone—ideally with such power that further stanzas in the renga could live within its world.

An ideal hokku presents one image, then another, then comments on their interrelation and informs on the season in which it was made. Some of the seasonal indicators, the *kigo*, are widely recognizable, while some are specific to Japan. To name only a few, there's snow for winter, frogs start singing in spring, a "sea of clouds" is common in late summer, and the Star Festival happens in autumn. Poets who wrote potent hokku began sharing them for others to use; these hokku, the establishing top of the renga, used by other poets, were all grandfathered in as "haiku" when that name became standard in the nineteenth century.

Like haiku, whatever else they are, to each of us, holidays are markers of time, they create a visceral sense of when you are in the year.

Recently my friend Amy, responding to the giant red and green plastic snowflakes arching across Court Street, remarked, "Can you believe it's the holidays already?" and what she meant was, only the holidays can convince me of time. We were wearing light jackets and there hadn't yet been a frost.

* * *

There's a baguette with eight Hanukah candles in it, all lit, and a mini brioche for the *shammash*—the candle used to light the others. I'm looking at a photograph I took in France, alone in my dorm room, decades ago, mid-December. I was in France for a college junior year abroad and I turned twenty that year; in fact, in the picture, I'd just days ago tipped out of my teens.

In the photo the baguette menorah is raised on a book, and seeing it, I remember it was wonky and wouldn't otherwise lay flat. The window behind it is two-tone white: the top of another cream-brick dorm building, and a rectangle of pale-gray sky.

I'd long misremembered the window as holding a sapphire sky, with a distant clutch of cypress trees like snake tongues flicking at early stars. I was wrong; no blue, no trees—the photo is a Mark Rothko not a Vincent van Gogh. I see burn char at a few candle holes in the bread, so this was not the only night I'd lit the bread menorah. I think the dorm walls were bright orange, but the photo is too dark to be certain. Anyway, there is the lithe, burning baguette and I remember my goofy joy about it.

What was I doing? I didn't believe in God, and it wasn't a party.

I recall that my mother had mailed me the candles. Only then did I think of the idea of the baguette menorah, and the rest was arts and crafts, and a scheme to make my mother laugh (this photo, sent home). Mine was a worried mother and I often added a touch of absurdity while mostly doing what she asked, but this wasn't entirely for her. I was keeping myself company, accessing community I had internalized. I was lonely that year and an alien.

I had too little French when I arrived to be anything like myself.

Honestly, I went to France to get out of my parents' house. When I was growing up my father taught at a nearby university and immediate family could attend for free. With home close by, our parents nixed the cost of dorms but encouraged a study abroad program that was a super deal for faculty brats.

Terrific idea, but I was as green as could be, and once there I was foreign and frequently terrified. This too explains why one *décembre*, newly twenty and alone in a probably orange room, I snapped this photo of said flaming-candled baguette. Lighting the menorah was not all jokes and craft, it was a jokey, crafty reprieve from exile. If I squint for objectivity, I see an as-yet-unmedicated depressed girl, two weeks out of her teens. Then if I ask myself, Do the light and scent of those candles matter? They do.

Your Poem

In your poetry book create a section for the holidays you celebrate and dedicate a page to each one. You can choose a poem that mentions your holiday, but you might find it melancholy. Or choose any poem that makes you feel the way you'd like to feel that day. Also, holidays are sticky for memories, and if a poem gets caught in one, for you, for whatever reason, put it in your poetry collection.

Plan a time to read the poem. If the holiday has a tradition of readings, perhaps insert your poem into it. Or read it alone. If you miss the whole holiday, the poem can stand in for the rest of it. The way life often goes is: didn't see any fireworks, didn't watch the parade, didn't kiss anybody at midnight—so you may be glad to have a meditation at the ready, as a companion and reflection.

We read the bittersweet holiday poem and it is a moment in another soul's Christmas, well-wrought so that if we read it over and over we are shoved out of ourselves, which allows us to be everyone else. Know that other nonbelievers are out here too, believing in life, and one another, and pressing the world for its meanings. With poetry for depth and history for perspective, it seems that the Interfaithless should have themselves a merry little Christmas, if their tastes allow.

* * *

Human beings set up calendars of cyclic recitations; we see it all over the world. The year is a circuit. Life is made of circuits of the Earth around the sun. Like a ritual you once did with your parents and now your children do with you. Adding a poem is a way to raise the volume of your intentions and to be surprised, again, by the inner life of other human beings.

We would do well to recognize the natural transcendent and ask ourselves which of its versions pluck the harp strings of our heart. Remember, when religion performs ritual, all those various ritual acts are enlivened by religious wonder. If we add the transcendent back in, through poetry that ignites us, paired with whatever acts and gestures make sense for us, we can continue with our holidays as usual, but new and improved. If we liven up our holidays with real meaning, they would liven us up, too. Party on, but when you think of it fresh you can gain some needed depth.

Returning to our experiment, wouldn't you think Jan Doe would be hurting at the end? It might seem like no big deal, but how long can a person or a culture celebrate without meaning and not come to feel empty and sad? If you want to change how you feel, it makes sense to experiment with putting the meaning back in, which means finding good words and setting up times for repetition. Of course, sometimes you're in the space station while Mecca rolls by far below, sometimes you're a nervous kid on her first adventure, far from home, setting fire to bread. (Thanks for the candles, Mom.) You work with what you've got.

7

On Scary Holidays

Facing Our Fear with Face Paint

*"How are we supposed to talk about death
without religion?"*

Ellen's girls are shocked by her Halloween costume. I'm on my stoop at the tail end of candy duty when the girls walk over, eager to tell me about their mother's bizarre getup.

Ten months ago, Ellen and her friend Sam were walking and got caught in a rainstorm. Sam stepped out into the street, against the light, and was hit by a car going too fast. Ellen heard the impact of grille and then windshield. Pow, crash. It seemed like he'd die, at first, but after a long hospital stay, then physical therapy, by summer Sam was nearly his old self. As for Ellen, at first she had spoken about the close call with death nonstop, then she stopped.

Now her teenage girls, Sophia and Mae, are explaining that when Mom was finally herself again they walked on eggshells to keep away from the topic, so she wouldn't relapse. That was difficult.

"There's a fair good amount of death in the news," says Sophia.

"And on videos, in video games, and just even *jokes*," says Mae, enumerating with double-jointed fingers—a finger of the hand holding her phone is pulling back fingers on the other hand to hypnotic degrees.

"And we're reading *The Great Gatsby* in class," says Sophia with a pop-eyed look of knowing that reminded me of the novel's own crash.

"Everywhere," says Mae, now scrolling her phone. "Death's everywhere. It got quiet," she adds and looks up at me.

"Right," I say. "Not talking about death can be the same as talking about it. Avoiding it makes you hyperaware of it." Here they deliver the response that sticks in my register of fine lines.

"So *you* get that we low-key didn't talk in the house last winter," says Mae. I hadn't until she said it.

Sophia adds, "All we ever didn't talk about was death."

The brush with death had only recently faded into the background for the whole family. Now, with this costume of Ellen's, the girls are saying they don't know what to think. We're all camped out on the stoop now, enjoying the night. The girls explain that Ellen had agreed to a group costume idea with her softball team. It seems that without thinking about it, she bought a "doctor zombie" costume with black tire tracks running straight across the bright green scrubs. She called it her "doctor zombie" costume every time, seeming not to notice that it was her "run over by a car" costume.

Sophia and Mae don't look much alike but when they describe their mom's costume they both do an eye-pop and jaw-drop look that makes them nearly twins.

"She still gave us her whole *Be careful crossing!* thing when we left," Sophia says. "Already wearing the clothes part!" She seems concerned for her mom and Mae's expression echoes it for a moment. They are scared. Then the moment is gone, and they are lighthearted teens again.

"I guess she had to touch the flame," says Mae, having fully traveled back from compassion to mockery.

"I guess she had to walk right up and touch the flame," deadpans Sophia in return.

But a fright had rippled quick between them. The season's accidental confetti shifts around us, orange wrappers of Reese's, blue papers of Almond Joy, and a rainbow of Skittles. Indeed, a historic Skittles battle must have here occurred. Or mishap. Or geyser.

When Ellen comes by later, just after her kids had headed off home, she tells me how much better she's doing. She looks undead. She isn't entirely oblivious about what she looks like, and that it is a bit odd, given her past year. Her workmate's makeup-artist husband did their whole group, and after her turn, when she looked in the mirror, she suddenly saw herself as dead.

She laughs at herself and says, "I mean, it wasn't my idea, but why did I say yes?"

I hesitate. "But you bought *your* costume, right?"

She looks down and it is like she is seeing the tire tracks for the first time. She seemed to try to back up from her front.

* * *

If you aren't being natural disastered right now, it's a safe bet that you will be later, or have a right close call with an accident, or violence. It's terrifying. How can we manage all the fears? Mostly, we attempt to put them out of our minds. It can work, for a while, but there is a cost in stress.

It must be good to get relief from this oceanic pressure sometimes, by surfacing your fears. Quite a splash, right? Switching metaphors (in the nick of time), it can help to occasionally give your suppressed worries an invitation to the revelry and a whirl across the ballroom, out in the open.

How Religion Helps

Many religions have a death holiday, where everyone remembers death together. Such holidays can be somber but also can be rambunctious fun. Either way, something serious is going on.

Consider the Mexican Día de los Muertos, or Day of the Dead. It is a Catholic holiday now, but the festival long predates the Spanish. The celebration was for the skeleton goddess Mictēcacihuātl, the Queen of Mictlān, the underworld, who watches over humanity's skeletal remains. She also swallows the stars all day, which is why she is depicted with open jaws. Aztec, Toltec, and other Nahua people saw mourning the dead as disrespectful, as the dead were still part of the community, alive in memory and able to visit during Día de los Muertos.

For the holiday, there are sugar skulls and a famous sweet roll iced to impersonate a femur. People paint skulls on their faces, hang up skeleton decorations, and gather for a picnic feast at family graves. Acrid, stinking orange marigolds are strewn in paths and thickly arranged on altars to help the dead find their way around for the visit. In the holiday's indigenous origins, it took place in spring. The Spanish moved the celebration all the way to late autumn to coincide with All Saints' Day, during Allhallowtide. They were lining up the two cultures' public death-memorial days. The "hallow" in the word "Allhallowtide" ends up becoming the word "Halloween." The content of Halloween, however, has its main source elsewhere.

Samhain is a Celtic holiday that included going door-to-door for treats, threatening tricks. Still today Samhain is understood by its Irish, Scottish, pagan, and Wiccan celebrants as the time of year when the dead can cross over and visit this world. For many centuries in Ireland the day included "mumming," that is, putting on small, costumed scenes, and *guising*, which meant dressing in dis*guise* to go knocking on doors, reciting verses, and demanding food. It gave people a night to think a bit about what they believe will happen when they die, while disguising themselves and getting into minor mayhem.

It's curious how playful people can be when cavorting with death. I suppose an abandon arises from the rank absurdity that all this build and battle ends in bones.

When a car accident shocked Ellen into a whole new way of being for a while, her daughters, Sophia and Mae, understood that the event had not brought death to their family in any real way. People dealing with post-traumatic stress from a specific life-threatening event remind us that there are levels to awareness of death. Scary holidays have existed for a long time because we love them and need them. They let our darkness have the run of the place a bit, a playful night in the streets as our own true fears and fantasies, whether we consciously know what our costumes and decorations are screaming about or not.

How Art and Science Help

Modern culture has many ways to have a moment of melancholy-with-intent or self-frightening. There's intense theater, thriller film, or music that is high in drama or decibel. There are video games of tremendous agitation with tension release in mock carnage and e-bedlam.

Consider our modern obsession with the undead from zombies and vampires to Frankenstein monsters and other awakened flatliners, whether roused by electricity or a shot of adrenaline in the heart. If watching the dead arise is an expression of our feelings, there's no shortage of material. These experiences may be cathartic, like opening a steam valve, but they are not generally linked to what we think of as our philosophy of life, unlike the ideal eerie experience within religion.

We do *have* positive rational philosophies about death. Many poetic, rational people hush their death angst with an idea that we can call *starstuff*. In the late-twentieth century, the physicist and science-popularizer Carl Sagan (1934–1996) explained that the elements that make up human beings were not made in the Big Bang—if there, forces would have instantly ripped them apart. They formed later, inside stars, and made their way to us; or rather, made their way to *be* us.

As Sagan marvelously explained, "The nitrogen in our DNA, the calcium in our teeth, the iron in our blood, the carbon in our apple pies were made in the interiors of collapsing stars. We are made of starstuff."

Today we often add that a woman did some of the key science on this. Cecilia Payne-Gaposchkin (1900–1979) was the first woman physics professor at Harvard. Cosmologists thought stars were made of the same stuff as Earth, and Payne-Gaposchkin spotted a conceptual error in the calculation. Stars were shown to be mostly light elements, perpetually crashing toward their centers, forming increasingly heavy elements; then finally running out of hydrogen, stars start collapsing in on themselves and exploding, only then creating the heaviest elements. Ones we need—in order to exist.

That starstuff is now planet Earth, which formed when such exploded-star debris joined together through gravity. Starstuff also made its way to Earth frequently before we had an atmosphere, through meteoric visitation. "We are made of starstuff" is a comfort to many because it finds humanity to be part of nature in a new way. The poetic insight is that we've *already been* the unconscious universe, we are home, not just in nature on Earth, but everywhere.

Your Ritual Draws on Both

If a holiday like this comes around and you want to participate, part of that could be taking in art that makes you cry, or scream, mourn the dead, or remember that you are mortal yourself. Music that gives you big feelings might be perfect, if you focus on death and its meanings for life, or at least assign the time as specifically open to such thoughts and feelings.

The graceful-life philosophers through history have urged us to remember death on the regular because it helps us see what we have. How will it feel the rest of the time if you put death thoughts on the calendar at least once a year, having made the holiday your own? As always, you can invent a holiday like this from scratch and see if you can get it off the ground, but the old ones have a lot to offer.

After all, if it weren't for established parties for the dead—I mean real parties with delicious food and an open bar, songs, stories, and laughter—who would dare invent one? It might seem disrespectful. It might seem bad luck to paint yourself dead at the end of October, if you weren't so used to it. If you and a few friends were the only ones, how would it look? Old rituals come preloaded with import and the camouflage of habit.

If you like the starstuff idea, maybe find a way to touch a meteorite and read your poem. If there is an ancient ritual in your tradition, or in your world today, you can join in with that ritual and make it more meaningful for yourself. Remember death by eating a sweet yet sour treat— if everyone has an excellent sense of humor, share sour gummy worms.

Taking in a strong flavor makes an impression. All those sugar skulls or chocolate bars alone can be a glucose jolt to the system. It's tricky work to conjure the meaning to such a shindig, so we bring in a professional.

Our Poem

Consider an arresting poem by one of my all-time favorites, Wisława Szymborska (1923–2012).

Could Have

It could have happened.
It had to happen.
It happened earlier. Later.
Nearer. Farther off.
It happened, but not to you.

You were saved because you were the first.
You were saved because you were the last.
Alone. With others.
On the right. The left.
Because it was raining. Because of the shade.
Because the day was sunny.

You were in luck—there was a forest.
You were in luck—there were no trees.
You were in luck—a rake, a hook, a beam, a brake,
a jamb, a turn, a quarter inch, an instant.
You were in luck—just then a straw went floating by.

As a result, because, although, despite.
What would have happened if a hand, a foot,
within an inch, a hairsbreadth from
an unfortunate coincidence.

So you're here? Still dizzy from another dodge, close shave,
   reprieve?
One hole in the net and you slipped through?
I couldn't be more shocked or speechless.
Listen,
how your heart pounds inside me.

"Could Have" ricochets around on its theme, danger anxiety, specifically the anxiety about sudden, violent death. It meditates on the role of chance in sudden disaster and the role of chance in escape.

Do you see the sneaky second line of the poem? It isn't like any of the poem's other statements. The rest of the poem suggests survival. A close shave, yes, but even the title suggests a miss. The second line of the poem holds a special place because it reminds us that these things do happen. They don't usually happen. Odds are tremendously in your favor that they won't happen to you. But they do happen to someone and line two holds that fact in place.

For me, the silver ball of "It had to happen" now pachinkos down to a lower level of meaning and here "It had to happen" refers to the things that *did* happen, whatever they were, to the poem's reader.

"Could Have" has been understood as a response to the Holocaust and how tiny daily choices were mortal choices. In his Holocaust memoir, the psychologist Viktor Frankl describes prisoners gaming their response to roundups—if the guards call for prisoners of a particular profession to step forward, some will guess the group is to be kept alive, and so pretend to fit; while others pretend not to, on the opposite guess. After a while you've watched guesses turn out wrong so often, you give up guessing and answer the truth.

"Could Have" is also read in terms of modern terrorism. It can be said that terrorism works exactly because the violence is random. In a city that experiences a minimal but real amount of terrorism, one is always and never really in danger.

At the start of the poem, the short-short sentences feel like the drummed-out phrases your brain allows after a flush of adrenaline. They are short like shortness of breath. The litany feels reasonable enough for a few lines, but from "Alone" to "sunny," we start to feel like someone's edging off their rocker. It feels manic. It feels post-traumatic.

The next five lines have more agency. Up until the repeated "You were in luck" lines, I take the "you" of the poem to be the poet. The voice still sounds internal to me, here, but now the experiences seem to be those of many people. Yes, it is an intellectual exercise, ticking off these possibilities, but in the first part of the poem all the claims are so passive and general that they are true of all of us. Now the drumbeat ramps up from anxiety to panic.

The items of salvation become so specific that they seem real, such as "a rake"—not usually anyone's salvation. It could be used to bat a foe or bar a door, but we don't know. Other items are so meager, like "a quarter inch," they wouldn't be enough to save you from survivor's trauma. When hiding for your life by holding your breath underwater, it is a lifesaver to have a straw or reed float by, which you can use like a snorkel, to breathe.

The next four lines feel like blinking at the wall while half thinking the nonquestion that begins, "What would have happened," and doesn't end with a question mark. That's a question that knows it isn't asking.

The poem's final stanza is uncanny. The poet seems to waken as if from a trance. She shifts into a new state of mind with more distance from the menace. She's surprised to have survived. She'd given herself up for dead. She's saying, *So I'm still here?*

The image of slipping through "One hole in the net" reminds us of birth. I think of conception, too, metaphorically, because of how unlikely it is for both sex cells to have made it into being. Before all the superior fortune you wish you had in the world, there was the first fantastic fortune, the implausible lottery win of being here at all.

There's an air of friendly teasing now. The experienced person who has been doing all the talking says that she couldn't be more shocked or speechless. Since that can't be true, since she is both knowing and chatting, it seals the sense of teasing. The poet uses a snarky voice to roughly soothe her own worry.

By a splash of poetic magic, the last sentence feels supremely honest,

feels so honest it makes you forget that irony even exists. We get an im-
perative verb, a command to attention, off on its own, "Listen." It soon
turns out we're not just getting serious, we're going internal. She asks
us to "listen," and it turns out she means *feel*.

> *Listen,*
> *how your heart pounds inside me.*

Maybe she's speaking from a place of authority when she tells us to
listen, but then she is seduced by sensation. In that last line she's coming back in sync with her whole self, tolerating the feeling. The poet is
not just talking to herself though. She's talking to us. She tried to be
distant but has collapsed back into her extreme empathy. She carries us
in with her, with that visceral leap to our pounding hearts.

Poetry Lesson: Romanticism and Its Transformation

European poetry is in an exciting battle—to this day—with Romanticism, an artistic movement that dates from early in the 1800s. The
Romantic movement was so devoted to nature that it can be seen as an
origin of environmentalism. Romantic art revealed humanity as minus-
cule compared to nature; its representative paintings have mountains
and bellicose clouds that dwarf their human figures into dewdrops.
By contrast, in the classical art of antiquity human beings were above
nature, except their own. And yet, in much Romantic discussion, the
"nature" of humanity was also seen as good. Such paintings are, after
all, firm proof that humanity is creative and awesome, too.

In the mounting horrors of the twentieth century, that conversation
began to look like a crushed old dollhouse in a wasted land. Across
the European world, from Russia to Ireland, the twentieth century saw
wars and genocide, starvation and state collapse. Bombs from a moon-
less sky to try to force surrender. Bombs set by locals, for terror. So
much death on purpose, so many died for nothing. Lived in fear, in
pain, lived with guns in their heads, died in sudden. As a result, a dark

poetry is what marks much of the territory's century. Dark like dried blood, or a rotten tooth. At times the bloody face with the rotten teeth laughs, but it reeks, and you feel hot and then cold.

By the late part of that recent century, and into our own, it was clear that Szymborska had made a new path. She lived through those atrocities, and reflects them, but she also lived beyond those ruined lives and worlds and transcends them by surviving into poetry. She strives to find a language for living inside all the violence and beyond it.

* * *

My Facebook status on September 20, 2016:

> The real story of the NY bomb is that my husband, John, and I were in a spat. We'd grunted goodbye at each other when he went off to work running a trivia night at One Star Bar on 24th and 6th. I was online, while watching TV with the kids, so found out pretty close to when the screen read, "A bomb went off on 23rd and 6th," and I called and reached him. Spat over. A terror love story.

Here's another story, but trigger warning for violence, gore. On September 12, 2001, an old student of mine attending Pace University, in downtown New York City, emailed me saying his apartment was next to the wreckage; he and his roommate in shock: "Can we come see you?"

"Yes," I said, and met them at Simone's, a cafe downstairs from me, sleek red-and-black lacquer. The decor was too hip for the mood. We were nearly alone in there. They said they had to tell me a bad thing. They confided that there was a finger on their windowsill. I was dumbfounded. "Go home to your parents," I urged, having ascertained they had somewhere to go. "At least for a few days?"

I didn't even have the presence of mind to tell them to call the police. It was the first day after, and we thought we were going to find survivors and bodies. It hadn't yet occurred to us that the finger was all that was left of someone who was otherwise just missing. Later that day I called my sister with the story and she told me the finger had to be reported. I called the guys, and they told me they'd already done it.

Then I hung up the phone and cried like a child for the rest of whomever it was. I'd clearly comforted the boys; they wanted to stay right there with me. I was likely murmuring some kind of comparison to history, or strength to be taken from some good idea, but I'd also missed the one practical matter before us, to get the finger to the authorities.

I won't tell you any more stories about the sense of close call all of us with proximity to those buildings felt. Or anyone with a history of being in them. Sorry, but writing that has made me think of one I can't help telling. I taught English to Japanese businessmen on the eighty-first floor of the World Trade Center while I was in graduate school at Columbia. I still remember the stores in the subway lobby I'd run past, already late, to the express elevator, switch to the local. Yup, express elevator, so it wouldn't take forever. On windy days they shut off the express because it would swing on its long descents and hit the sides. The buildings were designed to sway, or they'd have snapped off from the same forces. This is the sort of thing my dad was always teaching us, growing up.

For weeks there were flyers taped up on walls with photos of the missing, and details, they covered the bus stop shelters and kiosk walls. We all lined up to give blood for survivors and were surprised to be turned away. The pungent cloud of smell and smoke settled into crevices and stayed powerful for months. There were no bodies. We wondered what the smell was. We wondered where the bodies were. We couldn't imagine the answer. I couldn't imagine it and had to imagine it over and over. The smell was the molecules of bodies and the bodies were in our lungs.

I won't say anything else. I'll just tell you I think about the finger and I feel tears rise like a punch to this day. My student was sandy blond, his roommate was dark, his family from South America. The coffee was aromatic, lush. The air was charged with collective fear and shock, waiting for another blast to drop. That's what we all thought—that buses, pizza parlors, and cafes would be blowing up next. With provocation, I can still feel that expectation today.

Your Poem

It won't be hard to find a poem that engages with death. Poetry is consumed with how short life is, compared to how we feel about it. It's not
exactly that life is short; after all, many days are longer than we want.
It's that there is a clash between how important and real life feels and
how all that disappears with death. Personalities seem like mountains
and they disappear. Half the world's best-loved poems would serve to
contemplate mortality. Pick one and put it in your poetry collection.

Poetry is a place to let yourself feel, so that you keep growing, instead of getting stuck where you were the last time you let yourself feel.
In addition, fear, grief, and rage can be relieved by poetry's perspective
shifts and pleasures. You have to get to know the poem, live with it for
a while, leave it alone and come back to it. Maybe look up how others
discuss the poem.

The power of poetry to connect people to one another across time
and space, even when we are alone, hints at the inestimable reach of our
perceptions. We're aware of one another out there. Wouldn't it help us
to be even more so?

* * *

The regularity of such death holidays is an important part of their
function. It's easier to put feelings away knowing they will be invited
out again. The reverse is also true: when feelings are buried, they may
come out when called, if given a dedicated time slot, with a distinct
time to return to the depths. If you are already overly focused on death
and therefore don't think you need a communal death-remembrance
holiday, you might be surprised if you try it. One day of intentional
focus can absorb a measure of constant ambient worry.

Nature has long been cited as a comfort for the pain of fear of
death. The starstuff version of nature bypasses rot, and even the end
of humanity, warp-speeding us back into the cosmos. The stars made
us and someday we'll be with them again.

Today, we have the remarkable fortune of being able to distract ourselves from boredom and fear, a lot of the time. But the pile of what you are trying not to think about shouldn't get taller than, say, your eyes. People seem to need to confront the reality of death, to air this stuff out, to touch skull bone, to look in the mirror and see eye sockets and nosehole, or something of the sort, now and again.

Scary holidays do us good when they scare us a bit. To paraphrase Ellen's girls, sometimes we have to walk right up and touch the flame.

People need occasions to laugh about death with friends—when it isn't a funeral, so we are free to think about ourselves. When these happen around us, we can take a moment to raise a toast to the grass that may cover us and say a few lines of verse to help us stay with the wonder.

8

On a Day for Shame and Grace

Messing Up with Green Dress and Game Host

"Where do I go when I need to forgive myself?"

A bouncy middle-aged woman on a game show, bright green dress, wins big in early play. She lets out a "woo-hoo" and says she's going to buy a car that starts up on cold days. She mimes turning a key in an ignition that won't ignite.

Green Dress keeps playing, winning; knows the answers, lucks out on a gamble, quite a pot. Audience keyed up and squealing. One game left. Tall, dark fox of a Game Host asks if she'll risk it all or go home now with what she's won.

"What'll we do here?" asks Game Host, pivoting from Green Dress to the semicircle. "You were brave earlier; will we see that now?" Eyebrow up. "Play? Or take the money and go home?"

The audience shouts, "Play," in a wave and then another. There are also plumes of concern; the camera catches a young girl urging, "Take the money!"

Game Host says, "They want you to play!" Crowd erupts to a yowl. Green Dress clenches her face.

"I'll play!" she shouts, to a murder of applause. The game turns up a tricky question, but she makes an educated guess. A good guess. A possible guess. A wrong guess, and all the money gone. The audience moans in commiseration.

Game Host says, "Oh no, I'm so sorry." His face collapses. He can feel the icy air streaming in from the door seams of her bad car, and hear the motor grind.

Not Green Dress though, she won't have it, waving away the audience moans. She glares a headshake to Game Host, followed by a smile that seems real, and remains real in my recall.

"It's alright," she says, and pushes her face out. "It's alright! It just means I'm getting ready to be blessed."

* * *

How do we survive what so often seems to be the catastrophe of our choices? When Green Dress said it, I laughed and repeated it back to the screen: "It just means I'm getting ready to be blessed." I found it silly at first but then enchanting and it lifted my spirits. I was having a pack of hard days and her cockeyed optimism cheered me up.

Green Dress's response has stayed with me a long time. The vignette brings up the difference between the internal and the external experience of chance. From the outside, to a broad-seeing observer, a lot of what goes wrong isn't anyone's fault. There are known forces and unknown forces that push us into our office chairs, or scoot us behind counters, or button us into our uniforms. There are known and unknown forces that predict with whom we'll be watching TV ten years from now, down to our spouse's likely education level and whether that one more baby gets born. There are forces, apparently, that tuck us into airplane seats and lead us by the camera neck-strap to monuments, or keep us homebound; that push us along to play the stocks or sock our cash in savings.

Green Dress's claim, her faith, is historically interesting—*getting ready to be blessed*—because there isn't much theological backing for her thesis: it's a mix of American Protestantism and self-help. Things go up and down. When we're down, our job is to wait. We're getting ready to be blessed.

My memory ends with the woman's declaration, but we can imagine the drama further. Maybe later she questions her choice. Once she's away from the adrenaline of the crowd and the lights, she might get angry with herself for taking the risk, or for missing the question, or for both. Maybe Game Host goes home and has a bit of a cry. He feels sad for her, but also for himself, because he wishes he had her faith or her sunshine disposition.

Imagine with me that Game Host looks on the internet for comments that night, knowing that he shouldn't. People are launching accusations at him; they say he pushed Green Dress into risking cash she needed. The blowback is too much and he's fired.

On voice mail, his producer sounds gutted, says, "This is horrible and we're sorry, but people are angry. We don't have a choice."

Game Host mumbles to himself, with weary irony, "It's alright. It just means I'm getting ready to be blessed."

How Religion Helps

If Green Dress and Game Host look to religion, they won't find much boost for the idea of God as a novelist crafting obstacles to arrange for a more satisfying reward. If Green Dress was unflappable because she felt certain that she was *good* and that the good are eventually rewarded, that's another story. The idea that the good—the honest, the pure, the kind, the pious, the fair, the courageous—are rewarded is a more common notion in religion, and can be quite a comfort, if you feel you are super good. Such comfort can backfire, too, because there are so many ways to feel that you've been super bad. You can fail your own internal test.

More generally, the major sprain in the idea that the good are rewarded with a good life is the observable fact that the good are not always rewarded with a good life—think of all the people caught up in random disasters. Think of all the people who take a big swing at life, with decent odds, and encouragement from the wise, and lose everything.

If it was you who took a gamble, risked a lot, and lost, where would you go to get help with that feeling? The last time I was drowning in that feeling I felt like I had no way out of it, though I look back and see that I did have support, there were people I talked to about it. I had places, therapy for one, to go with my flailing despair.

We can easily imagine that if Green Dress is later angry at herself for risking so much, she might take her regret to church.

What can Game Host do with his regret? He has choices, with family from all the major faiths of Southeast Asia and Nashville, Tennessee, and no belief in religion himself. He thinks of the various techniques, mostly fasts and ritual bathing, that might be used by his family members if they felt a need for absolution.

Game Host's Father and His Sister Jyotsna:

Bathing in the Ganges removes all sin from Hindu believers, and they can increase that purity by entering the river in a certain tumultuous spot to extend the forgiveness into next year, for mistakes not yet made. For Hindus, Mother Ganga takes away your impurity, your wrongs, as she rushes you; you lift her in cups and spill her back into the river. When drawn or carved, Ganga has the form of a buxom beauty riding on a makara, a fierce swimming beast, crocodilian but enhanced, often with an elephant trunk. Seekers of solace venture to the Ganges in the thousands every day, and once every twelve years the Kumbh Mela festival returns and millions of people throng to the sacred water—it has been among the largest peaceful gatherings ever.

Game Host's Mother:

In observance of Ramadan, Muslims fast from sunup to sundown for a full month. In the words of the prophet Abu Hurairah, "He who fasts during Ramadan with faith and seeks his reward from Allah will have his past sins forgiven."

Game Host's Brother-in-Law Ananda:

Buddhists don't believe in sin. The Buddha advised that we work to let go of regret and shame, in part by letting go of the idea of the self. Tibetan Buddhism advises meeting one's shame as a sensation, with calm curiosity. Exploring the physical sensation of shame, clinically and imaginatively, can shift it.

Game Host's Sister Chesa and Brother-in-Law Tony:

Chesa converted to Catholicism when she married Tony. Catholics have Lent, a period of sacrifice. By choosing a delight to avoid for forty days, they purify themselves. They are encouraged through the year to go to confession, sitting in a closed space and speaking their sins anonymously. The listening priest gives penance—spiritual assignments like reciting texts or performing acts—and confers forgiveness.

Game Host's Sister-in-Law, Becca, and Nephews, Zack and Dan:

Jews have autumn's ten High Holy Days to apologize to anyone they have harmed throughout the past year and to accept offered apologies. The last of those Holy Days is the Day of Atonement, Yom Kippur, a full day of fasting, praying, and communally reading long lists of general apologies, in unison, for possible sins in case one slips the mind.

The main responses to shame in these traditions seem to be fasting and cleansing with water.

Consider this, too:

Game Host's Other Brother-in-Law, Ari:

Sikhism forbids fasting because it is not right to do harm to the body. Sikhs clearly state that nothing religious can be achieved through harming the body.

It's a caution to keep in mind. Maybe because we know that hard work hurts, we get tricked into thinking that pain itself can buy us forgiveness or success.

Communal fasting for the sake of inner peace can be effective. Believer or not, when you fast on an official fasting day, you can feel the company of other people's hunger, for food and for inner peace. Even better than that, at the end of fast there's often a boisterous feast. Ramadan ends with the joyous holiday of Eid al-Fitr. Cakes and pastries are so central to the celebration that the holiday is also known as Sweet Eid or Sugar Feast.

* * *

Water can help soothe confusion. Many religions require some manner of ritualized washing after contact with sex, death, or birth—or any bodily event you might want to separate from your more everyday self.

When traveling to a Shinto shrine, it is purifying to pass over water, and the more rivers one passes over on the way, the better. Derived from that ancient idea, the *sandō*, the path to the shrine, has built-in rivulets with little bridges. To enter the shrine, one stops at a *temizuya*, a pavilion with a water trough and ladles, so hands and face can be washed, in a ritual order.

Before leaving the house for a drive to a funeral, Jews set out containers of water for pouring three dousings over their hands, outdoors, before reentering the house. Jewish cemeteries have an outdoor faucet and a pouring cup there at the tap.

How Art and Science Help

People's happiness shifts with some predictability over a lifetime. Studies show that into our twenties we are relatively happy with our lives, likely because we are flush with hope and vigor; then our thirties and forties are rougher, also not surprising since in these years we learn about the binds of life and the grind to keep going; but then we report increasing happiness, for a couple of decades.

It seems that beyond middle age, regrets diminish. Apparently, we find the fun in where we've landed, and have rejected the untenable costs of the lives we once wanted. Still, most of us know regret, whether we grabbed the gold ring, or just enjoyed the ride, or stayed home to write songs about carousels.

Generally, we dream more lives than can be lived. A philosopher writes a book about midlife regret. He's set up an outstanding life, a professorship, a growing family. It's just that he wonders, *Did I choose the right adventure?* Using the structures of philosophy, he interrogates his own regret and finds a cognitive deficiency in the human ability to assess the past. It's almost an optical illusion. When we regret having chosen Job A over Job B, we are prone to compare what we know of a decade of life with Job A, with the same shiny Job B that we envisioned back when we knew nothing.

We forget to factor in the challenges we'd have met in that reality. But think about it. That other life would have had other illnesses, natural disasters, and ironic betrayals, its own unpredictable reasons to give up on exercising.

This cognitive deficiency should console us about specific times in our lives when we wish we'd stayed instead of bolted. We all have times we wish we had followed up on a job opportunity or a different life choice. We hang on to these things, these lost chances. Despite all the phone chimes of life that we do answer, we all have calls that, for whatever reason, we let ring into the air and never return. Isn't there something off about these one-off worries? Of course our specific choices matter, but always remember: we are never *choosing a life*, we are making choices in life. The variables are beyond us.

I know some of us—hand up—are still angry at ourselves for having missed a certain meeting (an ice storm coated the roads overnight so I missed my flight for a publishing meeting, and I believe my life split off there, to this day); that is, we are convinced we could have lived this life better. So allow me to take this philosophical idea a bit further, poetically. Consider that we don't know whether you'd have lived to this day in any other timeline. In this one, you did. Take the win. You might have been rich and dead, maybe famous and dead, but dead. Meanwhile the real you, in this world—lucky kid—kept stepping out of danger.

Your Ritual Draws on Both

An intentional hardship can be used as a way to show yourself that you are trustworthy, that you can see a challenge through. Populations through history have fasted or traveled to a river to feel better. It might be worth finding out what happens to you.

If you need to get clean, history suggests you *do* something. Hands don't get clean from thinking about clean, so why should hearts and minds? Swear off a habit for a week and find out who you are without it. Maybe splash your face three times with cleansed water, apologize to someone you might have hurt, or do a favor. You might visit a lake, swim in a river, an ocean, plunge down a slide, plummet into a quarry pool, or go out in the rain. Let the water around you lift the water inside you. Get a massage to help your fluids circulate. Without intention, all this is just bathing, thwarted desire, and getting some relief for your muscles. We can get to that significance with a poem.

Our Poem

Not all of Shakespeare's sonnets try for a huge run up into a mind-flip and then stick the landing, but one that does is Sonnet 29. It's an exquisite fit of self-hatred, ending with a flash discovery of a total cure.

Sonnet 29

When in disgrace with fortune and men's eyes
I all alone beweep my outcast state,
And trouble deaf heav'n with my bootless cries,
And look upon myself, and curse my fate,
Wishing me like to one more rich in hope,
Featured like him, like him with friends possessed,
Desiring this man's art and that man's scope,
With what I most enjoy contented least;

Yet in these thoughts myself almost despising,
Haply I think on thee, and then my state,
Like to the lark at break of day arising,
From sullen earth sings hymns at heaven's gate;
  For thy sweet love remembered such wealth brings
  That then I scorn to change my state with kings.

If great poems are delightfully arranged threads, this sonnet is impeccably woven cloth. You can kick at it all night and it won't fall apart, and four centuries later it will still keep you warm. The poet reports from a terrible time, swamped by disgrace and tight for the rent. He feels disliked, dismissed, and defeated. Alone and crying, he sees himself as pointlessly sputtering at a sky that has no capacity to listen— "deaf heav'n." He curses the brute facts of his situation.

He knows people who are all set up for prosperity ("rich in hope"), and aches with envy over someone's good looks ("Featured like him"), this one's popularity, that guy's talent, and someone's giant life. When he tells us that his usual pleasures lack all appeal, we know that he has been trying to comfort himself and failing. We hear depression in that, too.

Stewing in all this, he confesses to a near-complete self-rejection ("in these thoughts myself almost despising"), and then he happens to think of "thee," and everything changes. The idea is, you exist, and you love me. My state (of mind and situation) soars straight up like a bird to meet the morning sky. The sense of flying straight up, at first light, is enhanced by "From sullen earth," which describes the as-yet-still night-dark ground. Because of you, I wouldn't trade lives with anyone. Your sweet love outshines the state of a king.

Can we together contemplate the mind-scrambling idea that Shakespeare could feel so terrible about himself? That paragon of human success was writhing in self-hatred. He didn't know the future, but he knew he was excellent; he was at that moment writing a poem that still comes alive like a little being, once met never forgotten. Can an author be oblivious to that magic? I have to think he knew how talented (and had an inkling how timeless) he was, and yet still felt all of this.

In my mind I call Green Dress and Game Host to the gazebo near the trailhead of our imagination and give them the poem and ask them about all of this. "Even Shakespeare could be furious with himself," I instruct.

Game Host smiles (why not? It's my fantasy) and says, "I hear you. Whoever you are you can break your own promises and end up on the floor."

Green Dress shakes her head, asks, "Is all this still about me missing that question? My mother stopped driving, so I have her car now. It's nice."

She got her blessing. She's a forward-looking person. Up to a point, how you take things can be as important as the situation itself.

Poetry Lesson: The Sonnet

The sonnet began in the 1200s, as a Sicilian argument. The first eight lines were the "proposition" and then came a six-line "response." The response was the *turn*, the *volta*. While the philosopher-poet Petrarch was creating the Renaissance he picked up the form as a way to pose a claim and a retort or a rethinking. He set the rhyme scheme, ABBA ABBA followed by CDC CDC (or CDE CDE). There was a regular bounce to each line, *five* iambs, or iambic *penta*meter.

Thomas Wyatt translated Petrarch's sonnets into English and wrote his own in the early 1500s, and by the end of the century English sonnets were all the rage. Shakespeare's generation changed the rhyme scheme to ABAB CDCD EFEF GG, and Will did it so well that we call this iteration by his name: a Shakespearean sonnet. When later poets William Wordsworth and Elizabeth Barrett Browning went back to the older model, they called it the Petrarchan sonnet.

We haven't recovered from what Shakespeare did with the sonnet. He'd take his sweet time with the proposition, twelve lines sometimes, then deliver the turn and response in two lines, a lightning clap of new knowledge, epiphany in a bottle, and the final couplet a triumph in rhyme.

Sonnet 29 flows fast; it's a whitewater rapid to a waterfall, so we're airborne by the final couplet and land in the pool below. Despite storms of life's disgrace, all is answered in love. To hell with the skills I've missed, the sonnet suggests; to the dogs with the scope of life for which I'd hoped. I've got you, and I'd never hoped with any actual hope to have you. I'm already lucky, already what Green Dress would call blessed.

* * *

My friend Martha and I are visiting her grandmother, also Martha, who has made us all cups of hot tea, redolent of spice and sweet with cream, in her square, sunlit kitchen with its blue-and-green linoleum floor.

Young Martha laments having left college years ago, sighing, "I could have been a doctor by now."

Gran Martha says, "Sure and that would have gone wrong too."

The moment was magnified by the resemblance of the Marthas— pug nose, pretty eyes. After all, what can you do when your own face fifty years hence tells you there are no ropes worth showing? Frowns all around and then laughter. The laugh was at life's expense. On that crisp morning, bright yellow sunshine splashing pale yellow kitchen walls, the bond of injured laughter was sweeter than success.

As for a more personal story of disgrace, I'm not going to give a testimonial here, but the basics are in my poetry for anyone to see. I drank a lot for a while and know what the sear of shame is, and it's not gone. What do I do with mine? I went to meetings for a while and confessed it. I suppose there are lots of ways I confess my shortfalls. Maybe I try to be extra good to make up for them? I bob in the waves at the ocean and I go down slides with the kids at the water park. I sit with the bard on the dock of the bay.

Your Poem

What do we do with our shame? Find a poem with a direct message saying that disgrace can be survived, saying that it happens to a lot of people, saying you can find a group where having bad stories makes you feel entertaining and of use. Find a poem that makes you feel better. There are poems that will join you in lightening the mood around light sin, and poems to join you with leaden shoes in heavy remorse.

Our world has a problem with regret because it focuses on individual success and fortune. We tell children they can be anything, and it's not true, most children don't have a chance of becoming president, for instance, and while a lot of people do attain some internet fame, most who try do not succeed, and many never really try. Over time *can be* anything glooms to *could have been* and *should have been*. Poetry addresses this matter. Look for poems that use those "could" and "should" words and that challenge these ideas. Remember, if this has been a tough year, the woman in the Green Dress would wager that you ought to be getting ready to feel blessed.

You will find in poetry a voice for your most complex guilt and your simplest, childlike desire to have been kinder, to have saved more of the bees. Think of Shakespeare's Sonnet 29 and try to dream up his frightening fault or failure. See if you can forgive him. See if you can benefit from his hunch about value and let yourself be redeemed by the care of those you care about, the love of those you love. You can read it over and over, acquaint your body's rhythms to the mystery of how it stays knit, and you stay knit too.

* * *

Shakespeare couldn't have been Shakespeare unless he knew the shame he shows in Sonnet 29. It's a nice paradox that having known shame is a not uncommon component of greatness. They must have been low to go high. Shakespeare's lark, soaring up from darkness, is an image of transcending wreckage. You can't rely on these results *haply*, which meant "by chance," as in "*happen*stance," so it helps to prepare.

If there is any love or any moment that you would not trade away, for anything, it makes your choices "right" because they led you there. If you had children since your life forked off in what you see as "the wrong direction," you have to confront the fact that you have *these* children only on this timeline. Little Axe and Xe depend upon everything going a precise way from the Big Bang to whatever small bangs led to their births. You could have had kids in Chicago, if you had taken that job, but if you've got an Axe and Xe, you can confirm that real relationships are infinitely more valuable than possible ones. Imaginary children are fungible, like commodities or cash, any will do. Real children are not fungible, they are loved.

If you wouldn't trade away your actual children, you can't sensibly regret choices that led up to their existence. The lesson is not limited to children, but seems related to sacrifice and service. Had life worked out, you'd never have come to this good deed.

Expiating shame is a function of many religions. Of course many religions and graceful-life philosophies suggest not accruing shame in the first place, by acting with dignity and reserve. Some go the other way, advising we make peace with the consequences of a more reckless engagement with life. Either way we meet shame and regret, so it would help to have practices and texts in place to cope.

Some people think the universe treats them with intentionality. Some people feel like the universe's disregard is mirrored in the human world. I have to argue for a middle way being closer to truth. Both Green Dress and Game Host are better off remembering love, which can be constant, and luck, which never is. Thinking of the about-face turn of the sonnet's volta—*Haply I think on thee*—I become slowly aware of how it echoes that wonderful truth that life changes. Sometimes fast. Green Dress knew it. It is a blessing of the natural sacred that we get to try to know it too. If all else fails, let us recall the wisdom of the Marthas, and laugh.

9

On Sabbaths and Fools' Days

Rest, Creativity, and Solitude

"I don't know how to relax . . . or play.
I just know how to be entertained."

You wake up tomorrow morning and can't find anyone, anywhere. By all indications, you are alone on the planet. What do you do?

I've been asking people this for decades. It opens endless intense questions, and a few surprises.

So, back to you. You are alone. The electricity is out but you feel safe enough. You cry, you search, but then what?

How long would you enjoy exploring other people's homes? How about doing as you wish in stores, museums, famous buildings?

Would you read? What would you read?

Would you stay close to home or wander?

The reason I've been bothering people with this question changes. At first, I was mostly asking college classrooms, trying to induce an existential crisis in my students so we could talk about philosophy. While they were still laughing at the fun of the questions, I'd say, "Sorry to do that to you, but most of you were headed for an existential crisis anyway, so this way I'm here to get you out again."

I have also found myself asking this question to large audiences, most often when we're on the subject of suicide and discussing the poetic-atheist argument against it. These talks are philosophical, but they are also intensely emotional. Here I ask audiences to think about how it would feel to be alone on the planet because I want to give them an immediate reminder of what people mean to one another. Humans are social animals to such a degree that we can't be understood as individuals. The meaning of you is partly derived from community and sometimes when you aren't able to see your own worth, the rest of us can.

It's a shining blue-dome-sky of a day on a gorgeous campus and I'm being walked to the Little Theater where I'll speak to a group of English majors. It's sultry and slower than I'm used to. There's moss in the trees.

The students are crowded up waiting for the doors to open. A tall young man with longish dark hair and his long-haired dog lope over to us as we arrive, saying, "Professor Banks, sir, and ma'am, do y'all mind if Dave sits in today?"

Professor Banks introduces Rex warmly and asks if I'd mind the dog, adding, "Dave's quiet." I'm fine with it, and as the boy walks ahead of us, Banks drawls to me, "You heard right, the boy is Rex and the dog is Dave. They're real smart."

We pass into a cool, dim black box theater. From the low stage, as my eyes adjust, I see Rex on the far aisle with Dave in repose beside him. On the near aisle are a clutch of young women with nearly shaved heads, dressed in black. At center, a boy with blond fluffy hair is lit from behind with an errant spotlight, and I am thinking how beautiful they all are when someone in the lighting booth throws a blinding spot on me and yells, "Sorry." It's off fast, but it's too late, all is darkness.

I start talking anyway and put the question to the darkness. "What would you do if you woke up one day and found you were alone on the planet?" I can't make eye contact with anyone to nudge them into conversation, blind as I am, so I say the one name my brain gives me.

"Dave?" Dave barks. Right.

Rex laughs. He says, "I'll answer for him," which makes us all laugh. Rex says, "I believe you'd find out what you like."

I can see a few faces in the front now and a bit of the mostly full room. I find some eyes that look willing, the boy with a halo of hair, and say, "You? What happens to you, all alone on the planet?"

He smiles and says, "I'd be howling. I hate being alone." He pauses, adds, "Maybe I'd be partying from mansion to mansion."

Next to him, two companions seem surprised until the part about partying. The smaller one agrees with a loud chuck of laughter, "Ha, yeah!"

The bigger friend says, "Free everything." He pauses and adds, "Open pharmacies."

"You'd get bored," says a bald girl.

"You'd OD," says another, picking at her thumb.

"It would be wicked," says a third one, stirring her tall iced tea. "I don't know how to rest without being entertained. I suppose I'd find out."

"Come on now," Rex says, "Why would you need to get bored? You could do almost anything." Brightening, he adds, "Would Dave be there?"

One of the women in black says, "I used to panic when I was alone at home. I used to—but now I do feel bored when I'm alone. I feel dull and restless."

Rex says, "Forget it without Dave, but with Dave I'd go to the beach. Dave loves the water."

The girl picking at her thumb says, "The madness of the world must not be reconfronted every day."

This stops me. I sidle over and say, "First of all I love that. But, without people, what is the madness of the world that is so hard to face?"

She toggles her head and sweetly offers, "Carnivores?"

I agree heartily and lead us both to the next step. "And if there are none? Then the madness is finally just . . ."

". . . finally just death."

"So we're saying that death can't be faced fresh every day," I say.

She says, "Life can't be faced fresh every day because of death?"

Rex offers, "Or is it time we need distraction from?"

"Well, right," I offer, "I think that's the question. What would we do with time, without anyone else? Alone at the end of the world, we all would likely feel, at times at least, forlorn, forgotten, and meaningless, but some of us would also choose to feel important. We might decide that, though it may be random that I am the survivor, as survivor, I will keep alight some human flame. Maybe you need to have a project that you might not finish, you know? To make time precious, even scarce."

We talk for a while about their writing projects but we come back to the question I've asked them, about solitude.

"Wouldn't you go crazy?" asks the once-haloed boy in the dark.

Rex says, "Or maybe we're crazy now?"

"Maybe we have a crazy relationship to how we spend our time," I counter.

Rex parries, "Do you have a crazy relationship to how you spend your time?"

I allow that I do.

The girl with the tea points her straw at me and smiles, saying, "You want to be alone at the end of the world!"

Rex laughs, smiles warmly, and asks, "Do you?"

I'm flustered and realize these young people might have something, but all I manage to say is "Of course not, Dave."

Dave barks. Everyone laughs. I do too, but I'm embarrassed.

Dr. Banks opens the door and blinds us, saying the period is over but anyone who wants to can keep talking under the trees right outside. I stand on the stage to get my eyesight back before descending and I can't help feeling like a clown caught in the spotlights noticing suddenly that her jokes are all true. Wait, what? I want to be alone at the end of the world?

How Religion Helps

The Abrahamic religions compel people to take a specific day of rest, a day off from normal efforts. Jews rest from sunset on Friday evening to sunset on Saturday. Encouraged activities across Jewish denominations include worship at synagogue, hospitality and visiting family and friends over preprepared feasts with wine and bread blessings, singing, both reading and discussing the Torah, as well as sleeping and married sex. Jews welcome the Sabbath as a lovely woman, with candles on Friday night and temple visits in nice clothes.

Christians celebrate a sabbath day on Sunday, mostly, with some denominations celebrating on Saturday. For many Christians, Sunday means a church service with a sermon, a message famously inspiring, frightening (due to threats of hellfire), or both. Singing and listening to music and song can be one of the great features of these services. The Sunday meal, after church, is often the family's largest meat meal of the week. The day may be specifically nonsexual, and a day to repent of wine, rather than bless it.

Muslims take Friday as "the most excellent day" and hold that there is an hour on Friday when believers may be certain their prayer will be heard. Men are required to attend prayers at the mosque, while women have rituals of prayer and dress.

Other religions have rest periods on their own models. Hindus have many special days that are connected to a particular god and that are celebrated with temple visits and family rituals. There are resting holidays in Buddhist countries, but the religion has no regular day of rest set against weekdays of engagement and labor.

Connected to this time off from serious work, religions also provide models of playfulness, tricksterism, and foolishness.

Folk religions or traditional religions can be counted as the fifth major religion in the world by size. These religions are often tied to a specific region, tend to be oral rather than written, and may or may not be tied to moral or philosophical meaning. They can be a loose and changeable world of stories, some of which teach lessons. Their rituals praise and appease powers of the natural world and the gods and spirits described in their various stories.

Consider the Norse god Loki. Before Christianity arrives, Loki is a mischief-maker, though he becomes more aligned with the character of Satan later. In the early poetry version that precedes the prose, Loki merely messes with plans; plans of humans and of the gods. Loki inserts himself whenever someone decides to manage life through controlling all details. Loki's stories are reminders that we can overmanage the safety of our happiness such that we are not happy anymore.

One story tells that the goddess Frigg didn't want anything bad to happen to her son Baldr, so she worked her goddess off securing promises from everything in the world not to hurt him. Irked, Loki discovered that she'd skipped mistletoe, so he made a weapon from the plant and killed poor Baldr. The fact is, you can try too hard, care too much, work too hard.

How Art and Science Help

Weekends today are the result of collective bargaining, and both unions and government agencies protect people's right to days of rest. Do we rest on the weekends? Do you? A lot depends on what we define as rest and how you, as an individual, recharge and thrive.

I'd say that we have to be able to spend some time alone and offline in order to flourish. Certainly we need to be able to spend some time alone and offline if we want to be creative. I think of how travel time is marked off as leisure time by some hardworking people. That is not true for everyone as the glowing rows of open laptops attest. Many, however, see the journey part of even a work junket as special. I always see travel time as a time for puzzles, for pulpy reading, and for the arrival of unexpected thoughts and memories. You can be alone on the road.

Along with days for rest, many countries celebrate another kind of day off from seriousness, a day for jokes and tricks. Many are held on the first of April, as April Fools' Day, with traditions that celebrate both practical jokes and the art of invention. For example, Nordic newspapers often have a false story on page one on April 1. French and Italian traditions include the idea of the person who is the butt of the joke being an "April fish" and an April 1 trick-news story might include a reference to fish, as a wink to the wise. In Iran the holiday of Sizdah Bedar, on the thirteenth day of Farvardin, includes tricks and pranks carried out between friends and by the media.

Your Ritual Draws on Both

If your family tradition involves taking a particular day of the week and making it restful, you might want to pick up a bit of those traditional behaviors. In any case, many of us have something like an official day off, if not two, and we might consider whether doing nothing, just thinking, or doing something playful or creative is sufficiently part of the mix. A whole day might be difficult, and something like an hour or an afternoon might be a better fit.

Another idea is to reserve travel time for your mind to wander a bit, to allow for the poetic sacred to let the travel move you. On a train, bus, or plane, a long trip may be a strobe of solitude and company. Tell your story for laughs, tell your story for sympathy. A strobe of light and darkness. Sometimes you see the countryside, sometimes you see your face reflected in the glass.

We could take a fool's day on April 1—a day to be one's own trickster. You've heard of a day of rest? Have a day of jest. Do your art if you already have one, perhaps in some odd new way; and if you aren't usually an artist, dabble in art.

Also, read a poem. Poetry can be the domain of the tricky and the solitary. It's a way to spend time in that rarest of places, another person's mind, but with some order and artful design.

Our Poem

Here's a kicker by the Turkish author Nâzim Hikmet (1902–1963). Hikmet dazzled readers in his early poetry with displays of metrical perfection but, inspired by futurism in art and hopeful chaos in politics, he came to his own freer form.

Things I Didn't Know I Loved

it's 1962 March 28th
I'm sitting by the window on the Prague-Berlin train
night is falling
I never knew I liked
night descending like a tired bird on a smoky wet plain

I don't like
comparing nightfall to a tired bird

I didn't know I loved the earth
can someone who hasn't worked the earth love it
I've never worked the earth
it must be my only Platonic love

and here I've loved rivers all this time
whether motionless like this they curl skirting the hills
European hills crowned with chateaus
or whether stretched out flat as far as the eye can see
I know you can't wash in the same river even once
I know the river will bring new lights you'll never see
I know we live slightly longer than a horse but not nearly as long
*   as a crow*
I know this has troubled people before
*   and will trouble those after me*
I know all this has been said a thousand times before
*   and will be said after me*

I didn't know I loved the sky
cloudy or clear
the blue vault Andrei studied on his back at Borodino
in prison I translated both volumes of War and Peace *into Turkish*
I hear voices
not from the blue vault but from the yard
the guards are beating someone again
I didn't know I loved trees
bare beeches near Moscow in Peredelkino
they come upon me in winter noble and modest
beeches are Russian the way poplars are Turkish
"the poplars of Izmir
losing their leaves . . .
they call me The Knife . . .

lover like a young tree . . .
I blow stately mansions sky-high"
in the Ilgaz woods in 1920 I tied an embroidered linen
    handkerchief
            to a pine bough for luck

I never knew I loved roads
even the asphalt kind
Vera's behind the wheel we're driving from Moscow to the Crimea
            Koktebele
        formerly "Goktepé ili" in Turkish
the two of us inside a closed box
the world flows past on both sides distant and mute
I was never so close to anyone in my life
bandits stopped me on the red road between Bolu and Geredé
        when I was eighteen
apart from my life I didn't have anything in the wagon they could
    take
and at eighteen our lives are what we value least
I've written this somewhere before
wading through a dark muddy street I'm going to the shadow play
Ramazan night
a paper lantern leading the way
maybe nothing like this ever happened
maybe I read it somewhere an eight-year-old boy
        going to the shadow play
Ramazan night in Istanbul holding his grandfather's hand
    his grandfather has on a fez and is wearing the fur coat
        with a sable collar over his robe
    and there's a lantern in the servant's hand
    and I can't contain myself for joy
flowers come to mind for some reason
poppies cactuses jonquils
in the jonquil garden in Kadikoy Istanbul I kissed Marika
fresh almonds on her breath

I was seventeen
my heart on a swing touched the sky
I didn't know I loved flowers
friends sent me three red carnations in prison

I just remembered the stars
I love them too
whether I'm floored watching them from below
or whether I'm flying at their side

I have some questions for the cosmonauts
were the stars much bigger
did they look like huge jewels on black velvet
        or apricots on orange
did you feel proud to get closer to the stars
I saw color photos of the cosmos in Ogonek *magazine now don't*
    be upset comrades but nonfigurative shall we say or abstract
    well some of them looked just like such paintings which is to
    say they were terribly figurative and concrete
my heart was in my mouth looking at them
they are our endless desire to grasp things
seeing them I could even think of death and not feel at all sad
I never knew I loved the cosmos

snow flashes in front of my eyes
both heavy wet steady snow and the dry whirling kind
I didn't know I liked snow

I never knew I loved the sun
even when setting cherry-red as now
in Istanbul too it sometimes sets in postcard colors
but you aren't about to paint it that way
I didn't know I loved the sea
        except the Sea of Azov
or how much

I didn't know I loved clouds
whether I'm under or up above them
whether they look like giants or shaggy white beasts

moonlight the falsest the most languid the most petit-bourgeois
strikes me
I like it

I didn't know I liked rain
whether it falls like a fine net or splatters against the glass my
*   heart leaves me tangled up in a net or trapped inside a drop*
*   and takes off for uncharted countries I didn't know I loved*
*   rain but why did I suddenly discover all these passions sitting*
*   by the window on the Prague-Berlin train*
is it because I lit my sixth cigarette
one alone could kill me
is it because I'm half dead from thinking about someone back in
*   Moscow*
her hair straw-blond eyelashes blue

the train plunges on through the pitch-black night
I never knew I liked the night pitch-black
sparks fly from the engine
I didn't know I loved sparks
I didn't know I loved so many things and I had to wait until sixty
*   to find it out sitting by the window on the Prague-Berlin train*
*   watching the world disappear as if on a journey of no return*

19 April 1962
Moscow

The poem's title signals realizations of love and the poem is patterned out with such realizations interspersed with memories.

The poet is on a train, by the window. The first thing he says he never knew he liked is the night settling down on a smoky plain "like a tired bird," a metaphor he immediately rejects. This is the only time he tells us what he doesn't like; "I don't like / comparing nightfall to a tired bird." It's a writer's lament, in a mood of humor and doubt.

It feels like he's beginning again, trying to allow himself his epiphany; he hadn't known he "loved the earth." It should be straightforward, global as it is, but the poet undercuts this too with humor and doubt. "I've never worked the earth / it must be my only Platonic love." I laugh not only because he compares work to sex (which is what Platonic love doesn't entail), but also because he slyly thereby says that he has worked hard at all the rest of his loves, all his ideals and passions.

The loves he lists in the poem, though, are not things one works hard at. Rivers, for example. There's complex wit in "I know you can't wash in the same river even once." It is a play on the idea of the ancient Greek philosopher Heraclitus, "No one ever steps in the same river twice." Another of Heraclitus's famous statements is translated as, "Everything flows," or, "Everything changes." A moment further in time and the river is still the river, but the water isn't the same water; you are still you, but experience calms the mind. The body, too, acclimates to the shock of the cold. It's a sort of a trickster's riddle. The point is to notice how gradual change can be, so as to not miss it. Change is gradual and constant and every thing is really a process.

Hikmet's twist on Heraclitus seems to playfully deny the religious idea of washing oneself internally in a river. You can't get clean even once. Heraclitus lived in Ephesus in what is today Turkey, so the poet has a natural connection to him. It's stirring to hear a conversation across time in one place.

I am also swayed by the simple epiphany machine of the details of animals that live longer than we do, "slightly longer than a horse but not nearly as long as a crow." He worries that these thoughts are cliché, "said a thousand times before," and projects past himself with the phrase "and will be said after me."

He loves the sky. The first time we hear of the guards beating someone it is already "again." He loves the trees. Roads. Flowers. He's trying to write, but it's hard to be fresh. A memory arises.

Too bad that having a memory you would like to write up in a poem is only the first step. You have to keep up the belief that the memory is worth writing. He worries that "I've written this somewhere before"; and the even more meta, "maybe nothing like this ever happened." Well, yes. When we try to remember, there are levels of certainty. For instance, the poet "can't contain myself for joy," even after realizing that this memory might never have happened to anyone. About Marika with fresh almonds on her breath, note that her kiss isn't doubted.

What does he say he loves? The stars. The cosmos. The sun, the clouds, the snow, the moonlight, and the rain. The night pitch-dark. Sparks.

He loves the stars whether he's "floored watching them from below / or whether I'm flying at their side." He does this vantage-point shifting with the clouds farther down the poem and the spirit of Don Quixote turns them into giants. Of the stars he says: "seeing them I could even think of death and not feel at all sad." Is it true? It feels like a storm to say it.

Hikmet is troubled by the overdoing of beauty, but also when art refuses natural beauty. The sunset is cherry-red as one sees on postcards, "but you aren't about to paint it that way." In the same way, he's embarrassed to love the moonlight, "moonlight the falsest the most languid the most petit-bourgeois / strikes me / I like it." He doesn't want to love popular art, marred by capitalism, but it strikes him.

He wonders why he's having these realizations; "is it because I'm half dead from thinking about someone back in Moscow / her hair straw-blond eyelashes blue." Ah, I see. This isn't just enlightenment and nostalgia; it is also a sweet aching heart. The heartache of having loved and loving still even though if you let yourself see and feel everything you've had and lost you'd die of it. Pass on.

The last lines let us know he is sixty and the poem ends, "watching the world disappear as if on a journey of no return." Do any journeys allow return? He's en route. He seems alone. We're in this together. The date at the end of the poem is days after the date at the top. Writing takes time. So does the train. So do some of life's moments of vision and revision; here until sixty. The time this poem took happens to include April 1. Funny. You see the single and feel the double and listen hard for the rumble, rumble.

Poetry Lesson: Enjambment

If a line of a poem stops midthought, midrhythm, forcing you to rush to the next line to get the rest, it is called *enjambment*. It keeps the phrases of the poem distinct, so they carry their own meaning and yet are part of one sentence.

Breaking a meaningful sentence into two meaningful lines gives three meanings for the price of one. The rain leaves the poet "tangled up in a net or trapped inside a drop / and takes off for uncharted countries I didn't know I loved / rain." Does that enjambment mean that along with rain, the thing he didn't know he loved is uncharted countries? Yes.

* * *

"Hey, Rex?" says the big guy at center. "Why does it matter so much if Dave is with you?" Dave hears his name and with a tinkling of his collar tags sits up in a friendly state of attention. He settles his gaze on me, with about the sweetest dog face you can imagine, alert, goofy, just weirdly loving.

"*Ha!* The internet would be gone," exclaims the haloed boy's friend, he with the sharp chuck of a laugh. Then thoughtfully, "I suppose I'd stop writing. Or only a diary? Or only bang on a drum?"

"That's ironic," says a dark-dressed girl. "I get so many ideas when my phone is dead."

"You have to be alone to create, but you have to have people to create for," offers the boy with the halo of hair. Sighing, he spreads his hands out in an *I've set it all out for you* gesture.

I say, "Maybe we have to develop inner audiences who can't be taken away from us—people such as oneself, the dead, and the imaginary."

Dave lies back down as if exhausted by my absurd suggestion.

There's a jingle of his tags and a pause in the world while I just look at Dave. I tilt my head at him. He tilts his head back at me. I suddenly see that part of me does want to be alone at the end of the world. I want to be done trying to fit in, to stand out, to do enough. Can't I find a way to relax without radical solitude? Dave shakes his tags—jingle, jingle— and the world snaps back into action.

Pulling his hands into a clasp now, the boy continues, "Maybe alone you wouldn't fully create art." He pauses and adds, "That might be the least of your problems."

I give him a wan smile and feel almost infinitely tender toward him, them, everything.

Your Poem

Find a poem that speaks of rest and solitude, or silliness and tricks, or any poem with a train ride in it. Put it in your poetry collection. Look for a poem with a sense of a quest, across territory external or internal. Content can be less important than the effort of revelation. Poetry reaches across emptiness to connect our distant solitudes.

If not a train, find another sort of voyaging poem. Travel can be an opportunity to glimpse your double. Find a poem that allows paradox to create sparks in the darkness. Recall that to be inspired, often we must be disturbed. To chance and to fool are such good nouns, they had to also be verbs.

* * *

We emerge from the Little Theater into the warm, fragrant air; everyone is blinded again. I can just see Dave, gamboling about. I wonder what the days are like for him. I vow to be more like him, though I have zero idea how.

In Hikmet's poem, sorrow is lightened by the sheer unlikely joy of being kissed by a girl with the sweetness of almonds on her lips. What do we do with a day of rest? What do we do for a day of jest? We listen hard. I just remembered the stars.

There is no perfect train ride outside of poetry. Inside of poetry a poet can create a rhythm of dark and bright as when the train passes by track light after track light. Beauty strikes us. Sabbath, fools' day, and bang on the drums. Double, double. Chugga chugga. Something blissful this way comes.

10

On Earth Day and Rebirth

Climate Change Pain and Nature Festivals

"If we can stop poisoning the planet for a pandemic,
can't we stop it for climate change?"

She says, "It's like if you had a father who's a drunk and rough on your mom." She pauses to look in her bag for her vape.

"What?" I ask. We'd been talking about those memes of dolphins swimming in the canals in Venice and other marvels of nature rebounding without us during the pandemic.

"Right, and then his brother comes to town, or a job or something, and your father turns out to be able to not be a drunk for a few weeks, he can just stop."

She takes a pull on her vape and I wait. There's a bright moon and everyone is six feet apart. She says, "Right, the industries that are poisoning the planet, all the trucks and cattle and manufacturing of plastic junk, everything that is making the seas rise, they can stop, just not for you. Just not for what you care about."

"Well," I say, "that is a disturbing metaphor but I can't see anything wrong with it." She vapes and I tap my lip with my finger to think and remember the gesture could kill me.

"So," she says, "maybe we're the teenaged boy who is big enough to take on his father but doesn't know it yet and at some point soon he gets up and shuts it all down." She takes a hit on her vape. "Right? I mean why are we still cowering and letting him do this to her? This is life and death stuff, right?"

"I mean, right," I say.

Many people are twisted up inside over the fate of the natural world. We don't know what we can do, as individuals. How can we make a difference about a situation that feels far beyond our control?

How do we throw a Hail Mary without Mary?

* * *

In 1970 Walter Cronkite told the world about the first Earth Day on the evening news. He was the face and voice of objective information, a kind of national father figure who had no rival and was innocently and reasonably believed, and yet people weren't sure how seriously to take this thing. Cronkite wasn't laughing.

* * *

The new science of plants and their environments are showing us a natural world with "mother trees," vast fungi messaging systems, and other examples of vital sharing of resources. Suzanne Simard has led in both discovery and popularization of these ideas and offers remarkable proof that we can have a little faith in the forest. To paraphrase her, the forests are wired for cure.

Likewise the discoveries and writing of Robin Wall Kimmerer reframe the relationship between humanity and the rest of nature. We don't have to feel in charge of everything, of all the rescuing and all the wisdom. When we think of humanity as a junior partner with nature, in reciprocal care, it opens us up to new feelings.

European Romantic poetry worshipped nature and art in a way that was beautiful, but has potential for fanaticism, just like the old kind of worshipping. Without worshipping anything, we can learn more deeply from nature. I want to believe nature knows more than we do, and how could it not? I want to believe that learning other ways of being through listening can help us envision a way forward, and how could it not? So I am frightened and I feel helpless to help and I do hope that we will be saved by what we don't yet know about the natural world.

How Religion Helps

Religions tend to support care and such care often extends to the planet. There are significant exceptions. For example, in Genesis, the first book of the Bible, God explicitly gives humanity "dominion" over the animals and birds, land, sea, and sky, and "everything that creepeth" (1:30). Think too of the famed Genesis command to "be fruitful, and multiply" (1:28); and recall that throughout the Bible, God's top reward is a promise of megaparenthood, "You shall become a multitude" (28:3). With about eight billion people on the planet today, megaparenthood is not an ideal ideal anymore. Of course other parts of the Hebrew and Christian Bibles ask us to be stewards of a fragile Earth. The Garden of Eden, for example, was to be judiciously tended by A&E, but those values of dominion and expansion have been cited to justify rapacious consumption.

Other religions are founded on doing no harm, and would no more bulldoze a landscape than lop off an arm. The Jains are a quintessential example of selflessness and empathy for all that lives. Jain monks try to eat only what falls from plants naturally and dutifully sweep brooms as they walk, to clear any unseen critters from death by their footsteps. Hindu vegetarianism is tied to supernaturalist belief, at a basic level, because eating meat is made awkward by belief in the rebirth of souls across species. It is also an act of compassion, a choice to revere instead of devour.

Religions have nature holidays, days of rituals that turn our minds toward the outdoors. Some are fundamentally harvest festivals, others are spring or summer agricultural rites. The American Thanksgiving is today a celebration of abundance verging on conspicuous consumption, but it is also the place for families and friends to talk about what they are grateful for, and perhaps share readings of hope and thanksgiving.

The Jewish harvest holiday is Sukkoth. During harvest times farmers could not get back home every night, sleeping instead in a temporary

house, a sukkah, in the fields. Among the several construction require-
ments is a shade roof of natural materials so loosely applied that the
stars remain visible through the shafts of reeds or branches. Today that
means erecting a sukkah in whatever space avails, urban or otherwise.
It is a blessing to have at least one nosh in a sukkah at this time of year.
The little buildings dot the Jewish world for a week and it is a reminder
of the season of plenty.

The Tamils of India and Sri Lanka celebrate the Hindu harvest
festival of Pongal. It is three days of eating rice from the new harvest
boiled with milk and raw sugar, which is first offered to the goddess
Pongal. This is also a time for dressing up cattle, painting their polished
horns with bright colors and decorating them with garlands of flowers.
People make *kolam* art, which are pictures and designs made with rice
powder. There are parties and visits, and gifts are exchanged; Tamils
worldwide observe Pongal as a major festival.

How Art and Science Help

Indigenous American cultures celebrate natural forces in compelling
ways. The "Seventh Generation Principle" asks human beings to consider the needs of their descendants, to the seventh generation. The earliest record of the principle is in the Great Law of Peace of the Iroquois
Confederacy, and the idea is to plant a tree now so your future generations will have mature wood.

The Great Law of Peace of the Iroquois Confederacy governed the
Five Nations confederacy (later six) and was a marvel in the history
of democracy. It seems to have crucially influenced the formation of
the United States government. One definite vector is Benjamin Frank-
lin, who was public in his admiration for Iroquois governance. More
broadly, it was known as a system that wove power through three government branches.

Along with governing, the Great Law of Peace of the Iroquois
Confederacy organized the social and ceremonial life of the whole

confederated community, with celebrations featuring specific music, chants, dance, and trance. Coaxing oneself to feel natural can deepen connection to the natural world.

Earth Day was born in 1970 on the first anniversary of an oil spill off the coast of Santa Barbara, California, that killed thousands of seabirds, dolphins, sea lions, and seals. Rachel Carson's book *Silent Spring* had come out in 1962, documenting the harm caused to wildlife due to pesticides. The photograph known as *Earthrise* taken by astronauts in 1968 made people suddenly aware of the Earth as a fragile blue dot in space. Earth Day was born out of the idea of teach-ins, and is still a day for learning. It grew out of political demonstration and is still a way to show and share what we care about by pouring into the streets. It also arose from a need for hope and cleaning and it is still a day to clean and hope. It was first planted with the planting of one sad little Charlie Brown tree on the White House lawn, and it is still a day to plant trees. In 2016 the Paris Agreement was signed on Earth Day. In 2022 a billion people took part in the festivities.

The spread of Earth Day has had the free-form quality of a natural phenomenon—it's an idea, a date, and an unofficial flag—*Earthrise*, our planet as a wee blue circle against the wide sky. In fifty years, Earth Day has spun off and inspired an astounding number of initiatives.

Your Ritual Draws on Both

If your religion or national tradition asks you once a year to party for the renewal of Earth's bounty, perhaps use it to focus on the modern natural crisis. Read a poem and make a gesture to commandeer attention for the planet.

Let's think about how we might more robustly celebrate Earth Day, add a poem and a few physical features to increase the effect. If your harvest celebration or Earth Day has a full cabinet of holiday culture, embrace some of it, tweak it until it works, like any other art.

If the Earth holiday's cabinet is relatively empty, we've got to fill it up. Yes, we must clean beaches, plant trees, learn and listen, but what's for lunch?

* * *

For Earth Day festivals, we could all feast on the Native American food combo called the "Three Sisters": corn, squash, and climbing beans. Women did the farming, from start through harvest. Without plowing or tilling (which turns out to be bad for the soil) they created foot-high mounds in or around which are planted seeds for the three. Then in perfect timing the corn shoots up to provide a climbing pole for the beans, which support the stalks in high winds. The broad, prickly squash leaves minimize weeds in their shade; they keep the soil moist and the deer off. Beans fix nitrogen in the soil for their two sisters.

Protein makes the world. One gets the same amount of calories out of the Three Sisters as had you grown only corn, but more of it is protein, which means people can live on it. Three Sisters nutrition accounts for a population rise over the millennia as it developed and then a boom as this style of farming and eating spread. The surplus food created by Three Sisters crops allowed for urban life, and urbanity. The trip from Mesoamerica up through the northeast took only centuries. For a keystone example, Mississippian and Muscogee cultures came to flower from 800 to 1600 CE (when fatal Eurasian diseases brought massive death and cultural collapse). The Three Sisters were central to the Native American thanksgiving celebration. There are scrumptious recipes for Three Sisters soups and stews that we could serve on Earth Day.

Try to find ways to get involved. I think of Kimmerer's wonderful explanation, "Our elders say that ceremonies are the way we 'remember to remember.'" This remembering isn't always handed down continuously from parent to child. The remembering is more continuous across a broad community.

We've got the science, we need the heart.

Our Poem

We are shown the way by the former U.S. Poet Laureate Joy Harjo's "When the World as We Knew It Ended." Harjo is Muscogee (Creek) Nation.

When the World as We Knew It Ended

We were dreaming on an occupied island at the farthest edge
of a trembling nation when it went down.

Two towers rose up from the east island of commerce and
*   touched*
the sky. Men walked on the moon. Oil was sucked dry
by two brothers. Then it went down. Swallowed
by a fire dragon, by oil and fear.
Eaten whole.

It was coming.

We had been watching since the eve of the missionaries in their
long and solemn clothes, to see what would happen.

We saw it
from the kitchen window over the sink
as we made coffee, cooked rice and
potatoes, enough for an army.

We saw it all, as we changed diapers and fed
the babies. We saw it,
through the branches
of the knowledgeable tree
through the snags of stars, through
the sun and storms from our knees

as we bathed and washed
the floors.

The conference of the birds warned us, as they flew over
destroyers in the harbor, parked there since the first takeover.
It was by their song and talk we knew when to rise
when to look out the window
to the commotion going on—
the magnetic field thrown off by grief.

We heard it.
The racket in every corner of the world. As
the hunger for war rose up in those who would steal to be
    president
to be king or emperor, to own the trees, stones, and
    everything
else that moved about the earth, inside the earth
and above it.

We knew it was coming, tasted the winds who gathered
    intelligence
from each leaf and flower, from every mountain, sea
and desert, from every prayer and song all over this tiny universe
floating in the skies of infinite
being.

And then it was over, this world we had grown to love
for its sweet grasses, for the many-colored horses
and fishes, for the shimmering possibilities
while dreaming.

But then there were the seeds to plant and the babies
who needed milk and comforting, and someone
picked up a guitar or ukulele from the rubble

and began to sing about the light flutter
the kick beneath the skin of the earth
we felt there, beneath us

a warm animal
a song being born between the legs of her;
a poem.

I'm always surprised by the power of the final uplift. The poem was first published in an anthology responding to 9/11. Writing this, I went back and forth over telling you that fact before giving you the poem. It helps clarify the symbols used here, especially at the top of the poem, but can obscure the poem's broader scope.

Without the specific timing, what "world" is ending? Reading the title today the "world" ending is the result of climate change—as I write this it is 108.7 degrees Fahrenheit in Paris, France, the hottest it has ever been. "We were dreaming" is about being oblivious to the coming disaster. Is it also about being dissociated, in the psychological sense; numbed by past trauma? Awareness that the poet is an Indigenous American may lead us to our first understanding of the country as "occupied." An "occupied island" is an island with an outsider army on its territory. It can also mean an island that isn't emptied, perhaps by reason of being submerged in the Atlantic. The poem allows us to time travel in more than two directions.

"The farthest edge" of a nation hints at New York City, among other island-like edges, such as Washington, DC. The phrase also conjures the furthest edge of awareness. The second stanza tells us, "Two towers rose up . . . went down." But its story begins with twentieth-century conquering, awesome but aggressive, male in reality and symbolically—towers, men, brothers. This second time we find the phrase "it went down" we see it was consumed whole by fire, oil, and fear. True enough of the two World Trade Center buildings, which we always called "the Twin Towers," but also true of the natural world today.

Note all the lines about watching and awareness: "We had been watching since the eve of the missionaries . . . We saw it . . . We saw it all, as we changed diapers and fed the babies. We saw it . . . We heard it . . . We knew it was coming." The tone is both insight and shock. This shock is historical, but the poet is also one of us, in today's world. Today, we all do a lot of passive watching; looking on, looking back, unable to change much, or anything.

The Tree of Knowledge in the Abrahamic religions becomes "the knowledgeable tree" such that the tree itself has knowledge. The phrase predates the recent tree science, which observes the ways that older trees store knowledge and supply it across the forest when needed. The truth was espied "through branches" as "through" a screen door, but also "via" the wisdom of trees; as well as stars, sun, and storms.

Nature long suggested something was coming, but now nature says it has come. The "conference of the birds" highlights the social intelligence of animals, extended to the planet with "magnetic field thrown off by grief"; both are compelling phrases. Our "tiny universe / floating in the skies" is a tender switch-up of our usual observation that the universe is large, and we are tiny.

The poem began with the towers rising; now we rise to see them falling. "We" is getting complicated again, as it seems to be a family or group of friends in New York City. Then the destroyers in the harbor suggest that "we" is any person who had suspected that violence against the United States "was coming." Toward the end of the poem, the world ends. Then a human pulls an instrument out of the rubble and begins to sing. The song is "about the light flutter."

What light flutter? The strange and electrifying moment of quickening in gestating a baby—or interacting with nature, or making art—when we notice the world outside one's mind acting on its own, fluttering into reality, a shiver in your belly, the warmth of an animal, like lines of verse that take the poet years to understand. At the end of this poem, the Earth saves itself.

Poetry Lesson: Allusion, Romantics, Ecopoetry

The poem tells us that world had been loved for some specifics that are also profound symbols, like "sweet grasses" and "colored horses."

These symbols also refer to stories that are not specifically mentioned, so they are what we call *allusions*. If I say *King Lear* is heartrending, I am making a *reference* to Shakespeare's tragedy. If I say "Howl! Howl! Howl! Howl!" I am making an *allusion* to *King Lear* by quoting from it without making that explicit. Those howls are marked on many people's memories.

With allusion, the people who miss the meaning never know it happened. So why not always make a reference, rather than float an allusion into the ether? The reference is a handoff, the allusion a hopeful throw. So why? Because the experience of understanding an allusion brings up memories and connections. Also, the person who does understand the allusion has been flashed a secret message in plain sight of everyone. It feels special, perhaps vague in meaning, but clearly a sign.

Kimmerer's book *Braiding Sweetgrass* shows the importance of the plant "sweetgrass." In Iroquois myth it is the first plant brought by the first person on Earth, Skywoman, who fell to the world carrying a sheaf of the vanilla-honey fragrant plant. Sweetgrass is best planted not by seed but by placing the roots into the wet ground. As a botanist, Kimmerer showed that the old Native knowledge about the plant was true: harvest it and it thrives, ignore it and it may disappear. The science confirmed the poetry. Kimmerer turns it back into poetry, offering it as an example of a reciprocal relationship between humanity and nature. It allows us to see humanity's role as capable of being a positive force in nature, functioning in integral ways like the other animals, though recent on the scene.

The famous painted horses of the American West date back to the 1500s. Native American tribes created new breeds of wonderful character, slightly wild, which are today registered by lineage and color.

Horses with a colored marking only on the top of their heads, called medicine hats, were prized as protective in war and other dangers. They are part of much literature. Among the Plains Indians, stealing horses from another tribe was an honorable sport for young men, a way to gain experience and make a name for oneself. I think of the poet and novelist Sherman Alexie's poetry book *I Would Steal Horses* and the first line of the poem of that name: "for you, if there were any left."

Poets writing about nature today may see that work as part of the relatively new genre called *ecopoetry*. Some define ecopoetry as a part of the political, ethical response to humanity's attack on the natural world. Others define it more broadly, including poetry that simply cherishes nature.

The ecopoets are responding to the present crisis, but they can also be seen as a continuation of the ideals of the Romantics, the artistic movement that began in England and France in the late eighteenth century. Romanticism can be seen as a rebellion against two modern tendencies rejecting the coldness and arrogance of science, and the cruelty and filth of the factory. People were raising up art and nature as better guides for life than science and industry. They celebrated passion, wild nature, and unfettered imagination.

The story of Romanticism begins with the chance meeting of two poetry-loving young rebels, William Wordsworth and Samuel Taylor Coleridge, who published their poetry together in a book called *Lyrical Ballads*, in 1798. Separately, both went on to write a few of the best-loved English poems of all time. They both lived long and grew into establishment figures, while a second Romantic generation flared, brief but brilliant, with the poetry of Percy Bysshe Shelley and John Keats.

This poem by Coleridge is an excitement toward the natural world with an advertisement for the world of the imagination:

Kubla Khan
Or, a vision in a dream. A Fragment.

In Xanadu did Kubla Khan
A stately pleasure-dome decree:
Where Alph, the sacred river, ran
Through caverns measureless to man
  Down to a sunless sea.
So twice five miles of fertile ground
With walls and towers were girdled round;
And there were gardens bright with sinuous rills,
Where blossomed many an incense-bearing tree;
And here were forests ancient as the hills,
Enfolding sunny spots of greenery.

But oh! that deep romantic chasm which slanted
Down the green hill athwart a cedarn cover!
A savage place! as holy and enchanted
As e'er beneath a waning moon was haunted
By woman wailing for her demon-lover!
And from this chasm, with ceaseless turmoil seething,
As if this earth in fast thick pants were breathing,
A mighty fountain momently was forced:
Amid whose swift half-intermitted burst
Huge fragments vaulted like rebounding hail,
Or chaffy grain beneath the thresher's flail:
And mid these dancing rocks at once and ever
It flung up momently the sacred river.
Five miles meandering with a mazy motion
Through wood and dale the sacred river ran,
Then reached the caverns measureless to man,
And sank in tumult to a lifeless ocean;
And 'mid this tumult Kubla heard from far
Ancestral voices prophesying war!
  The shadow of the dome of pleasure

Floated midway on the waves;
Where was heard the mingled measure
From the fountain and the caves.
It was a miracle of rare device,
A sunny pleasure-dome with caves of ice!

A damsel with a dulcimer
In a vision once I saw:
It was an Abyssinian maid
And on her dulcimer she played,
Singing of Mount Abora.
Could I revive within me
Her symphony and song,
To such a deep delight 'twould win me,
That with music loud and long,
I would build that dome in air,
That sunny dome! those caves of ice!
And all who heard should see them there,
And all should cry, Beware! Beware!
His flashing eyes, his floating hair!
Weave a circle round him thrice,
And close your eyes with holy dread
For he on honey-dew hath fed,
And drunk the milk of Paradise.

This is one of the first poems I fell in love with when I was still a child. I loved the language, the rhythm and rhyme, the variety of tones of exaltation, and the drama of the phrases. Coleridge had been reading descriptions of faraway places, then came to this poem in an opium dream. Nature is much farther away in this Romantic poem than in today's free verse nature poetry. Certainly nature feels much closer in the Harjo poem. I laughed when I noticed that the central drama here is also about natural forces bursting into being and changing everything. Both poems trust the power of the Earth.

This one is by Shelley and is a vivid warning against arrogance:

Ozymandias

I met a traveller from an antique land,
Who said—"Two vast and trunkless legs of stone
Stand in the desert . . . Near them, on the sand,
Half sunk a shattered visage lies, whose frown,
And wrinkled lip, and sneer of cold command,
Tell that its sculptor well those passions read
Which yet survive, stamped on these lifeless things,
The hand that mocked them, and the heart that fed;
And on the pedestal, these words appear:
My name is Ozymandias, King of Kings;
Look on my Works, ye Mighty, and despair!
Nothing beside remains. Round the decay
Of that colossal Wreck, boundless and bare
The lone and level sands stretch far away."

It's another of the first poems I ever loved. Shelley had been reading, too. His world of wisdom was also a mix of a little information about a faraway land, and a love of imaginative creation. The message is as fresh as ever. Even what seems permanent and real can disappear without carefulness and care. Beware, beware.

* * *

What a strange nightmare. When I was young, the ocean was *the* big. The ocean is so big we gave it five names. It's so big you lose jet planes in it. Now it has a floating island of garbage. It's no longer clean enough to drown our sorrows.

I look at maps that project climate-change flooding. A lot of them show that the beaches I grew up going to will be entirely underwater. When I was a teenager, I could make the trip to the beach when I wanted, walking the half mile to the bus at the Freeport station on the Long Island Rail Road. Jones Beach is where I felt best, where the world was sufficiently beautiful. The ocean, the floating, riding waves. The breadth of the sand is immense at Jones.

All summer on that sand the same life was lived out in the open, a city without walls, beach blankets were our floor plans. Nearly naked yet at our ease we read paperbacks and magazines, ate our cooler-packed lunches, oiled up, drank soda or beer, listened to radio stations, competing or synced with nearby boom boxes. A boy would walk by calling out, "Frozen Snickers here, frozen Milky Way." Then a man, "Hey, beer here." It went on for miles.

It is terrifying that so many of the climate-change maps agree about what is happening. There is hope but there is so much inertia. The boardwalks will for a time hover just above the waves, and then they will go under. In peril from flooding, too, is Coney Island. Will the Wonder Wheel be spun by waves, scooping water into the cars we rode up and around? First I rode it with my parents and sibs, then with my cool friends, then me and John and the kids as they grew.

What about you? River rising? Even if your personal world seems safe and dry, it's a cataclysm; it is too late to save many species of animals, because we've crowded them out. Paradoxically, it's unbearable. All the more need for a sacred moment.

Your Poem

When holiday features are slim, as with Earth Day, poetry can help create dimension. There are all sorts of poems that can turn our attention to the natural world. While Earth has always felt fragile to some, poetry has made a profound response to the current crisis. Many such works can be found in collections of nature poetry or ecopoetry.

Maybe the forest will teach us what we don't yet know and that will help. We'd have the perfect right to go insane, but let's keep trying to help. What can we do but try? The trying is the sacred. Despair is reasonable, but remember how often we have been surprised by the tenacity of nature.

* * *

It's a few years later, I'm in final edits, and Portugal just hit 116°F, its hottest day on record. We need poetry and the poetic sacred in order to feel okay about doing the right thing in the face of hopelessness. Celebrate the harvest holiday of your religion, or region, and use it to honor a more reciprocal and nuanced relationship to the Earth's bounty.

LIFE CELEBRATIONS

11

On Weddings

Metaphors of Unity in Mud, Ribs, and Fire

*"I can't believe the things we've agreed
to say just to get married."*

The line was delivered deadpan, followed by a beat, then a sudden blaze in his eyes. He's telling me, and the rest of the Decline of Religion Conference audience, that his fiancée's family goes to a progressive church, and he's agreed to have the wedding there. "I'm an atheist. She thinks about religion less than I do. She wouldn't even come to this." He was charming us but was clearly in distress.

In my talk I'd explained what I call "drop by and lie religion"—how so many of us ignore metaphysics until the most important days of our lives, at which point we show up in a space designated as sacred and say things we do not believe. It's bizarre.

The fiancé riffed on the extent of his "drop by and lie" relationship to religion, and we watched him go into a bit of a tailspin listing the religious services he'd accepted for his coming nuptials. Candle lighting ceremonies, audience participation, Jesus in the vows.

He said, "I assumed that was how you get married." In many ways, he was right.

Weddings mean a lot to people, on a lot of levels. They are important for private reasons we may never tell and public reasons we may never hear spoken. Yes, we are driven by love, but we are also driven by fear and pressure. Yes, we are hopeful, but we are also not idiots and are aware that marriage is a dicey proposition.

A wedding is likely the most ritual-dense event about *you* that you will experience in your entire life. Even if you are given a birth ritual party and a funeral, you can't dance at either. This is your one day in the spotlight of ritual. Hidden in what we do and say there, weddings reveal the mad magnificence of modern expectations. It is rare in history, anywhere, for the ideal marriage to include equality, best friendship, selfless support, and ever-rekindled hot sex. It is a lot to ask of one relationship, and that's before you throw in today's engaged parenting.

Every culture has its own version of marriage, but all ask for the couple to become new people in momentous ways. With exceptions and to varying degrees, when the rite is complete:

1. You have a new family.
2. You've promised never to have sex with anyone else.
3. Your own parents are emancipated from the care of you.
4. You're expected to have children.
5. You're domesticated.
6. You're in it forever.

These are colossal expectations. You may end up calling two new people "Mom" and "Dad." You may get a new name, representing a new clan. (People will guess you are Irish, Mrs. O'Shea, née Cozzi.) For some, monogamy is a huge challenge, and even for those not overly taxed by the idea, promising you'll never have another first kiss has a bittersweet bite. Some of us want the world to see us as settled, but like it or not your condition has changed.

Your parents' metamorphoses can be as hard to fathom. I was recently at a party where a woman with a neat, gray coif and a fierce bearing said her daughter had married, and added, sotto voce, "I'm glad I'm no longer the emotional front line." The observation is commonplace, yet what had changed? And how? It is amazing that a day can alter long-standing habits and perceptions.

Much change in life is gradual, but some changes, like the frequency of parental phone calls, can shift dramatically after a moment's vow.

How Religion Helps

Religions provide a template for the wedding, a series of acts taken, and texts read aloud, to move through the event. The symbols in those acts and the stories in those readings can help humans know the time of choosing is over, down to their flesh and bones. For Jews and Christians, the classic wedding reading is in the Bible, Genesis 2:4–25, wherein Eve arises from Adam's loneliness and rib. In the story, God first answers his man's sighs of solitude with a zoology of animal pals, but Adam is still alone.

> So the Lord God caused the man to fall into a deep sleep; and while he was sleeping, he took one of the man's ribs and then closed up the place with flesh. Then the Lord God made a woman from the rib he had taken out of the man, and he brought her to the man.
>
> The man said, "This is now bone of my bones and flesh of my flesh; she shall be called 'woman,' for she was taken out of man." That is why a man leaves his father and mother and is united to his wife, and they become one flesh.

It's quite an operation, for both of them.

We slit you open and snap off a bone, wake you up, and tell you it's your wife, and to love it forever. Or try being a person's rib, turned into a person, delivered of, and to, a waiting lover. This origin story for the married couple leads into superb love metaphors: "bone of my bones," "flesh of my flesh," and "become one flesh." It's so radical, yet tender. There is a measure of violence in transformation, a tearing; he has to leave his mother and father to become one with his wife.

Change is hard and requires an imaginative leap. Speaking of it poetically helps make it true. We may find the rib story too sexist to salvage, since Adam comes first and Eve is made for him, but as we drop that keen image of marital solidarity, we should take stock of what we are losing.

Hinduism, too, has a spectacular expression of marital unity, the oneness that is always still two. The wedding rite, commonly called the *Saat Phere*, meaning Seven Turns, and officially called the *Sapta-padi*, the Seven Steps, includes a corresponding list of marital promises and acts. Before a fire the vows are read out and sworn to, and then the couple walks seven turns around the fire. In North Indian weddings:

> We have taken the Seven Steps. You have become mine forever. Yes, we have become partners. I have become yours. Hereafter, I cannot live without you. Do not live without me. Let us share the joys. We are word and meaning, united. You are thought and I am sound. May the night be honey-sweet for us; may the mornings be honey-sweet for us; may the Earth be honey-sweet for us [. . .] As the heavens are stable, as the Earth is stable, as the mountains are stable, as the whole universe is stable, so may our union be permanently settled.

The exquisite "we are word and meaning, united" shows how two can be one. The vow has each of the pair assign "thought" to the other, and "sound" for themselves, which can be read as promising to be the voice of each other's needs and notions. At the end they claim permanence through a simile with things that change but change rarely or slowly. The sky is stable, but comets and eclipses do happen. The earth is stable but occasionally quakes.

The mountains? There are seashells up there. Things change. It recalls the strange "till death do us part" in many ceremonies, which seems to open up the afterlife for nightlife and can raise spirited dispute on the romantic logistics of heaven and some of its ghosts. Perhaps we can see these as metaphorical air holes for marriage's more gaspy captives.

It is lovely but as with the story of Adam and Eve, ancient religious texts can be hinky these days. Traditionally, the vows of the Seven Steps tell the woman about all the chores she'll have to do. Edited for such egregious sexism, the vows are still daunting. Bride and groom promise to be kind partners, but also to live a healthy lifestyle, to make money, to raise great kids, and to ever strive for self-improvement.

It's an optimistic plan, which is nice, but optimism can be pressure. For Christians, Paul's First Letter to the Corinthians has a feel similar to the Hindu Seven Steps. A standard wedding text for a long time, 1 Corinthians 13 (the "love is patient, love is kind" piece) asks a lot of love. It also leads directly into one of Paul's more misogynist musings, 1 Corinthians 14.

Even if modern people cut around the chores in the Seven Steps and stop Paul before he says that women should not be allowed to speak in church, these texts are still problematic for a lot of us. The marriages they describe are too demanding. Instead, poetry can step in for the reading.

How Art and Science Help

What do we do without religion's template for the wedding? Perhaps nothing; some couples tie the knot with all the fanfare of tying their sweatpants. But swanky or slight, a lot of us want the day to have a shine to it. We want it memorable. We may also sense on some level that we want to be transformed.

Come to think of it, this is how I consoled the man at the top of the chapter who had already said *yes* to it all. His fiancée surely had her reasons for saying *yes* to it all, and it may be that without all the to-do, her clan won't see her as married. On some level, too, she may be hoping all the froufrou transforms her into someone who can do this wife thing.

The idea that "rites of passage" are important for human happiness and development, distinct from religion's story about them, is over a century old. They are first described as such in *Rites of Passage* by the Dutch-French anthropologist Arnold van Gennep, in 1909, and with lasting insight. Beyond the observation that secular rites matter, Van Gennep explained that, religious or not, rites of passage are not mere markers of change but functional "passages." By carrying out their steps, one will arrive at a new state. Van Gennep spoke of the rite and its party as a "liminal" (doorway, in between, neither-this-nor-that) space where usual rules are suspended for all. Indeed, carnivalesque behavior from the guests is part of the ritual.

The "modern traditional" is a real term in the wedding industry, and cultures around the world have them—versions of services that feel classical but are disconnected from partisan origins. We, the Interfaithless, benefit from the fact that believers could never agree on what they believed, so when their populations start marrying each other, in times of mixing (through new trade and travel, or war or other upheaval) they cut the dogma of origin stories and leave symbolic acts. Weddings come out of the church and the church comes out of weddings.

What's left is a script of symbolic doings and sayings, a script, and the lead actors are also the principal audience. The action starts with the procession, which can seem religious as a march to the altar, but which also raises emotion, as two families flow down a center aisle to pool in one delta up front. They feel the act of coming together and those attending are witness to it.

The parents of the couple convey their child to the altar and then step back. That step back enacts their new task: to stand down. And there is the vaguely arcane locution of, "Do you take this . . . ?" "I do." It seems we retain old phrases because in stiffening with age they take on the creak of liturgical speech. Which is to say they're old, and rarely used other than in oaths, so it makes you feel serious, then married. Hinduism's Seven Steps entail physical actions, along with the seven turns around the fire, such as placing flower wreaths on each other. They are traditionally carried out under the auspices of religion, but more secular versions are popular now.

If you grew up seeing people get married in a particular way, you might be drawn to doing it that way yourself, and likely it will help you feel married. You may want to tailor it, though.

Your Ritual Draws on Both

Established rituals can help you feel married, but there's a balance. You don't have to feel like you are in someone else's badly written play.

If you like symbols, you don't need religion to justify them. You can light a candle or step on a glass without offering a rationale. If you want to, you can revise a ritual's meaning in the wedding program so that your guests understand. You can write, *We use our separate candles to light the central candle symbolizing our life together!* so everyone knows that it isn't a religious act; or, *We are each stepping on a glass today, to celebrate breaking into our new future together!* Any poetic statement suggests, *This is not being done for religious reasons.*

There's a reason people fall back on the traditional routines—they're ready and waiting. They don't have to be invented. The participants and the guests *recognize* them, in both senses of that word. To make a clear statement about big changes, it helps to speak to people in language they expect. But there's a cost.

Fitting these to your beliefs and circumstances can be enormously rewarding, in the moment and in memory ever after. Anyone might fret about upsetting relatives or looking silly to friends, but you have a right to arrange for a wedding that suits you. People incorporate symbols from various allegiances into their ceremonies. Many religions in the ancient world were *syncretistic*, accepting the worship of new gods with no insult to the old ones, especially in cosmopolitan centers like Alexandria. You can too.

Weddings manage the paradoxes of love and law, change and sameness. This person whom you met at a random party, or your parents picked, or you found online in a rare mood to swipe right, is now *part of you*, legally, socially, in all future biography, and soon yet more physically in your children or whatever family or world you raise together. Wedding rituals and poetic imagery structure the passage from random to real, from happenstance to happened.

These rites can be minimal and still do the trick, but they don't have to be. The wedding gestures that you love but that perhaps seem off-limits to a nonbeliever may not be any more religious than you are. Maybe you both once were, but not at birth and not anymore.

Our Poem

The Chinese poet Guan Daosheng lived from 1262 to 1319. She was a highborn artist, and, in this poem, "You and I Song" (known more often as "Married Love" in English), she is writing to her husband. It is a wedding favorite.

Married Love

You and I
have so much love,
that it
burns like a kiln fire.
Grab a lump of clay,
mold a you
and a me.
Then smash them
into pieces,
mix the pieces with water,
and mold again a you,
and a me.
I am in your clay.
You are in my clay.
In life we share a single quilt.
In death we will share one bed.

The poem is narrative, which is to say it tells a story, and some wedding guests will follow that story and enjoy it, but some won't. It's hard to follow a poem being read to you in a fancy, excited crowd. One eyeful of bridesmaid side-boob and anyone risks losing the thread. Some couples put their poems in the wedding program, which helps a lot, but you can do more.

In the theater of the ceremony the poem can be an axis, an exceptional moment. You just need a bit of explanation. How? Well, the delicious part of the poem likely goes by too fast, so start there. By discussing the part of the poem you like best, you are able to repeat it a few times.

For this poem one could say:

> I read poetry all the time, but I can't always follow a poem new to me being read aloud, so I thought I'd say a few words to explain. We chose this poem because, in it, love is shown to be so many things. In the poem, love is sweet and also terrifying. It is sweet that our love is a fire that burns so bright, and sweet that the howling separateness of human life is so profoundly solved here, and that we get to sleep together for life. The terrifying part is that it burns like a fire, that we are broken into pieces and smashed and molded, and that we will end up one animal in two separate bodies. But we're into it.
>
> We also love how the poem is so neat and tidy, but the material it chooses to stand for love is clay, essentially mud. Love is both sweet and terrifying, but either way, it's messy. What do you expect? We're on planet Earth. Today, everyone here, we are all one clay, all one mess of love, joined forever in the hope and promise of this moment, together.

Or just:

> We love how this poem says, "I am in your clay. / You are in my clay."

Or maybe:

> Married love is known to be a bit of a challenge, but we talked about it and we really don't want anything from each other except to keep hanging around. What I want more than anything is for you to see me and feel, *There is my rest, there is my home.*

When you are near me, I feel respite, I feel the rest of me, the rest of you, and I'm whole.

Guan Daosheng's poem to her husband in thirteenth-century China says our love is like a fire, and in that fire we bake the two of us, and then we smash them up, mix the dust with water, and make the two of us again. In reality this joining together happens through time and curiosity, patience and empathy. The metaphor is profound connection and also a kind of freedom and trust.

It also shows that love is a mess, a serious mess. There's a lot of destruction and remaking. Total destruction, total remaking, new substance, remade form. Married people are separate yet united; strong bonds can go along with fierce contrary forces. An old world can be made new through the lunacy of love.

Guan is today considered China's greatest female painter as well as an influential poet, though not much of her work has survived the centuries. A woman poet of acclaim was unusual, but her husband was the government official and famed calligrapher Zhao Mengfu and he published her work in his anthologies. He was known for breaking rules in order to bring her with him on his work trips, but he often had to go alone, and this poem was written to him while he was away.

When Guan died at fifty-eight, Zhao grieved hard and followed soon after, and though married before, he was buried with Guan; reality and poem tucked in neatly together. Her work survives because of the savvy of a few empresses who collected her works.

Poetry Lesson: Chinese Classical Poetry

China is a powerhouse of world poetry. We speak of it as classical and modern with the fault line at 1912. Classical is thus a gigantic category, but it doesn't hurt to know that Guan wrote in the Yuan dynasty (1271–1368), which saw a rise of "song poems" written to be sung to existing tunes (as is done in Christendom with hymns). Yuan poetic style lasted into the Ming dynasty (1368–1644), and that mattered a lot because in the Ming poetry exploded in importance. The start of modern Chinese poetry is the end of the Qing dynasty (1644–1912), when China's poets took a bolt into free verse.

Classical Chinese poetry speaks of daily-life doings, and it was part of daily life. Friends and lovers kept in touch by sending lines of poetry back and forth, and powerful men exchanged poems to bond and impress. The form was usually short lines, of five and seven characters, juxtaposing images that sound and feel stirring together, and leaving much to the reader's interpretation.

The scholar Jennifer Purtle's literal translation shows implied words in brackets, so the first two lines are "Thou [and] I, / Excessive [are our] passions, [and] many." Purtle says the poem would have read as "racy," and a brazen statement of female desire. The relationship described in Guan Daosheng's poem also speaks to the union of author and reader, over time. We get mixed up in each other.

Your Poem

There are lists and collections of wedding poems and a lot of them are not the best poetry. They are clear and chipper and there's an ocean of them. If you love them, you can use them, because surely this is a day for happy daydreams. But note that harder works of art will help more in rough times. There are great poems that are cherished by poetry readers and nonpoetry readers, such that they've become cultural liturgy. The great poems hurt a little. Do you want to cross choppy seas on a comfy but soakable, sinkable bale of hay, or a wood-hard vessel?

The truth of a marriage is that some drown, and many are bruised. Too much metaphor? What I'm trying to say is that good poetry includes some ambivalence on any topic because feeling many ways about things is a part of the human experience. When poets include both optimism and fear we have reason to trust the optimism, since they were honest about the fear.

The poem "i carry your heart with me(i carry it in" by the early twentieth-century American poet e. e. cummings is wildly popular at weddings, to the point that the poem is cultural liturgy. A friend told me his wedding cake had the poem written concentrically around it, traveling down the tiers. It isn't an easy poem, but it's beautiful even before you spend a lot of time with it and find an understanding.

> *i carry your heart with me(i carry it in*
> *my heart)i am never without it(anywhere*
> *i go you go,my dear;and whatever is done*
> *by only me is your doing,my darling)*
>   *i fear*
> *no fate(for you are my fate,my sweet)i want*
> *no world(for beautiful you are my world,my true)*
> *and it's you are whatever a moon has always meant*
> *and whatever a sun will always sing is you*
>
> *here is the deepest secret nobody knows*
> *(here is the root of the root and the bud of the bud*
> *and the sky of the sky of a tree called life;which grows*
> *higher than soul can hope or mind can hide)*
> *and this is the wonder that's keeping the stars apart*
>
> *i carry your heart(i carry it in my heart)*

The poem opens and closes with a heart inside a heart. With the lost Biblical image of unity in love, Adam's rib becomes two hearts occupying one space. The words are at once caretaking (I'm carrying you for your sake) and talismanic (I'm carrying you for my sake). Love here is even deeper inside the body than ribs, in that tenacious thumping muscle they cage.

The interior of the poem is a brightly frenetic report on this cardiac fusion. To love is to know the world through the beloved's eyes, even when apart. There is a feeling that we will be apart a lot. The degree of mutuality expressed in "whatever is done / by only me is your doing, my darling" is nearly creepy. Fear is flagged in the tiny, set-off line "i fear." A hint of fear in a wedding poem can be a safety valve against the pressure of scheduled joy.

The poem's multiple parentheses feel like ever-greater confidences. There in the plant world's sexless striving, we find the hunger of human root and human bud. He says that love can reach past a jumble of physical and emotional limits but in calling this "the deepest secret" he acknowledges that optimism is not obvious from experience. How can we hope to exceed our own limits and love's renowned limitations? The "tree called life" grows and carries us higher. The poem's final, "i carry your heart(i carry it in my heart)" seals us up, like Adam, shy one rib and ready for love.

Cummings was inspired by the imagism of American poets Amy Lowell and Ezra Pound, a clean descriptive style animated in part by new contact with Chinese poetry. Also, after a trip to France, he was influenced by surrealism. For all that is new in his free use of language, the poem is essentially in the shape of a sonnet, and is Romantic about love and nature. The e. e. cummings and Guan Daosheng poems are images of marital unity that seem to promise that love survives *anyway*—despite the realities of fears and separations, growth and recombination. These feelings arise together, true love is like true courage in that there is no real sense to the word unless you are scared; unless you are risking more than you're holding. Consider poems that reference specifics about your wedding day. Don't worry about being too on the nose, if you get married in a barn, and you read a poem with a barn in it, it adds a sense of inevitability. It's memorable. If a poem you love has a bleak part that could feel incongruous with the day, hang a lantern on it: "We love this poem because it contains joy and despair, light and darkness." Some people trim off disturbing lines, but there is much to be said for letting the poem have a note that plays against the day's cotton-candy utopian dreams.

* * *

I was married while standing on a huge dictionary. At six feet five, my husband is an inch taller than Lincoln was, and I'm five feet three. John and I are word people—books and puzzles—so a massive *OED* was a nice way for us to see each other without neck strain, but it meant more than that. The role of wife was worrisome, for me, in the eyes of society, as my work as a scholar and writer seemed under natural threat by the condition. So we literally hoisted me up on words.

* * *

Your wedding seems like a good day to tell the truth, or try. At least it's a good day to avoid dealing out all hands from a pack of lies. A wedding is a group project, so you have to find a balance between pleasing others and doing things in a way that seems sensible to you. In whatever way you can, though, make sure some things are said about marriage that are both inspiring and real to you. To my mind, it's okay if parts of your wedding strain your taste, if you'd rather not make waves.

I think "drop by and lie" ritual can be better than no ritual at all, for many, and if you are in that situation, you can include a few sweet rebellions, details you'll look back on and smile. Stand on whatever book you want to. May it bring you height and words.

As close as word and meaning, rib and ribless, heart in heart, hand in hand. Twenty years in, marriage-wise, it's funny how easy it is to forget how mixed our clay is. He's puzzles and I'm poetry, but when one of us isn't there, who's the likely expert in the room, on puzzle and poetry matters? When you're super mad at the dear you married, the accuracy of the poem's two singular beings glows bright; you are separate from your situation. You could take whatever it is you have become on the road and find out if it works as a solo act.

But we're in it, right? And in it, the potential for transcendence through intimacy over time is an unmitigated good. It doesn't have much to do with being understood or fulfilled, but of being shared in body, heartbeat of living, and getting where that gets you. I, for one, look everywhere for signs of what I'd love to be true, which is that love and meaning grow, as with Adam, while we are sleeping. Think of it! He didn't even know. Neither will you, neither will I. If we want to try to stay together, we might think about the metaphors that make us feel united yet untied. Anagram! See what things have come to? Love's got puzzles in my poetry. Why not find out what will happen to you?

On Welcoming Babies

Snowstorms of Surprise

"I can't believe we did this."

"We almost had the baby in a snowplow," said Sameer. Taller than his friends, Sameer is usually reserved with his body. Now he's bouncing on the balls of his feet. He laughs and adds, "I don't know if we can do this." Of course, that's no joke even under normal circumstances when your switch flips from not-a-parent to parent. Almost no one has normal circumstances.

This case was extra-off-kilter. It was Sameer and Eliza's first baby. First babies tend to come late, as they knew. Eliza wasn't due for two weeks. They'd trusted in their town's speedy storm cleanup. Yes, the "blizzard of all time" was announced and snow flurries had begun outside their living-room window. Yes, she was having pain, but they'd eaten spicy food last night, of course it was that; it had ruined her sleep.

So this morning she's drowsing on the couch, not making sense of the periodicity of waking in discomfort. As she falls asleep, she sees three girls outside, their long hair loose, playing in the snow. Pain, and the snow jumps higher; she shifts position, watching, then she's back asleep. The sunlight moves across the wall an infant's length, she wakes again to pain and this time someone moaning. The girls are gone and so is the city. It's all darkness and snow. She wonders, "Was *I* the one moaning?" Now there's a new pain, a whiteout of pain. Subsiding.

When she can speak again, Eliza calmly shouts, "Sameer, it's happening."

Sameer runs in, already soothing: "No, it can't be yet."

"You're not in charge!" says Eliza. Then she stands up, adding with less certainty, "I'm in charge."

As if in answer, her water breaks.

They live mere blocks from their hospital, but no cabs or other cars are traveling.

"Why?!" yells Eliza, though she can see for herself that the roads are impassable. They're back inside deciding what to do when a snowplow slowly rolls into view. Sameer runs out and flags him down. Honored to help, the driver battles them through the storm with squinting eyes and a heavy foot, and they make it to the hospital with only minutes to spare.

A month later Sameer whisper-shouts at me, laughing, "Nobody said to worry about this happening!" Outside snow is falling again, but now we are all home with their baby girl. He grows serious and says, "I can't believe that happened." Then he picks up a tiny pair of pajamas and says, "I can't believe any of this."

"Nobody can," I say. "All new parents are shocked."

"I hope we can do it right." He brings us mugs for the hot chocolate I'd brought over in a thermos and adds, "I hope we can do better than our parents' generation. We both had secretly cool parents . . . publicly strict." He shakes his head and says, "Not good. One star. Do not recommend." Dipping a ginger cookie into the cocoa he tells me that their parents felt that they had to meet religious community standards. Sameer and Eliza wanted to live by a different kind of standard.

"But wait," I ask, "if your parents don't need you to raise her religiously, then you're done being pushed around, right?"

Sameer puts down his cocoa, waves a hand until he can swallow a bite of dipped cookie, napkin-pats his mouth, and exclaims, "It just changes targets!" He puts both hands up, palms facing me, and says, "My mother already brought her a toy stethoscope."

I bark like a seal, his eyebrows shoot up, silent pause, hilarity all round.

* * *

One hears "I can't believe we did this" from new parents for reasons both elated and forlorn.

The elated reasons are that new parents can't believe the detail of the tiny person, can't believe that they are in charge, can't believe it all came true. The forlorn reasons new parents say, "I can't believe we did this," is because new parenthood can feel merciless. Both elated and forlorn reasons can make those first days and weeks feel like you are falling down a hill, so often are you struck hard by what will not yield, and so regularly do you have a little throw-up on you.

Outside religion today, the shocks of new parenthood are not well-cushioned. Even inside religion, the age-old comforts often don't fit today's needs.

How Religion Helps

Some religions have small rituals for the day of birth. Muslims have a ceremony called *tahnīk*. Baby's first taste is to be a smidge of mashed date or honey. An imam or a chosen loved one places the smudge of date and says a few words of jubilance and prayer. The rite is commonly explained as giving the baby its first taste of the sweetness of life and a time to ask that his or her life be an asset to the religious community. There are further various explanations by region or doctrine; for instance, Bangladeshi Muslims hold that the ritual will make the baby speak sweetly.

In Tibetan Buddhism a woman helper ties off the umbilical cord with string and recites:

Oh, my child, you are born out of love,
May you live for a hundred years,
May you see a hundred autumns,
May you live long and be glorious,
May the nine evils be destroyed,
May you have prosperity, happiness and wealth.

I love "May you see a hundred autumns, / May you live long and be glorious." Tibetan Buddhism has a ritual cleansing at birth, to get rid of spirit threats that hover at the doors into life and death. A few days later friends and family gather from near and far, bearing prayer scarves as gifts for mother and baby. Two prayer banners are hung outside the house, one to protect from evil and one to bring luck.

The party is mainly in the courtyard; the baby is shielded from most people for over a month. Buttered tea is served, and barley wine, and there's a feast of fluffy pancakes; music, chanting, and dancing. These rites predate the first wave of Buddhism into Tibet, in the seventh century CE, and go back further centuries into Bon culture.

The Jewish bris is held eight days after birth. In branches of Christianity that believe in infant baptism, most christenings take place within two weeks of birth. The major religions hail from a time before obstetrics. Natural birth may have been as healthful as the modern medical version, in ideal conditions, but conditions weren't always ideal. Both infant and maternal mortality were high, in childbirth and in the first week after.

Our religions today were shaped by those realities of possible death, and they schedule their official baby-welcoming parties for a week or so *after* the baby's arrival, when it is safe to say that mother and child survived.

These days, even when nonreligious people like the idea of a traditional gathering, the strict traditional timing can make it tough. Just after giving birth is an impractical time to throw a party, so it works best when there's a system in place, with people who know the recipes and where to rent folding chairs.

Especially if there's more than one religion in the picture, tensions flare around these rites and it can feel as if they are all about religion claiming the baby. You get to choose, but it isn't always easy.

How Art and Science Help

Today *tahnīk* has delightfully morphed into bringing candy to the maternity ward, a custom many nonreligious Muslims still enjoy, literally and symbolically presenting sweetness to the newborn. Honey is not advised for infants today, and many have let go of putting anything in the baby's mouth.

The secular world hasn't created anything like a singular baby-welcoming ceremony that serves the functions we've seen in religious ceremonies. But let's consider the idea that we *do* have a robust baby ritual, obscured from our notice by its timing and as-of-yet shallowness: the baby shower. The baby shower might seem odd as a poetic-sacred baby-welcoming party. For one thing, the baby isn't there yet. Consider, though, that these days, due to advances in medicine, and a boost in average daily nutrition, births are remarkably safe. Now one *can* have a party before the birth, in confident expectation of the miracle.

Baby showers may seem like a bad moment for the sacred because these showers have a reputation as consumerist and silly. For one example, note this banter between hosts of a New Year's Eve television show in 2020. Anderson Cooper teased cohost Andy Cohen about his baby shower having been just a party of "you opening presents." What Cooper missed, because we don't spell it out, is that the gift-opening ritual is a crash course in taking care of babies, in *up to the minute* consumer reports from our peers. Many parents-to-be blush at the intimacy and unfamiliarity of the gifts and explanations (breast pumps will often do it) and don't enjoy the unwrapping, but later recall that when they opened the duplicate gift of a curved feeding pillow, people hummed and said, "Don't return it, you'll be glad to have two," and it will be true.

The medically enabled timing shift (an earlier party thrown in confidence of a good outcome) works with product-aided modern parenthood. Historically, new mothers needed extra hands when the baby came, to wash diapers, make food, and rock the baby. In modern consumer culture we meet up before the birth and present the expecting couple with gadgets to make the newborn days easier—with or without an invasion of older women. The childish games, perhaps involving baby food or bottles, help us fathom the coming life change. Still, hidden depths aside, if the shower is to be our baby party, it should be enhanced with insight and beauty.

Your Ritual Draws on Both

We might consider adding a bit of ritual and poetry to the hospital visits that close family and friends already do. A select few are often invited to show up when you are in that wild state. It could be nice to have something prepared for visitors to whisper to the new baby, and sweets, perhaps honey sweets, might be brought in to snack on. There are poems that could do a lot of good in that moment.

As for the tensions of the traditional gatherings, a flip in perspective can show us nonreligious benefits to having some sort of baby party—whether before or after the birth. For instance, as humans we are born and toddle into privileges hotly defended from anyone showing up in any other way. Think about it. Why should an intergenerational family of nine suddenly cede one tenth of its resources to this wee newcomer? Baby rituals can inspire powerful figures to recognize your child and his or her rightful portion. With a few gestures to the poetic sacred, birth rites have the power to solidify birthrights.

There's an emotional, psychological benefit in witnessing this. I've heard from new parents who allowed a religious ritual as the path of least resistance but found themselves moved by people's admiration for the baby. Wayward siblings get on planes for you; illustrious local figures make an appearance and beam at your baby in a way they don't beam at your other projects. The family's old grouches smile and take personal pride in the pride's new cub. This valuing of your baby can prove transformative in the moment and sustaining later, when you are bogged down for weary stretches in the diaper trenches.

You can opt for an Interfaithless version of your family's baby-welcoming party, using the same timing, same food, same music, but no priest. Ask key people, in advance, to hold the baby during a recitation or ritual. If you want, create a climactic moment, with the crowd coached to respond, "Welcome to the world!" Or to draw out the gooey goodness of that last one, write a few lines of welcome, listing a few things you think they might like. Here, I'll take a crack at it.

My darling! Oh, welcome to the world! Welcome to the strange and endangered world, welcome to its sweet mother's milk and to its weird sleeping dreams. Welcome to its mangoes and apples, to its bread. Welcome to you, sweet child. Welcome to a universe already expanding, to red oleander, to oranges, to yellow stars, to pale green leaves just born in spring; welcome to blue lakes rimmed with violets. Welcome to the story of the Big Bang and whence it flew. Who knew, all along, we were waiting for you?

A benefit of designing your party as a translation of a religious one is that classic ritual motivates people to travel. Just as it is bad form to miss your niece's christening, so it will be bad form to miss your niece's poetic christening, or metaphoric mitzvah. Common terms for these today are "naming ceremony" and "baby welcoming," and these will gather the healthy and willing, but if you want the lame stragglers, try a postreligious flourish. Your invitations can echo traditional ones, in physical material and speech pattern, but with a poetic-sacred twist. Perhaps write a simple, "This a sacred party to welcome Baby Raya to our family, histories, and songs."

The classic "baby book" comes from the same era as "formula," so named because doctors were supposed to examine your baby and then give you a formula so that your baby drank a personalized potion. Mom did her part by recording baby's intake, growth, and development. Over time the booklets sold to hold those notes grew inspirational and more interested in sweet memories than in health stats. True they often have only a few pages filled in, but aren't those few pages precious to us?

What if we kept using these baby books but filled them with poetry? Maybe we could ask our friends to bring a printed poem of the physical dimensions of our baby book and tape each to a page when they come to visit.

If the only thing you like about a religious celebration is the music, make much of the music and drop much of the rest. In any case, think about music that feels poetically sacred to you and music that could add a zest of your history to the party.

Our Poem

At baby-welcoming ceremonies, religious or otherwise, it is common to include a poem in the day's proceedings. If you don't believe what is said in the ritual, or if you've cut the religious texts, it can be important to hear a *believable* sacred-toned portrayal of what you're going through today and why your tomorrow is going to be okay.

At Sameer and Eliza's baby party a friend read an eight-line wonder by the Persian poet Jalāl ad-Dīn Rumi (1207–1273). It is a popular choice for baby welcoming, worldwide. Rumi gave it no title, so we call it by the first line.

> *You were born with potential.*
> *You were born with goodness and trust.*
> *You were born with ideals and dreams.*
> *You were born with greatness.*
> *You were born with wings.*
> *You are not meant for crawling, so don't.*
> *You have wings.*
> *Learn to use them and fly.*

The first lines defend children against those who would presume to instruct them in potential, goodness, and dreams. The poem also assures the new parents of their own innate know-how.

Reading this poem at a gathering can also serve as a message from the new parents to the controlling authority figures in the room, saying we should love children as they are. Saying, *It's our turn now*. Saying, *Back off*. The poem prizes the morality of a child's heart above the dry old authorities. Another meaning evoked by baby-party context is that with every birth, greatness is born again for all of us. Tell your guests that—they might need to hear it. Having delivered gifts in the first five lines, the poem commands that we use these gifts. "You are not meant for crawling, so don't" at a baby party is funny. It also amplifies the fantasy of the next lines' flight.

The poem says we were born with so much greatness it has to be partly saying that we can kick back and bird-watch or play a video game. The poem gives us that, but now we see there is another message in it, that you were born for better.

You are not meant for crawling, so don't.
You have wings.
Learn to use them and fly.

Subtly insulting, the poem tells its readers that we are living on our knees in order to tell us we can fly, and by some law of life, must try. Subconsciously, if not otherwise, the message gets through. Read at a party, all people will hear is ebullient validation and inspiration in surprisingly short, clear, normal sentences. People will feel better. People who need to reassess, may reassess.

Poetry Lesson: Rumi and Persian Poetry

Eight centuries ago, a poet used eight short lines and since then millions of people have been moved to recite them and pass them along. Persian poetry is one of the highlights of world literature, especially in the lyrical golden age beginning in the thirteenth century.

Rumi is a founding figure and constant star. He was a Sufi, the mystical sect within Islam. Sufi poetry was intended to be read as love poetry *and* as a mystic's diary of a passionate quest to deeper awareness of the unity of all. Rumi wrote of transcendence but with a careful avoidance of the specifics of religion or sect.

His wisdom is uncanny and popular in many languages. Here are a few compelling examples of his wit and insight.

"Your task is not to seek for love, but merely to seek and find all the barriers within yourself that you have built against it."
"The wound is the place the light enters you."
"If you are irritated by every rub, how will your mirror be polished?"

As the Rumi translator Shahram Shiva writes, "Rumi is able to verbalize the highly personal and often confusing world of personal growth and development in a very clear and direct fashion. He does not offend anyone, and he includes everyone." It seems spectacular that a poem written eight centuries ago is meshing with the latest thinking on raising happy, healthy children, and that the newest forms of welcoming our children are so welcoming to these excellent words.

* * *

I've heard of some surprising paths to compromise. At a lunch between conference events I put my tray down near a woman sitting on her own and, as it turned out, she'd attended my talk and had a story for me. Her husband's family had a tradition of brides later using fabric from their wedding dresses to make christening gowns. She'd heard about it obliquely when an aunt was pleased that she'd chosen a casual wedding dress, as it makes it easier to cut up in a few years.

"Huh?" She thought she'd misheard. "Cut up my wedding dress?"

"Oh yeah, it's what we all do. Three generations, we use the skirt fabric to make christening gowns for the babies." The mention of babies felt hugely embarrassing at the time, and intrusive, "Babies!" she repeated to me at the table, adding, "Plural!" and hitting the table with her hand. Bam! Rattling our silverware. They weren't even sure they wanted children. So she'd heard about it, but had "filed it without comment," she explained, gesturing such a filing job with a swooping glide of her hand to the rear of her skull.

She had essentially forgotten about it a few years later when she and her husband gently let the families know their baby wouldn't be baptized. They met unexpected resistance but at last realized that the quirky dress-to-gown tradition was the loss most grievous, and held a christening-gown party with no christening. She let the aunts do the sewing, it turned out cute, and there were photo ops, toasts to the baby's health, and gifts.

"Everyone was happy enough," said my lunch companion.

"'Happy enough' is the best you can get with 'everyone,'" I said. We laughed and I thanked her for the ingenious story.

Such compromise is a reminder to examine carefully what matters to the people you'd like to please, including yourself. Much ritual seen as religious is a fundamentally poetic, artistic amplification of the natural sacred.

Your Poem

Baby-welcoming poems that imagine the baby into the future help us understand that a mewling ball of blanket is a person. If you are family, that ball of blanket may be at your funeral, may be the person who comes through for you when there's no one to drive you to the market or help you put on your pants. A poem that imagines the baby into the future hints at this heart-rattling truth. A poem may also point out the colossal mercy and heartache of parenthood, that the child's stages keep changing.

If it is hard to find a poem that you vibe with enough to read aloud, find one that has a line in it that you love, and tell your audience that the poem grabbed you there. Look for poems that speak of transformations and evolutions. At a first-time baby shower the expecting couple may be hyper scared, or in joyful ignorance. She may be suffering physically; he may be at pains to keep it together. The poems can help us see ourselves in a wonderful great chain of really being here.

At a celebration on the day of birth, a poem should acknowledge the upheaval, what they've been through and what they are feeling. For celebrations a week after the birth, consider poems that revel in the joys of parenthood, with gentle hints about the struggle.

People seem to like list poems for baby-welcoming events. You can find one that fits your mood or sketch up a list of things to tell the baby about yourself. Have fun with it. If you got to the hospital on a snowplow chariot, or if it was an otherwise difficult birth, you can acknowledge that with some chaos in your list. I'll try another:

Welcome! Welcome dear child to our absurd and precious world,
to our corroded world, to the opulent and the scarce, to the un-

derworlds of feeling, to forgiveness and remorse, to love, to the lean and taut, and the slack relaxed. To the wonder of flying squirrels and hanging bats. Welcome to cows and cats, storms and facts; to parallels and swings. And why we are all so happy, and why sad singers sing, and that the sea is hiding fish, and that all wings have dreams, and dreams have wings.

* * *

When our daughter was born, we only caught our breath to have a naming ceremony on her second birthday. Not ideal, but it was still fabulous. A friend who taught at a humanist Jewish school said some words and led us in song. My husband read a little poem I'd written, a list poem specific to our girl. We ate deli. My sister-in-law said she'd never been to one of these and I told her no one had, we'd made it up.

"Can we do that?" she asked.

I bounced my head to show I shared some trepidation and then said what that humanist teacher had once said to me, when I'd asked a similar question, "Who's stopping us?" She also said, "The orthodox wouldn't recognize any ceremony you'd be comfortable with, so why are we wincing?" Now I believe the right answer is that not only *can* we do it, but also we *should* do it. It's good for us. For the baby, someday, the pictures and story of the day, and the poem, may mean a lot. The Interfaithless can all do different rituals, but in the same spirit. When we all invoke the poetic sacred by drawing from the same canon of renowned world poems, we'll feel one another's support.

* * *

If the old ways seem awkward now, we'll need to find new ways to celebrate—especially for when we are flabbergasted and baby-blasted by love and wonder, scared half-daffy, and clinically exhausted. We can't believe we've done this. Or that we can give all that needs to be given. Yet, we can't believe our luck so far, either, holding the tiny new being. All year long we see the light in the garden break fire against the greenery and stone, hope and spleen, and can't believe the luck of it, to be so situated as to see the light like this, just as it is today. You deserve a moment to stop everything and celebrate it all.

In this crazy, mixed-up world, we are all snowplow babies. Then summer comes and the greenery displaces snow with the boundless intention of youth with something to prove. A hundred autumns, a call to be glorious. The garden is ephemeral, yet Brooklyn is perennial. Something between the garden and the light is Brooklyn. The garden is what is created by our strange, sustained astonishment, after all these years.

A poem often published with the title "A Jewish Blessing" includes the lines "In every birth, blessed is the wonder," "In every love, blessed are the tears," and "In every transition, blessed is the beginning." These blessings condense paradox into words and they aid the magic of transition by getting us to say the word "transition." Here is to love and to creation, to what doesn't last, to holding and letting go, and to the brutal unsettled beauty that marks us forever and then moves on.

On Coming-of-Age

Seijin no Hi, Quinceañera, and a Different Drum

"You don't have a nationwide party when you turn twenty?"

Kei scrolls through brilliantly colorful photographs and bursts into tears, laughing. I'm delighted seeing her come alive like this.

She says, "You don't have anything like this?"

Japan's Seijin no Hi is a rite for the passage into full adulthood, at twenty. On the second Monday in January, everyone who turns twenty that year gets dressed up in ornate kimonos and complex hair, or in suits of inventive chic, and all gather at the town hall for a day of congratulations and entertainment. The crowd outside beforehand is an immense swath of loveliness. It can be frosty in January, and many kimonos are accented with fur. Tokyo Disneyland hosts a Seijin no Hi every year with celebrity guests and pop acts. At smaller, local celebrations there may be slideshows of teachers and the kids growing up, as well as bands and dancing.

Kei said she'd looked forward to dressing up, checking out the show, and then going out drinking with her small group of friends. Twenty is the legal age to drink and smoke. News reporters say, "How do you feel?" to the stunning, uniquely dressed young people waiting to enter the gala and it isn't rare to get a response similar to what Kei said she had expected, early in the evening. "I just want to go out and drink like an adult, in public." More than a few add an intention to get hammered, as young adults anywhere might say on such an occasion.

Later, though, one can hear multiply in the streets a shout of joy peculiar to unexpected reunion, often in layered voices as groups meet groups, punctuated with solo shouts of awe.

"At Seijin no Hi," says Kei, "what turns out to matter is meeting people from across our entire lives. In childhood we have many schools and activities and sometimes never see friends again." Modern childhood has us so often marooned with age-mates, in ever-shifting schools and activities. When the streets are packed with people exactly your age, you spend the day seeing nearly everyone you ever knew.

Seijin no Hi is credited with a historical antecedent in the year 700, when a young prince received a gift of adult clothing; but today's practice was started in 1946 to encourage the generation coming of age after World War II. Imagine turning twenty in Japan in 1946. And what world are we asking young people to take over today?

Classically, coming-of-age is about demonstrating acquired skills and gaining responsibility and the right to take part in the group's culture. Today there are so many skill sets for young people to acquire, so many kinds of responsibilities and attainments, it is hard to imagine choosing one as the mark of the "grown." Yet this abundance of maturity markers makes it that much more significant to have a big moment of welcome into the big world. This celebration can also help parents and mentors start letting go, and prompt them to sum up some advice.

Making notes on coming-of-age rituals I soon tired of writing "coming-of-age ritual" and switched to the acronym "COAR." COAR nicely recalls the word "roar," reminding us of lions; and "core," a center and support; and "*cœur*," French for "heart"; and "*corps*," French for "body," which, in English, became "corps." Coining COAR was about brevity but has influenced my rethinking about this. A new word can help us update ideas.

How Religion Helps

Many of us may think of a COAR as a single event marking a teenager's passage from child to adult, in the eyes of the group. In popular depictions, it is often a one-time event centering on a test of skill and endurance, sometimes terrifying, whether killing a lion in the Kalahari Desert, or killing a Torah portion in Scarsdale despite stage fright unto fainting. It's more interesting than that. Coming-of-age ceremonies around the world mark any or every stage of growing up. Sometimes coming-of-age is about adulthood within religion; and the ritual test is a display of religious skills, or the child's first pledge to the religion. Sometimes they instead celebrate nonreligious achievements, like school tests, life skills, or just a physical maturation, like hitting a given height.

Finding so many persuasive ages for COAR, three age ranges for celebrating emerge.

> Ages 6–8: You're not a baby anymore and can take part in serious doings.
>
> Ages 13–16: You're a young adult, know of sex, and are not naive to loss and lies.
>
> Ages 18–21: You're that legal age when youth can neither restrain you nor explain you.

Historically, people rarely knew their birthdays or even their birth years; before industrialization, life wasn't sufficiently calendar-based for it to be of interest. As such, these COAR celebrated maturation and development as observed by grown-ups around the young person. That may sound more sensible, but development happens in various physical and mental ways and any given marker will fail someone; Margaret Mead thought it unfair that taller girls were given more work in Samoa. Even today some COAR have an age range for celebration, at the discretion of teachers or parents. Within such age-range limits, sometimes the young person decides the when, as with the lion-confronting warrior ritual in the Kalahari.

In Roman Catholicism, first communion is at age seven, that being "the age of reason"; they then celebrate "confirmation" between ages twelve and fifteen. In the official teaching of the Church of Jesus Christ of Latter-day Saints, the minimum age for baptism is eight, "the age of accountability," and anyone younger than eight "is an innocent." The Jewish bar or bat mitzvah is at thirteen, with the Orthodox girl's bat mitzvah at age twelve. In Islam, children join the regimen of daily prayer at age seven, and at puberty begin practicing the religion as an adult. For the Baha'i, fifteen is the "age of maturity," when youngsters are welcomed into the world of prayer and fasting.

The Hindu samskara rituals celebrate baby's first outing, and every little coming-of-age, from first solid food and on through the touchstones of life. There is one rite for reaching the age for religious rites, and later, another one for reaching adulthood. A cardiologist I met on a plane—we were both doing crosswords—told me that his Hinduism meant going to pujas maybe once, twice a year to see family and catch up on any juicy news. "We love blessing things," he said jokingly, "and dressing bright and fancy." He explained that he didn't think he'd do any of it on his own, but added sweetly, "but I let them bless me." We grinned at each other and went back to our puzzles.

How Art and Science Help

Outside religion, today, we celebrate growing up with birthdays and their festive rituals. Birthday parties write the word "Happy!" on cake and light it on fire. They sing you a song with your name in it. You get a wish and blow out candles to make it come true. There may be helium balloons, those colorful freaks of gravity. There are fancifully wrapped gifts. It's merry, but specific birthdays could have more specific meaning, perhaps with the addition of a poem.

A wonderful example of a meaningful birthday is the celebration of a quinceañera, a girl turning fifteen, a practice thriving in many Spanish-speaking cultures in the Americas. (It's a common error of American English to use the word "quinceañera" to mean the party, rather than the girl.) The bash can be as elaborate as a wedding and has a rich store of rituals. A central one is the "Tree of Life," in which the quinceañera presents candles to fifteen people who have influenced her, making a speech about how each helped her grow into the young adult she is.

In some countries there is a church component to these parties, but they aren't at base religious. Instead, the fete is only a century old and began as a lighthearted social ritual to welcome a teen girl to makeup and stockings, talk of young men and old warnings.

The twenty-first-century quinceañera is altering some long-standing rituals, such as the Changing of the Shoes, wherein girls switched from slippers to high heels, because neither the symbolism nor the footwear was making the birthday girls happy. They still do the ritual but go from one pair they like to whatever shoe they also like but that feels more grown-up—including tough boots.

Germany has a specifically nonreligious COAR for fourteen-year-olds that is remarkably well-established. It's called the *Jugendweihe*, or Youth Consecration, and it began in 1852 as a humanist replacement for Christian confirmation. Nonreligious families wanted an analogous event for the life lessons and coming-of-age gala that the Church had long arranged. So, they set this up. It may be hard to imagine a sizable nonbelievers' association so long ago, but it seems that in German cities by 1850, atheism was ordinary enough to inspire such innovations. There were even different varieties. Arthur Schopenhauer's philosophical, idealist atheist *World as Will and Representation* came out in 1818; Ludwig Feuerbach's historical, materialist atheist *Essence of Christianity* was published in 1841.

To prepare for *Jugendweihe*, teens take humanist classes, go on nature walks together, and make visits to London or Paris, all of which culminates in a nationwide bash. The custom took bad turns in World War II and later with East German state control, but today *Jugendweihe* again champions humanist values. The Humanist Association of Berlin-Brandenburg prefers to call the event a *JugendFEIER*, meaning "celebration" (emphasis theirs) to distinguish it from the idea of consecration, and generally make a fresh start. The experience requires some effort and yet is hugely popular. In 2018 in Berlin 10 percent of the youth population took part in the classes and events leading up to a party in town halls and movie theaters with celebrities, live music, and other acts.

The key personal ritual for the young people is the solemn bestowal of "the gift book," a specially made orientation handbook for life in the here and now, updated every few years, by experts and peers, arranged by the humanist associations. There teens find life advice about finding joy in nature, art, science, and love. The book contains a portrait of their generation, and the world they will set out in. We're all born in medias res—why not take stock together? Who wouldn't want a book that sums up the world you are stepping into?

The teen Germans, waiting with sweet pale faces, are called up to the stage and given a book and a flower, the back of the audience sniffling with pride in the darkness, and all we can ask of the young is to keep on surprising us with their fresh eyes and zest for life.

Your Ritual Draws on Both

If your religious tradition includes a COAR, consider taking part in it, with adjustments. You can make all the ritual's texts copacetic with your beliefs, or just add enough poetry that the young person is genuinely inspired and encouraged. People seem most romantic about their childhood COAR circa age seven, recalling the dress-up and drama, stage-size symbols, and the sense of the uncanny. Perhaps a candle ceremony with an exciting recitation evocative of wonder.

I would hate for these ideas to give any kid homework they don't want, or additional attention that they don't want. In particular, in many religions and locations, sexuality was once a major part of teen COAR, but these have largely become private matters. Some young people will welcome a revival or an invention of a COAR ritual. Others perhaps have sufficient challenges already that could be more memorably celebrated. The gift of a poem on significant milestones can be formative.

You can put a poem in a greeting card for your young person. Or type it small (they have good eyes), fold well, and tuck it into a gift wallet, or a locket, or other portable pocket.

Our Poem

Consider "Jabberwocky" by Lewis Carroll (1832–1898). It's a marvelous work at any age, but especially for the young.

Jabberwocky

'Twas brillig, and the slithy toves
  Did gyre and gimble in the wabe:
All mimsy were the borogoves,
  And the mome raths outgrabe.

"Beware the Jabberwock, my son!
  The jaws that bite, the claws that catch!
Beware the Jubjub bird, and shun
  The frumious Bandersnatch!"

He took his vorpal sword in hand;
  Long time the manxome foe he sought—
So rested he by the Tumtum tree
  And stood awhile in thought.

And, as in uffish thought he stood,
  The Jabberwock, with eyes of flame,
Came whiffling through the tulgey wood,
  And burbled as it came!

One, two! One, two! And through and through
  The vorpal blade went snicker-snack!
He left it dead, and with its head
  He went galumphing back.

"And hast thou slain the Jabberwock?
  Come to my arms, my beamish boy!

    O *frabjous day! Callooh! Callay!"*
        He chortled in his joy.

    '*Twas brillig, and the slithy toves*
        Did gyre and gimble in the wabe:
    All mimsy were the borogoves,
        And the mome raths outgrabe.

Between the doubled first and final stanza is the cryptic terrain of a tiny inner epic. Epics are long by definition. This one mimics the steps, but in miniature. An elder teaches a youth about dangers. Next stanza he's grown, armed, and out there—looking for his life-defining fight. Searching is hard and he rests. When I read this as a child the lines where he rested, "And stood awhile in thought," so drew me into the picture that I can still feel leaning there, sword at my side, one foot up on the tree behind me, gone to thought. Losing heart? "Uffish thought" sounds frustrated to me.

Into this stillness crashes the Jabberwock. We've heard of its claws and jaws, now it arrives with eyes of flame. We feel it coming closer and in a single, singsong stanza the battle rages and our man is gloriously, gorily victorious. In that stanza's final line, the hero gets home. To think that took Ulysses ten years.

Then comes the stanza of joy, an ultimate childhood fantasy of heroism, group salvation, and parental accolade. The elder's "Callooh! Callay!" picks up the glee of "Hip hip hooray!"

Children note in words and acts that normal adult adherence to the daily usual is a kind of insanity, but they also know it's rare anyone achieves wonder outside the rules. As such, kids receive genius-level nonsense as proof against boring adulthood, and we are lucky to partake in that when they do.

Poetry Lesson: Ballads and Nonsense Poetry

"Jabberwocky" is known as a nonsense poem, perhaps even the best of the form, but nonsense in poetry isn't truly nonsense at all. It's also a ballad, a poetic form not strictly defined by rules but recognizable by a cluster of traits.

1. Ballads usually tell a story,
2. usually have songlike regularity in short rhyming lines, and
3. usually have a touch of chorus-like repetition.
4. Often ballads are in quatrains, meaning four-line stanzas, with an ABAB or ABCB rhyme scheme.

Ballads were dominant in Ireland and Britain from the medieval period and eventually grew popular across Europe and then in the Americas and Australia. It's said to be the natural form of English-language poetry. "Jabberwocky" calls back to the book-length medieval ballad *Beowulf*, in which a young knight must battle a human-eating monster named Grendel. Carroll's poem sketches that triumph with a triumph of economy. Who knew you could tell that story so fast?

The young should be offered the ride of high fantasy. Most other poetic epics, whatever their genre, will be more uffish throughout, frustrating I mean, and rife with failures. Tales with setbacks and melancholic endings are praised today for complicating the old fantasy-style children's stories, but precisely which texts supply that bedrock fantasy? Where is the original win we are all deconstructing? It is in "Jabberwocky," for one.

Whether the poem is already an old friend with your young friend, or the youth is new to it, receiving the poem at a COAR may connect this young person to the poem in a way that feels special for life.

There's more about the poem that might be useful to have on hand. Carroll wrote and published the first stanza on its own, with companion notes of etymological silliness. In these notes, at times, he seems to be genuinely guessing why his mind handed him these rhythmic sounds; at other times, I'd say he's just making things up. I am further persuaded that this interpretation is not to be taken as settled because when Carroll later published another decoding of the same words, he's not always consistent with his early definitions.

The story of the Jabberwock went from stanza to full poem because friends and family loved the lines and begged for more. Carroll obliged, writing the rest of "Jabberwocky" and making the poem central to the *Wonderland* sequel, *Through the Looking-Glass, and What Alice Found There*. Alice asks Humpty Dumpty to help her decipher the poem (again only the first stanza is decoded).

In both this explication and the earlier version, Carroll says "brillig" is a time of day: about four o'clock in the afternoon when people start "broiling" food for dinner. I'd previously read "slithy" as "sly" and "lithe," but Humpty, making sure Alice knows that two words smushed into one is a portmanteau, says the condensed words in this case are "lithe" and "slimy," a gross image compared to mine. I see no profit in arguing with a talking egg and move on.

Translating the stanza with Humpty's definitions reads as follows: It was near dinnertime, and the lithe, slimy, spiraling snake-badgers were twirling around ("gyre") and screwing themselves into the ground (to "gimble" is to move as a gimlet, a corkscrew tool) around a sundial. Alice here guesses correctly that "wabe" implies a sundial because time goes a long [way be]fore and a long wabe hind; also on the scene were flimsy and miserable ("mimsy") borogoves, those being birds already normally thin and shabby-looking, but here further abject, with "feathers sticking out all round—something like a live mop." The "raths," green pigs, who Humpty guessed were called "mome" because they were far "from home," they were lost, added the egg with sagacity. And what, Alice asked, is "outgrabe"? It's an awful screaming. The far-from-home green pigs were screaming.

Carroll's version is dark. Nasty, frenetic beings are spiraling madly around time, while tattered and half-bald old birds molt feathers from tired fashions, and the lost green pigs repeat their awful cry. In my mind "mimsy" is upbeat, because it sounds like "whimsy," rather than "miserable" and "flimsy," and we don't have to believe Carroll's definitions. I do find them delish for their syntax, and because right below the surface of a joyous poem, there is a companion in despair. It's such an imaginative, absurd despair.

Both "Jabberwocky" and *Beowulf* are remembered as pinnacles of accomplishment, but there is more to it in each case. After Beowulf kills Grendel to stop him from eating people in town, Grendel's mother shows up raging for vengeance, and even when that battle is dispatched, at last enters the dragon.

Likewise, in the paternal warning stanza in "Jabberwocky," there are two more monsters, still out there, the Jubjub bird and the Bandersnatch. Even in the primal vision of triumph, where a battle won feels like a good job done, there's a hint of how life really comes at us (it keeps on keeping on).

Your Poem

To find your own poetry for a younger COAR keep in mind that young kids love the fabulism of "Jabberwocky." Few poems have as many invented words, but fabulism is one of poetry's regular styles; you'll find ample stores from which to choose. Maybe try an advice poem, whispering in urgency. Consider the Rainer Maria Rilke quote I spoke of in the introduction, which is from his book *Letters to a Young Poet*, and which floated down and saved me. Not all advice poems must meet that feat; indeed, any one that moves you might mean the world to the young person you give it to, because you gave it to them.

You might want to include a brief explanation with the poem. This can be your chance to say what you hope will be remembered. If it's hard to start with praise or advice, just write that the poem moves you, for its sense of play, home, or whatever, and that you want them to have it too.

Here's a sample:

This seems like a good moment to welcome you to the next part of your life's big adventure. I know you are going to be great! You are already great, and you just keep leveling up. We couldn't be prouder. The advice I want to give you is advice you only dare give special people because no one else will be able to hear it anyway. You already know it, but I want to throw a floodlight on it. Follow your own intuition, but also pay attention to what you do that seems to help people. If after much toil you win the day, who will say "Callooh, Callay"?

Also—and no one wants to hear this when they are young and running out there—but there will be times of uffish thought. It can be hard, but I believe in you. It is a big world and I hope you let yourself learn about it slowly. I know you are going to be magnificent, as a friend, as a person with kindness to others and to themself. I know if you want to swing a lasso to the moon and pull Greenland out like a sink stopper, you can and you will, and I await the cleaning bill.

For all of us, even in good situations, it can be confusing and painful just being a person. There are actual honest-to-goodness triumphs in life, but only if you notice them. The frumious Bandersnatch is still out there, but it's still time to Callooh Callay today. You are my beamish young person already. Beamish as can be. The triumph of most note is a matter of the heart, what it loves, what it keeps. Stay curious. Take rests. Be kind. Make a mark on the paper and see if you don't feel better. There are going to be mistakes! As Rumi said, "There's a crack in everything, that's how the light gets in." Read your poem.

We call out to the past and when the past calls back, we are startled to hear a living voice belting back from back there. The intimacy matters as much as the advice.

* * *

When I was ten years old, a teacher gave me a poster with lines from Henry David Thoreau:

Why should we be in such desperate haste to succeed, and in such desperate enterprises? If a man does not keep pace with his companions, perhaps it is because he hears a different drummer.

Let him step to the music which he hears, however measured or far away.

To me it said, "Stay weird." Did I enjoy learning that I was noticeably out of step? Conflicted. Mostly yes. I liked being singled out. But it kept happening. Over and over grown-ups called me a "different drummer," smiling sideways. They'd tell me to not let anyone change me. Year after year, every teacher from third grade on.

I hadn't thought of it in a long time but writing this brought back the image of the poster, eight-by-fifteen parchment, from that teacher. Written in calligraphy; eventually curling old tape on the corners. It mattered that it was chosen for me. The quote still feels quite mine. In ninth grade, I was sitting in the back of the room in History wearing black and talking in class and the teacher called out my name.

"Yes," say I, outer moose, inner mouse.

"You're what they call a different drummer. Cut it out."

Well, slap me silly. There's a coming-of-age for you. I was old enough to find this hilarious and actively filed it away as material, I suppose for this book. Then I guess the nineteenth century finally ended on Long Island and I stopped hearing the term. Folks found more modern ways to call me a weirdo.

* * *

I think of Kei setting out on the seas of life with a sense of her town and her friends as a kind of bedrock dock to which one ever returns. Consider the lines before and after the standard version of the Thoreau quote, above. It is from the end of *Walden*. The preceding line is: "Let everyone mind his own business, and endeavor to be what he was made." And the lines after: "It is not important that he should mature as soon as an apple tree or an oak. Shall he turn his spring into summer?"

History happens to everyone. It hurts to live in interesting times, but it's not only a curse. Sometimes we have to accept that we are in a story that is larger than we are. A story about a generation, a time. The advice is be your own authentic self, but also try to go along with your times. The story is, you are born into a freaking nuthouse—world wars, new diseases, Bandersnatches—but so is everyone. So try, but don't beat yourself up if a wave comes in. They come in.

Truth is, I don't know anything. Childhood is a bit of a hypnotic trance from which we awaken, alone and together. We were children a moment ago. Thinking of the changes we have grown used to, it becomes clear there are a lot of acts to a one-man show these days. Looking back through time and space, I see us all running around in desperate haste to succeed at times, other times drumming our own drum. The world is in flux, as it usually is, but maybe more. What can we do but tell them, *Go get 'em*, then step back and find out how they rebuild the world?

On Love Poetry

With Sappho, Pushkin, Keats, and *Dirty Dancing*

"I'm rational about everything but love."

It's April and the cherry tree behind our apartment has been in bloom a few days, a lush pink puff. The bright dark pink has already faded to pale, and the perkiness of its whole being seems to have relaxed like a gaggle of pink bridesmaids having finally collapsed on a sofa and kicked off their shoes, worse for the wear and crushingly beautiful. We've arrived at the few days when pink petals begin to flutter into the air.

A woman who was my graduate student, Liz, has come over to sit in the garden and catch me up on her projects. She's a lot younger than I am but I find her remarkable. As always, she gives clear expression to opinions I hadn't understood before, on subjects from manual labor to hip-hop, to Dante's inner circle.

I admit it is I who asks what the story is when she mentions a boyfriend. Further, when she asks, "Are you really interested?" it is I who say, "Yes! I'm deep in domesticity, let me live some young romance vicariously." I listen for a long while after I realize the story is unintelligible. There are too many details, and the timeline is drunk. Liz realizes this and says, "This is boring, right? But what should I do?" She says that she can reason or work her way out of any problem but love.

The petals are falling in their slow pink fantasy, and I say I have a story for her and refill our cups with tea. The story turns out to be only the beginning of a drama with my friend Eugene, who calls himself Eu.

I knew Eu from college in New York, a long while ago, and we've met to catch up because I'm briefly in Los Angeles, where he's been living.

We are eating an early lunch in a restaurant on the boardwalk and happy to see each other; he's still gorgeous and still with the bright eyes, but it's bad timing—he's just heard grim news. His uncle is sick and likely dying. Eu has to come to New York City to stay a while, to take care of him. They are close—Eu's father left when he was young, while this uncle had no children, and he stayed around. Also the uncle is wealthy and is leaving it all to Eu. It's wealth, not just money. That sort of gift creates a bond.

Eu's father also started life with a fortune but partied it away on private planes and lawsuits. I can't tell what Eu is living on, but he's published film reviews in good places; he still does insane rock climbing, wins prizes at it, but probably the uncle already helps. Eu admits he might be waiting for the inheritance for his life to start. And yet this news feels like bad news—he loves his uncle, hates hospitals, and says he hates the city. We'd reveled in New York City together when we were young. But revels do end.

He's still single. He raves and rants that marriage is a boredom trap but speaks like a man not bored but thwarted. I tell him I'm not bored. He says he needs to live a life that can be changed by whim. He doesn't smile when he talks of this whimsy life.

I joke about his famous animal magnetism. Way back, Tanya met Eu at an engagement party we were all at and boom! Fell for him hard. She was maybe twenty-two, and he was about thirty. She was so pretty, and wonderful, but I knew she seemed like a kid to him. She seemed like a kid to me. She was idealistic and romantic, not to mention baby-faced for her age. He was running around with women who could teach him dangerous things.

I say, "Listen, I do know Tanya must have been a special case, because she was such a rom-com monster."

His face squishes. He says, "You don't know the half of it."

"That so?" I say, thinking of the half I do know. I know they met when someone asked a few of us to carry the fruit bowls and carved

melons out to the tables. I remember the late sunlight hit the fruit arrangements from the side, each a little temple of color, a rainbow pile
lit up against the darkening green.

Eu sees her face and says, "Wow, who are you?"

Tanya answers, "'I carried a watermelon.'"

Eu says, "*Dirty Dancing*." He beams. "I carried a watermelon, too."

That was it, she looked into his smiling green eyes and gone,
gone, gone. They were near each other at the dinner and talked about
movies and mountains. Both were witty and delightful, but that's it;
one evening, in public, and Tanya talked about being in love that same
night.

He pulls down his jaw with every facial muscle below his nose, and
then he says, "I bet you know about a quarter."

I'm stunned. You will perhaps agree that "a quarter" is the wrong
amount to know about a thing like this. I air the complaint.

He says, "That watermelon turned out to be a lot to carry."

We get the check and go down to the boardwalk. He says, "Don't
get the wrong idea." I shake my head at him because he hasn't given me
any idea, right or wrong.

He laughs. "I just mean it changed my life. No. Legitimately, it's the
legitimate place my life started."

I skeptic-face him, *legitimately*. Tanya was in love with him for a
long time—a long time—so I was certain that he disappeared for all
those years. Since that time nothing. I thought I'd know. Today Tanya is
a full-time writer and what I call an indoor cat. I look at the white-gray
cloudy sky and mock-moan, "I'm the one person who visits L.A. and
doesn't get sunny weather."

"What, this?" he asks, with surprise. "This will burn off in an hour."
Then he says, "She wrote me a letter, after we met the first time—at that
dinner."

We are both staring out at the slate-blue ocean rolling in, but now I
turn to him. "We all know about the letter. Remember?"

"Right, okay, but did you read it?"

I shake my head, no, but concede the point. "No, but I can imagine.

I remember how she was. She watched *Roxanne* and *Moonstruck* on a loop."

"*Eternal Sunshine*," he responds, with that big smile. "*Splash*," he says, and laughs. "T was looking for her merman, and I was he."

"But you didn't even answer the letter," I say.

"No, true. But I came to your birthday party and talked to her." I stay quiet so he'll talk.

"The letter she wrote, it was beautiful, it was, but there was no way to answer it. I was a lot older than her, and she was proposing everlasting love, I'm telling you, she swore herself to me body and soul." He rubs his face. "She could write like a demon even then. She said that true love happens in a flash, and is rare, and we should be together. She'd leave college if I wanted to keep traveling." He looks at me hard and says, "I couldn't work out the right thing to say."

I move on. "I know about the sermon you gave her at my birthday. She called it 'the sermon.'"

As for that, mostly he had told her how lovely the letter was, and how she was so amazing, but that he had no plans to settle down with anyone; that he cheated in the few relationships he'd had and would likely cheat on her if they tried it. Then he cautioned her not to do this again, that some men would take advantage of receiving such a letter.

I suppose what rankled, for her, over time, was that he did not even respect her singular choice, that he thought she was reckless rather than a good judge of character, that he thought by twenty-two she couldn't possibly know a rare chance at a rare love when it happened to come to your friend's engagement party.

"That's the last chapter you know about?" asks Eu, his pretty face going through a series of plastic exercises. The face arranges itself around the smiling green eyes again.

"There's more to it then?" I ask, trying to not show my excitement. What could it be? I see Tanya, we're friends, I'd know. Unable to wait, I joke, "You realized you were in love and came back for her?"

He squints like the sweetest, sourest memory is rising through him. "Something like that," he says.

* * *

Liz nods and says, "Missed chances, wrong directions."

The wind blows and we are showered in pink petals as we agree that love is damnably difficult stuff. If you don't believe in fate, how can you pick one person out of the billions? How can you know it's real, and when to go all in? As the years pass, how can you make it work if it's such hard work? How can two people keep choosing each other? How do you know when the dark clouds are here to stay, and when they'll burn off in an hour?

How Religion Helps

Religion helps people deal with love, sex, and marriage by giving them rules, advice, and stories. Love stories from religious texts have examples of joy and pain that help people process overwhelming feelings. Too, religions have soothing promises about one's one true love being pre-ordained supernaturally, or supernaturally ordained once chosen. Religious leaders can find someone for you or bless whomsoever you find.

Take a look at this romantic story and how it shows desire and power in motion. It is an unusually erotic piece of the Hebrew Bible, or Christian Old Testament, Song of Solomon 5:2–16. The speaker is identified as "fairest among women."

> 2 I sleep, but my heart waketh; it is the voice of my beloved that knocketh, saying, "Open to me . . . my love, my dove . . ."
> 3 I have put off my coat; how shall I put it on? I have washed my feet; how shall I defile them?

She hears him trying the door, "and my heart was moved for him." She listens, softens, gets herself up, and opens the door, "but my beloved had withdrawn himself and was gone." She goes out looking for him, calls out to him, "but he gave me no answer."

7 The watchmen that went about the city found me, they smote me, they wounded me; the keepers of the walls took away my veil from me.

She tells her girlfriends that if they find her beloved, "tell him I'm sick with love." The ladies are not stoked that their leader is so thirsty. They ask what is so special about him. She says his hair is black as a raven, his eyes are like the eyes of doves, his lips like lilies, "his belly is as bright ivory overlaid with sapphires."

15 His legs are as pillars of marble . . . his countenance is . . . excellent as the cedars.
16 His mouth is most sweet: yea, he is altogether lovely. This is my beloved, and this is my friend, O daughters of Jerusalem.

The beauty of the poem has kept company with many a longing lover. Note that he came to her door, and she didn't rush to him. Her reasons for delaying were fussy, her cleaned feet, her hung robe. She says that she got up only for his sake. But having been too slow to catch him, she was now willing to risk more than dirtying her feet. Romantic love doesn't stay still. It's volatile. Its weight changes direction.

Hinduism is specific about ways to turn this volatility into happiness. There are five stages to love, and they are inclusive, so that mature love contains them all.

1. First is romantic, erotic love, called *kama*. Temples are carved with bosomy women in complex embraces with flexible men. Texts cheerfully note that desire and pleasure are often the first aspects of romance.
2. In time, romantic love develops to include *shingara*, which means rapturous intimacy. It's about getting to know who the other person is.
3. Next is *maitai*, which is described as being like maternal love; selfless care for each other and family.

4. In *bhakti*, this generous love expands beyond your loved ones to include everyone, the whole world.

5. The final step is *atma-prema*, or unconditional self-love, based on realizing that you really are a blameless part of this world you've learned to love so much.

If you want to sidestep the whole love and sex circus you can find support for that, too, in religion. Buddhism generally suggests it's best to leave *kama* out, seeing it as a time-consuming distraction at best, and often a lot of stress. Christianity stands out as being anti-sex in much deed and text. Since a lot of us are, at times, locked out of romantic love and sex, the Buddhist and Christian rejections can be nice. They do have their limits, especially when they teach sexual shame.

What religion does well is to depict a lot of different versions of romantic success. Its laws can make people stay around longer, so the relationship has a chance. It celebrates long relationships. Religion gives you things to do. The big ones are simple.

Get together with someone who grew up the way you did.
Give of yourself. Remember the big idea of love.
Give it some time. Mark the passage of time.

Religions have rituals to mark the stages and events that tend to roll out in committed romantic love. Further, each religion has love rituals that are specific to some sects and some regions, delicious little behaviors to keep things dividend-ing and diverting. Another thing religion gets right, as always, is that it asks you to repeat the same texts and stories, on a daily, weekly, and yearly basis.

Giving it time can do so much for love, and chance will have its hand in the matter. If you are lucky, bad things with happen (I know, it's oxymoronic, but I mean it) and you will stick around for each other through them. After you do that, there is gratitude and trust. If you get through fights, you may learn to get through them faster or with less fear. If you are terribly lucky you will get to a place where you can fight dark and still say, *What, this? This will burn off in an hour.*

How Art and Science Help

Social science has shown that a series of somewhat ritualistic acts can significantly increase the chances of two people falling in love, acts such as prolonged eye contact, and responding to a series of intimate questions. Companies arise left and right asking you to swipe left and right to be matched, in harmony, for life. Yet there is so much touch and go. And how does it feel? It's touch and go.

Religions have theories of love. Cultures have theories of love too, as do individuals. It pays to broaden ours, to let into our consciousness more and varied models of relationships. It would suck to find out on your deathbed that when it comes to relationships most people are less demanding than you were. Love is stories. Relationships can come back from hell if they have a model for it. It is cultural liturgy in America to respond to a breakup with ice cream. Also cultural liturgy is the "boyfriend bonfire," in which one ceremonially burns items that belonged to the ex-beloved.

Which reminds me of the story I was telling you and about how Eu was pretty roughed up by life. His best friend had an accident and died while they were in a stupid argument; he blames himself. I asked if it hadn't been fun being so rich? He gave me his warmest smile and said, "Yes but no." He had indeed inherited money and land, but when his father died, he left him debts, the land isn't free to sell; he'd had an illness, moved to California to get healthy. One night he goes to a party in Hollywood and she's there, the center of attention. Tanya. She's married. He's surprised to learn her husband is a year *older* than Eu. They have a family and are comfortable and happy—happy enough.

Eu and Tanya sit talking much of the evening. It's as it was, he makes her laugh, she makes him concentrate. At the end of the night he actually says, "Run away with me." He begs her to run away with him. There's no time for her to respond. She says nothing. As she is helped into her coat, she thinks everything. He allows her the long moment of triumph, watching her eyes and mouth smile wryly, shake it off, then suddenly, again. His face, animate as it is, goes through all the shapes of naked regret and tuxedoed adoration.

He writes to her immediately, asking again. He writes a few times before she responds at all. Finally, she agrees to meet.

She tells him that he was probably her life's great love, but *no*. She loves her husband and their family and life. She isn't even tempted. Their eyes meet and it is clear she is tempted, and they smile, and laugh, but she said *no* and he saw she meant it.

He says he did not cry until later, and often. He says, "I couldn't get over it. I mean, can't, really. That's the real reason I'm single now."

I look at him like he has eaten my parakeet.

Your Ritual Draws on Both

Looking for love is a singular struggle. It is a time for much witchy-ness. Looking for love is a stage full of symbology, of a particularly magical nature. Staying in relationships has some witchy-ness too. Unlike the sphinx, true lovers must be able to occasionally survive being solved.

When I get back to New York City, of course, I tell Tanya I've seen Eu. Before I say anything, she tells me the same history he told me, but for a point. She'd read his film reviews all along, and before he reappeared in her life to be rejected in the flesh, she had rejected him in print. She says that he stayed seduced by the romantic version of life, whether idealizing versions of it or demonizing it. She'd wondered if *he* had always been essentially a pastiche of romance movies. It happens to everyone. You realize later that someone was trying to love you and you weren't that interested. Then you were very interested indeed, and they've moved on.

The story I've been telling you is basically true, but I've bent it slightly to fit the story of the most famous poem by Russia's most famous poet, Alexander Pushkin (1799–1837). The poem is called *Eugene Onegin*. Eugene and Tatyana, often called Tanya in the poem, are dealing with romantic novels, not film. "Tatyana's letter" is key to Pushkin's story, as is Eugene's "sermon."

We have played a lot of literary moments. Certainly, we have known longing. There is no substitute for this kind of codified wisdom and poetic stories. Yes, watch rom-coms, but also read Henry James's *Washington Square*. Do things always work out in the end, for everyone? For the longest time we just don't know. For the longest time it's touch and go for all but the most fortunate few. Things don't always work out in the end. As is true with the Capulet and her Montague. If there are gestures or guidelines in your family's religion that help people with love, there's nothing wrong with considering them. Nonreligious celebrations of the couple's "firsts" and anniversaries, of children, of the children's firsts can help keep things going.

I think you should have access to a love potion. I don't usually even play with magic power, as I don't believe in it enough to play, but love was an exception. I felt highly uncertain about love for much of my life. I was raised to get married and have children and for the longest time I couldn't figure that out. There was the joy of youth in trying, but even then, I was anxious to know how I was going to solve the problem of myself. Then at some point I tired of wondering what the hell was finally going to work out. Somewhere over all those varied years, I made a few love potions and rituals for myself and others. It was total play, but with the reasonable intent of changing how we felt.

I like to start from the mood of Shakespeare's witchy spells. That means that without going so far as "eye of newt," you conjure a weirdness. You want a for instance?

Here's one I've written just for you. It is a simple *Love Please Come Again Potion.**

Into a small blue cup, mix a walnut shell's worth of apple-cider vinegar with the amount of grape juice that would fill a hamster (I don't mean satiate a hamster but fill the skin of one wherefrom the hamster had been removed). Add crumbs rubbed from the bottom of a slice of cake. Do not eat the cake. Add water until the cup fills above the rim. Say your love poem while care-

---

* If you've never been in love before, it's the same potion but at the end you can eat the cake.

fully drinking this libation creation. Do not spill. When you have finished drinking, face east (if above the equator; if below, face north), and shake out the sillies. If you perform these acts with your whole heart, your love life will improve within forty-eight hours, or possibly longer, if it works at all.* Good luck.

Human beings hope. Among the things we hope for are some ethereal features of experience. We hope for love, acceptance, for everything to turn out okay.

If you were pregnant as a house and you passed by an ancient statue carved for the protection of new mothers and easy births, would you take a few steps over and bring your hope to it? My pregnancies were a lot for me and they put me in this hyper-hoping mood in which I didn't believe I was asking anyone, but at times, I asked. *Let him be alright. Let her come true.* For romantic love I don't remember ever asking the sky for help, or any totem, but I lit more than one candle in hopes for my own heart's peace. I was, at times, placebocally willing to do what I could to gather the pieces.

Our Poem

Our poem comes from one of the greats of twentieth-century Russian literature, Marina Tsvetaeva (1892–1941).

I'm Glad You've Lost Your Mind Over Someone and It's Not Me

I'm glad you've lost your mind over someone and it's not me,
I'm glad I've lost my mind and it's not over you
and that the heavy globe of the Earth
will never float away from under our feet.
I'm glad that we can be silly and funny—

---

* You can double the spell's power if you take a shower and leave the house.

can act however we want and not worry over what we say,
and that neither one of us blushes like drowning in a wave,
when our sleeves happen to slightly touch.

I'm also glad that you casually kiss someone else in front of me,
and that you don't curse me to hellfire for not kissing you.
I'm glad that my sweet name, my sweet, is not
the name you speak, not day nor night—in vain . . .
and that never will they break the silence of the church
by singing out over us: Hallelujah!

I'm grateful, with all my heart and hand,
for your knowing not that you are in love with me,
and for all the peaceful nights,
for the rarity of our being together at sunset hours,
for our nonwalks under the moon,
for the sun not being over our two heads,
because you've lost your mind—oh well—not over me,
because I've lost my mind—oh well—not over you.

Friendship is a romance of its own kind. The poem has areas that are easy to read and understand, and areas that are difficult. This forces us to have two experiences of the poem. The clear part is—to cite an astute teen reader to whom I gave the poem as research for this writing—a BFF poem. A poem about best friends (forever). They "can be silly and funny" together and relax. It's relatable. Anyway, that's what my other teen said, when I showed it to her. We love being with good friends because we feel at ease and authentic with them. When you are being your true self, it's relaxing. No one is frozen out of authenticity by fear of a misstep. Anyway, that's what I can see clearly, at first. It's what my teens saw, at first. But we can feel that there is more, that a certain ambiguity crept in at some point.

To my mind, a close read shows her to be in love with him. From the opening lines of the poem there are hints to suggest that she is not *at all* glad he has fallen for someone. English translations fashioned by

Russians make the following distinction clear: he's lost his mind over someone; she's just lost her mind.

After that tricky opening pair of lines, her next thought is also stated as a negative, so we have to pay attention in order to follow what is being said, which distracts us from the strangeness of the claim. The protestation is flimsy compared to the weight of the image, the Earth falling beneath them. Don't we usually call that flying? I'm not inclined to believe someone who says I'm so glad he and I aren't crazy in love and rising up into the sky together. It feels like a strange thing to say unless the opposite is true. I think the lady doth protest too much.

The next lines draw me in though. With their conversational tone and directness, I find myself open to believing her again. It is nice to be with our friends after the hyped-up state of being with our affairs. She makes such a good case for friendship that we are surprised when she hits us with the self-directed sarcasm again. "I'm glad," she says, "that neither one of us blushes like drowning in a wave, / when our sleeves happen to slightly touch." Recall what that feels like, almost drowning in the chewing maw of an ocean wave. You are being rolled. You can't control your arms, your legs, your head, what you know is (a) not which way to go to find the sky, and (b) that you might die.

Once I head into this reading of the poem, the second stanza eggs me on in the same direction. I mean, if any of these things were true, you wouldn't mention them, surely not with such extremes. Maybe I'd say, *It's good that I don't mind seeing you kiss someone and nice that I don't have to worry about you wanting more from me. If you are up nights suffering over someone, I'm glad it isn't me.* But who is actively glad about what she says she's glad about? Especially when she gets to the part about being glad they won't marry; why add the "Hallelujah!"?

It's only at the top of the last stanza that we are sure we have been stabbed, and we know it partly because she's already running in to sew us back up. Wait a second, we say, why claim that your friend is in love with you but unaware? And that you are grateful? It makes more sense if she is in love with him and she is only hoping that he is at least unconsciously in love with her.

I believe she may be, at times, grateful for peaceful nights. Especially after the tumult of a romance, we can be ground-kissingly grateful for quiet. I still think we are hearing straight talk, to some degree, when she is glad for the rarity of their sharing a sunset. Perhaps it is the negative phrasing that makes me suspicious, uncertain. It starts me thinking about lovers at sunset; so I think that is what is on her mind, too.

Finally, the poem has such a strong sense of them as lovers walking under the moon that it exists, whether as fact or fiction. The best she can do to deny being in love is that she's pleased that their walks under the moon remain fictional. The next line seems like a mirror of that moon line, but with the sun. Curiously, it isn't. Because the sun *is* over their two heads. The final lines also look like they mirror each other, and the difference is subtle. I don't know how it works, but to me they read: You have a crazed crush on someone, it's too bad it's not me. I've lost my mind, oh well, [wistful whisper:] not over you.

This poem was written in 1915; we have the yellowing paper on which she wrote it and placed the date.

Poetry Lesson: Love Poetry

It is hard to write a poem about romantic love that is both happy and any good. True love is fascinating from the inside, but frequently the experience looks a tad naive from the outside. When we are crazy about someone, and they are wild about us, we are true believers.

I can think of a few poems that center on that over-thrilled moment of new-love bliss. They solve the problem by being explicitly stuck in time. Sappho's shivers of longing happen in the instant she is struck by hotness.

I think of the English Romantic poet John Keats as writing more about time than about love, but it came up a lot. His sonnet "Bright Star" is a best-loved love poem.

> *Bright star! would I were steadfast as thou art—*
> *Not in lone splendor hung aloft the night,*

And watching, with eternal lids apart,
  Like Nature's patient, sleepless Eremite,
The moving waters at their priestlike task
  Of pure ablution round earth's human shores,
Or gazing on the new soft fallen mask
  Of snow upon the mountains and the moors—
No—yet still steadfast, still unchangeable,
  Pillow'd upon my fair love's ripening breast,
To feel for ever its soft fall and swell,
  Awake for ever in a sweet unrest,
Still, still to hear her tender-taken breath,
And so live ever—or else swoon to death.

It is one sentence long and the volta, the change in argument, comes right in the middle, with a "No." In the first half he says he wishes he could be Polaris, the bright star around which the whole sky seems to turn. He wants to timelessly watch Earth roll by. But "No." Instead, he wants to stay forever with his head on his love's breast, feeling it rise and fall with her breath. Presumably she's asleep. He's too excited to sleep. He decides that instead of the whole world as it ever changes, forever, he'd like just this breast, just this moment.

Love poetry is not at the center of contemporary poetry. One reason that love poetry makes many poets check for the exits is that we trust art that is about ambiguous feelings and romantic love poetry isn't.

Much great love poetry, then, is partly about how difficult love is. Sappho is the great love poet of the ancient world; indeed, she is the great poet of the ancient world—she was called the greatest at the time. In one poem she is lovesick and prays for Aphrodite's help. She imagines the love goddess appearing to say, of the longed-for beloved,

if she's escaping
Soon she'll be chasing; if she's refusing
your gifts, she shall give them. . . .

Let me go loose from this merciless craving.
Do what I long to have done: be my own Helper in Battle.

Note the volatility. She is not wishing for love perfected, but for the vector of the chase to change direction. Let her chase me instead of me having to chase her. At the end of the poem, she wishes to be done with "this merciless craving," and echoing Homer who lived a century before, she asks Aphrodite to be, once again, "my own helper in Battle."

Marina Tsvetaeva's poem has the same crestfallen beauty, to me, and I like the twist of seeing deep friendship caught up in the emotional mix. Love isn't always a battlefield, but it is hard to know when to be honest and when to hold the peace.

Many of the people who consume romantic comedies and novels that revolve around broken hearts gloriously mended, with swelling music in the background, know perfectly well that this kind of story is a tiny fraction of the truth about love.

When we read the film reviews of mournful love stories in award-winning independent films, we trust them. We know that if we see the painful film there may be a life-altering image of resilience installed in our hearts, for life. We believe the sad movies but don't buy tickets for them, and buy tickets for the rom-coms, though we don't believe in them. When it comes to love, we hide from the truth and pay for the lie.

* * *

Why is romantic love so difficult? Perhaps it's the paradoxes. I can't solve them, but I can attempt to sketch them.

Why don't you assign a rating, 0, 1, 2, or 3, for each of these, to indicate how much of an issue the particular love paradox is for you, personally.

1. The paradox of love is that it can be so intensely one-sided and can then switch sides.
2. The paradox of love is that it comes with strong feelings of "forever," and yet, often after experiencing these feelings, we leave.

3. The paradox of love is that we want someone who fixes the wounds of youth, and yet we also fall for people who repeat those wounds and hence bring us to primordial passion.
4. The paradox of love is that it is so ethereal and generous and yet so deeply embodied and hungry; angelic and yet animal.
5. The paradox of love is that we know the ones we love, know them in a profound way, and yet we may lose the ability to see the way they appear to others.
6. The paradox of love is that it can be so fixated on a single person out of billions, even over a whole life, and yet for many people it happens with a few different* people over a lifetime.
7. The paradox of love is that when a romance is over, even when you want the affair to end, your body may choose to grieve it most grievously.
8. The historic paradox of love is that in the history before modern times most people either had their spouse chosen by their parents or had choice, but it was limited by class and religion. You were always limited to the people you might possibly meet on foot, by travel, or connection. Until now, the problem of love has never been an abundance of choice. The paradox is that scarcity was a problem for love, and as it turns out, so is abundance.

If your number is sixteen or higher you are an intuitive, philosophical being with high love prospects. If your number is between fifteen and ten you know how to play the game, but you are above it, a prince among men. If your number is nine to five you are bright as a new penny but might want to look around a bit more. Those in the four to zero camp should see their counselor immediately.

Joking. The point of the numbers you gave these are to get a good look at what you are thinking and feeling now, and importantly, to come back to these paradoxes in a while and see if your concerns change and how static or dynamic are your feelings about love.

---

* Sometimes quite different.

Your Poem

When you are looking for a love poem to offer or to savor yourself, don't be troubled if you don't agree with everything the poem says—or seems to be saying—about love. You can offer the whole poem but specify that it is the charisma of a single apt phrase that made you share it.

The truth is, it's better if the poem you share has parts that disturb you. Go ahead and pretend they don't exist when you are giddy in love. The other parts of the poem will come in useful when a bad romance day hits us with its cricket bat of sadness.

By the same broken token, when choosing a poem for your own savoring, it is much better if the poem bothers you in spots. Those irritants change over time and remind you of your former selves in ways that are otherwise unlikely to happen. You can't map a projection forward without charting a few plot points. Plot a few chart points.

For your poetry collection choose a poem to contemplate when you are thinking about love. The question of love poems to offer to people you are trying to seduce, ahem, people you have fallen in love with, is more complicated. Your beloved does not want a used love poem. There can be a poem that you share with many, ahem, friends, as long as you introduce it as a poem you have loved and shared for a long time. If you want to do something that makes a person feel that a poem is specific to him or her, I think you have to find a new poem. I know, I know. It's all touch and go. So make a commitment to a poem and stay with it.

* * *

Literature can coax us through poetic experiences of love that are mighty instructive, and it is a curriculum hard to communicate in straightforward prose. It's not just that people you trust will break your heart (they will); and that it doesn't all work out for everyone (it doesn't); and that when love does work out, it requires a remarkable degree of compromise (it does). It's the degree to which we fail to understand the other person, the gulf of unknowing between us all. A love isn't all about understanding. It's about knowing and getting known anyway.

Two people don't become one, brains don't work that way, the motormouths that they are, they never stop inventing schemes of personal interest, and imagining the possibility of their own need for mistrust. Literature teaches us that everyone has such a Chatty Cathy of a brain. They stream different kinds of chatter, very different sometimes, but here is what is always true: no one's actions and thoughts match up neatly, whether it is because we are trying hard to be good, or because we are lying.

So it's about getting to know and be known anyway. Let's all go sit under the cherry trees in spring and tell each other our stories and let the petals grace us. The season of cherry-tree petals is a fast one, but it comes back every year.

Outside religion, the Interfaithless need poetry to remind us of the grace of various stages and varieties of romance. Anyway, it is way grander and less lonely to suffer love's longing with the likes of Sappho, Pushkin, Keats, and Tsvetaeva, than without them.

15

On Funerals and Memorials

Erasures and Messages

"What did we read at the funeral? He's still in my closet."

The woman I'm talking to in Cobble Hill Park says she reads a lot of poetry and when I tell her about this book she lights up. She starts listing poems she's heard at funerals and poems that might be good for funerals. She has lots of ideas and seems energized by the proposition of thinking deeply about such poems. Then she says, "Well, Irving."

"Irving?" I say, drawn in because it was my paternal grandfather's name.

She said, "We didn't read anything at the funeral. We didn't have a funeral. He's still in his boxes in my closet."

"Boxes?" ask I.

"I had him divided for me and his sister but then his sister passed."

* * *

"I don't do funerals," began a student of mine in his late twenties. He was coolly dismissing religious myth, but his voice dipped into a minor key as he continued. "My friend was killed, hit by a train, summer after high school."

"And it was a bad funeral?" I asked.

"No," he said, pulling a long drag off his cigarette. "I mean, I don't know. I didn't go. Me and him had stopped going to church . . . we grew up in the same church and we both quit going. I didn't want their lies. I knew he didn't care if I went to his funeral—he's gone. Maybe he wouldn't have wanted me to go, you understand? Since we'd left together?" So he didn't go to the funeral.

I say, "That makes sense." When there's a long pause I add, "Sometimes people have trouble realizing the person is really gone, though, when they don't attend the funeral."

He nods. I nod. He fidgets. Then he says, "I have a dream about it. It's like a recurring nightmare but more numb." He describes trying to wake his friend for school—no panic, in the dream, just frustration and a faraway inkling that something might be really wrong.

* * *

Musicians are weaving the *Moonlight* Sonata like a shroud over the bowed crowd. The air is sweet with gardenias and warm on my skin. It's a clear night and there is no moonlight, so the sky is a blast zone of stars. I'm at a memorial doing moral support for a friend, whose boyfriend lost his father. I'm minding the meatballs when I discover that the college-age young man next to me is the boyfriend's younger brother. He says, "I'm having a terrible day."

I'm eating, mouth full, and just manage, "I'm so sorry."

"He would have hated what the minister said, all the heaven jags he went off on," adding: "The meatballs are good?"

"I'm so sorry," I say again, covering my mouth with my hand. "The meatballs are delicious. Lamb, I think. He didn't believe?"

"He did not believe," repeated back the young man with dramatic intonation. "It shouldn't matter since he isn't here to hear it but it feels wrong." Then he waved at the stars and the air and said, "But still, where is he? You know? Where is my father?"

* * *

There's big news in deathways, big news that people see in their own lives, perhaps in flurries of change, but they often don't realize it is happening more commonly, like an avalanche.

In our era, much of the world is experiencing a precipitous decline in burials, especially in the West where burial was long dominant. In the

United States, the cremation rate in 1960 was 3 percent. Half a century later, in 2015, it reached 48 percent—an astounding shift.

It happened for two practical reasons. The first is that cemeteries around urban areas are full or nearly full. The second is that burials are expensive, often thousands of dollars more than cremation. But crowding and expense problems have been met in the past without compromising religious burial. For instance, people adopted the once unthinkable idea of a cemetery outside walking distance. When cost was the hurdle, working people invented the insurance industry, as "burial clubs," which pooled funds so that whoever dies has all the standard rites.

What has changed for us is how we feel about the pressures of scarcity and cost, and that seems to be about the fading of religion. We can see this geographically. Where Christianity is still strong, like Rome, Italy, and the American South, burials have held on, while in nearly postreligious Scandinavia, cremation is the rule. Cremation is also the rule in the American West, land of the "nones"—so dubbed for the box they check on religion survey questions.

Reports from the National Funeral Directors Association cite waning religion as key to the change: "A surge in the number of Americans that no longer identify with any religion has contributed to the decline of the historically traditional funeral in America—and the rise in cremation as the disposition of choice."

How Religion Helps

Religions are the stewards of death. In many times and places, when there is a death, the family contacts clergy, and clergy orchestrate the symbolic, the practical, and the unspeakable. Religions require particular acts and recitations that may have ornate fantasy elements, yes, but also minister to the human needs of the grieving. That means time. Religions provide behavioral templates for the bereaved, which can create more space for recovery than some people would find without regulations that apply to all. That way even mourners who are usually ridden hard by a boss or neurosis are mandated time for R&R, whether the boss or neurosis likes it or not.

Funerals have declined along with burials. We could have merely added a detour to the crematorium, followed by cemetery or mausoleum, but it seems that funerals were too linked to religious comforts that didn't comfort anymore.

Some people are racked with ambivalence for not sinking the money, but in the moment they chose not to have a funeral. *This* time in history when circumstances made the old traditions hard, people stopped doing them. They either didn't believe in God, or didn't believe in following organized religion. They also didn't feel overwhelmed by the expectations of society or the needs of family who believed. No god was asking for it. There just wasn't enough there there, to bear the bother.

Let's tally up what the classic American model gave us and what we get now, and see what we've been choosing and what we've been losing. A common funeral has features that serve psychological functions, often directed by a religion, but are by now *cultural liturgy*, by which I mean doings that ring of the poetic sacred on their own.

1. *Visitation*. Casket in the room, often open. You see the dead face, an indelible memory. Perhaps you press your fingers to a still lapel. Even a closed casket has a dramatic presence; nearly glowing with what is inside it, empty and full.

2. *Funeral Service*. Clergy's speech frames death and grieving. Eulogists surprise us with facets of the person we hadn't known, while stumbling verbs into the past tense. The deceased may have chosen the music or readings. A guest book for signatures helps people know it matters that they made the trip (even if there's a crowd) and for the grieving family it creates a sacred memento of the day.

3. *Procession Drive*. You ride to the cemetery in a many-eyed snake, each car with lights on to help the group cohere. Up front, the laden hearse leads. We're in transit. We're in shock. When cars make way for us, we feel the gravity of who we are

today, death and grief. Onlookers make way for us, motorcade of what makes madness of all usual traffic.

4. *Burial.* Puts the corpse into the ground, hides it, and yet, paradoxically, also localizes the death, making it visible. Principal mourners begin the burial—with a shovelful or handful— another sensory fact, indelible memory to stand as proof. The feel of shovel handle or cool lump of earth bring out a bright reek of upturned soil. Then comes the sound of dirt hitting casket, *thum-thump*, and the salty bite of tears and sweat.

5. *Gathering at the House.* The primary mourners are accompanied home. People say grief truly hits when everyone goes home. This helps us recognize that the casual after-burial gathering is a crucial liminal time, a final in-between place before the clock of *after* starts. Friends bring abundant food so the bereaved are relieved of cooking for a while, a job that once included stoking a woodstove. Meals are easier now, so the practice is today more memo than meal. *We know you feel dead but we want you to live. Eat.*

It is common for religions to schedule multiple rites in the year after a death. It can be helpful for mourners to know that such a schedule stretches out in front of them, so that a mind in the stopped-clock shock of grief can envision the future. Such rituals often culminate in an event at the end of the first full year.

A year after the loss, Hindus celebrate the anniversary of a death with a priest coming to the home and conducting the sraddha rites, which include offerings of *pinda*, cooked rice pressed into firm shapes, and delicacies including favorites of the deceased.

In Judaism, after the death of a parent (or at times of a close relative) one says the mourner's prayer, the "Kaddish," every day for eleven months. You need a minyan, a group of ten, to say the Kaddish, so mourners must gather with other people, even if they feel like being alone. With the death of a parent, there's no one between the grave and you anymore. Whatever else changes for you with this loss, you may need some help with that new condition.

How Art and Science Help

The Interfaithless have access to similar care—supportive ritual, poetry, and community—but it's not automatic, nor widely respected as supernaturally ordained. Important parts are left out because we don't see their purpose.

In the West, cremation and burial are equally accepted, but notice that if you go with burial it comes with thousands of years of cultural messages, first and foremost, the message requiring that people close to the deceased attend, whatever it takes. In paintings, literature, and history, a lonely burial is the very image of sorrow. Compelled by such imperatives of cultural liturgy people overcome distances and resentments to gather at the grave.

In the East, cremation is the rule and has its ritual obligations. In the West it's new and hardly has any. Some crematoria now feature family-viewing rooms. That's nice for American Hindus, as Hindus in the United States long ago transferred the family duty to light the bier into the push of a button setting the casket in motion; that used to mean standing in a dingy corridor. Mostly the West isn't ritualizing the cremation process itself.

Because countries have laws for the quick disposal of a body, uncoupling that physical event from the memorial gathering sweeps away traditions that were epiphenomena of the old urgency.

The benefits of the new model are delayed, but significant. Without the old time constraint, cousins across the country don't have to abruptly miss work, ditch plans, and take red-eye flights. With time to prepare, memorial parties now often feature an artful array of photographs and mementos, special music, and slideshow videos. These too have become cultural liturgy, established poetic ritual—at least for today. They are normal but not demanded or divine.

They work. Photographs can move mourners to face the reality of the loss. They can also console. When grief is compounded by the unfairness of an early death, it can be a relief to see evidence of a full life—love, friends, accomplishments, and idiosyncrasies. Images of travel seem especially suited for this task, maybe because world travel is childhood's fantasy of adventure and midlife's fantasy of retirement. If the lost friend got some travel in, maybe he wasn't so terribly fleeced by fate. Maybe he did alright.

Quintessential objects of the lost loved one may be on display, perhaps around a large photo. The hat they wore, award they won, wool they spun, maybe his helmet, or her fancy hairpins from that updo bun she tried to wear, always coming undone. This poetic shrine benefits from having more time than a burial allows.

The burgeoning norms of ash scattering seem to allow even more time to pass after a death than memorials—years sometimes. Those who have ashes at home, waiting, often scold themselves for it, calling it laziness. But is it? Since the scatter ritual often puts the remains far away, life with a box of grandma is a stage in knowing and letting go. That linger era is a corollary to one of the most positive aspects of the new deathways, the ash-scattering trip. Travel for the purpose of spreading ashes can send mourners on a physical adventure to a loved place. It's usually in nature. Burial feels like we are protecting the body, tucking it in, while scattering ashes feels like we are enchanting a place with sacred powder. Either way, we put the ghost there.

Your Ritual Draws on Both

If you have a model of ritual that feels right for you, derived from religion or not, I'd say observe those rites; take the assist. The ritual that you experienced in childhood, intimately or remotely, has might and can take your weight. By "remotely" I mean that, for example, you saw it in a movie and it struck an inner chord, and it took hold in you.

If no existing model of grief ritual appeals to you, build a starter ritual around whatever your lost loved one used to do. Make a list, as his or her interests and habits come to mind. Jot down what appeals and also what repulses, since you may desire a challenge, and tastes do change. Maybe through these acts you'll grow together into the future. Memorials might benefit from more ways for attendees to add to the keepsake record. If there is a display of things that represent the deceased, friends could add an object to the shrine, either just for the day or for the family to keep. It can be anything. Or bring a photograph, drawing, quote, or poem.

If your religious background, or theirs, suggests a food or drink, have some on hand. For instance, the arrival of the dear departed's favorite delight, say, a platter of warm almond croissants, can create a moment of communion. Consider other sensory experiences. Perfume or essential oils can invoke the beloved and can bring a repeatable sensory kiss to the event. If there is memorial music from your history or your relationship, listen to it. If not, again, consider the opportunity to create a new association; music you play at a memorial can become sacred through that experience.

Unlike their religious counterparts, such memorials have no required readings. It is a big loss and worth the effort to remedy. What do we want from such a reading? Gravity and grace, and maybe a moan or a howl.

Our Poem

The Chilean poet Pablo Neruda (1904–1973) is megafamous for his love poems, and this sonnet meditating on his own death also finds redemption in adoring romantic love. This is from his book *100 Love Sonnets*.

Love Sonnet LXXXIX

When I die I want your hands on my eyes:
I want the light and the wheat of your beloved hands
to pass their freshness over me one more time:
to feel the smoothness that changed my destiny.
I want you to live while I wait for you, asleep,
I want your ears to go on hearing the wind,
for you to smell the sea that we loved together
and for you to go on walking the sand where we walked.
I want for what I love to go on living

and as for you I loved you and sang you above everything,
for that, go on flowering, flowery one,
so that you reach all that my love orders for you,
so that my shadow passes through your hair,
so that they know by this the reason for my song.

The poem starts with a storytelling opener, "When I die," but with "I want your hands" there's a temporal slip where "I want" refers to what I want right now, or as I die, or after; so by the end of this very first line the variety of meanings takes off exponentially.

The first line says: *In the moment after my death I want your hands on my eyes.*

And it says: *I want you to be the one to close my eyes when I die.*

And: *I'm scared of death and I want you to shield my eyes from it.*

And: *Dead bodies are so dead that people can touch the eyes.*

And: *When I'm gone, I want you to use my eyes to see the world.*

That last one sharpens focus as the poem continues.

In the second line, why "wheat"? What is "the wheat" of someone's hands? Well, wheat has a golden-brown complexion, kernels of firm flesh, and is often pictured sun-warmed—with its fibers lit up like a haloed mane. It's an incredible line, "I want the light and the wheat of your beloved hands." The words "light" and "wheat" have multiple meanings. The word "light" can mean easy, surface, gentle, as light housework and a light dusting of snow. It can mean revelation, as in "I saw the light." Sunlight and firelight are warmth. The spotlight is attention. The interrogation lamp discovers the true story. Smart people are bright. The basic meaning is worth stating, too: the light is what we see. The word "wheat" is just "wheat" but is still rich and deep. Bread is life. A few interpretations echo:

"the light and the wheat"
the warmth and the sustenance,
the easy and the home,
the illumination and the earth,
the truth and the food.

His love's hands have a "cool touch," which is sometimes translated as having "freshness"; either way they refresh him. I think of fever or feverish distress and the comfort of a cool hand (of mother's cool hand) on a warm brow.

What do we make of line four—"to feel the smoothness that changed my destiny"? How can her "smoothness" change his destiny? Maybe she led him to a frictionless way of being.

Note that grammatically, the whole poem is three long sentences. Each says "Quiero" ("I want"), wanting her to keep wanting life, implanting the bywords of the living, *I want, I want, I want.*

If a reader believes in an afterlife, he may see it in the first line of the second stanza—"I want you to live while I wait for you, asleep"—if not, that line says that the gap separating the living from the dead will soon enough be forged by us all. As for Neruda's beliefs, biographers note his atheism or agnosticism and also that Catholic images suffuse his poems.

In the original Spanish, the double-flower line reads "por eso sigue tú floreciendo, florida," a bloomer blooming, an efflorescence.

She must live with all her verve and fire, as a gift to him. The poem says that her future joy is "ordered" by his love. It's both a fantasy that he will orchestrate her happiness after his death, and a kind of logical proof: his love "orders" her happiness because her élan is evident in his adoration, and such élan must always grow, always "reach."

In the penultimate line, "my shadow" is an apt name for a posthumous friend, as "shade" was once common for "ghost" as a literary device; there are shades in Homer's *Odyssey*, and in Latin, *umbra*, in Virgil's *Aeneid*. "My shadow" can also mean "my influence," as living in a father's shadow, or "my darkness," as living in an emo vampire's lair.

Passing "through your hair" suggests "comes to mind," by proximity of brain to coif, and it is also the slightest kind of contact, a lift in your hair.

Just as the poem's sentences say, "Quiero," "I want," three times, so the three final lines all begin "para que," "so that." It's a construction that imitates rational argument being used to manage a riot of senses and emotion.

Returning to the poem's first line after reading it through, I find peace and comfort in the melding of their hands and eyes. There is no dread here, just: *You are my sight and my bread.*

Poetry Lesson: Sonnet, Erasure Poetry

The poem is a sonnet. It has fourteen lines and makes some kind of claim for most of the poem, and then turns on that claim like a tiger who liked walking with you but got hungry.

At the end, the poet shifts from saying I want you to be happy, which might be an act of generosity (real or aspirational), and begins asking for her help into the future: please "go on flowering," and show the world what I was talking about in all those poems.

If you want, you can write on your poem and find new messages in it. When a poem results from this we call it an *erasure poem* and you can do it with any starting material, from *Moby Dick* to a comic strip. Put a few copies of your poem into your poetry collection. Now you can mark it up while keeping a clean copy. Underline, argue in the margins. By crossing out words, maybe even most words, you'll create a new meaning. Like any form, the point of an erasure poem is that constraints lead us to places we might not go if left in a state of freedom. It's a way to learn new things about yourself.

For those with a taste for this sort of play, it can be a nice way to be creative and ask yourself questions. It can be a playful oracular poetry. Or try sharing your poem with someone and telling them about it. Writing about a poem always gives me a deeper personal connection to it, as happened with this Neruda poem. You don't have to write about your poem, but you do have to get to know it by doing more than reading it.

* * *

At my grandmother's funeral I heard my mother say, "Bye, Mommy" (in a voice so young I flinched), as her handful of dirt echoed *Pum Pum tum*. At my turn I said nothing, and the dirt struck, *thum*. That's where Grandma Dolly is. Tucked into the earth among her people.

We had no funeral for Grandma Molly. She was the one who listened to me without being game-stompingly negative, though she was the famously mean one. Her ashes are in my parents' patio garden, but I've never thought of her as there. My grandmother lives in my heart now, where I bet she likes the temperature.

* * *

"We haven't spoken to his family since the funeral." I looked from her lamenting eyes to his face, which registered their dismal surprise.

At a seminar on "Death and Dying and Secularism" at Columbia University, a married couple told me about the funeral of his beloved and proudly realist mother. Services had been arranged by religious family.

"Every comfort they offered made me sadder," he said.

She added, "They erased her."

"Though," he said to her tenderly, "that certainly did remind us of who she was. It was like we could hear her voice again—disagreeing!" We laughed. I avowed that comfort comes to us in the strangest of ways.

Consider a song popular at funerals, "Hallelujah," by Leonard Cohen, also well-loved in a Jeff Buckley version, among others. The lyric cites biblical passions, David "overthrown" by Bathsheba, Samson double-crossed by Delilah, and the personal revelation that all went wrong. Still, all he can say of life is "Hallelujah." Musing that there may be a God up there, he says all he's learned from love is tricks and competition. The song clarifies that his "Hallelujah" is not some pilgrim's claim to have seen the light. This hallelujah is cold and damaged. Baffled. It is still, by definition, awed and thankful. It is "hallelujah."

In interviews, Cohen fought religious assumptions. "'Hallelujah,'" he said, was "a desire to affirm my faith in life, not in some formal religious way but with enthusiasm, with emotion." He added, "This world is full of conflicts and full of things that cannot be reconciled. But there are moments when we can reconcile and embrace the whole mess, and that's what I mean by 'Hallelujah.'"

Your Poem

A funeral poem is a poem to read aloud at a service or other memorial gathering—so a public poem. But such a poem may also hold that space for us when we are alone, remembering the funeral, or in the absence of a funeral. To choose a funeral poem for your poetry collection, use these four functions as a guide.

1. Help us know the dead are dead by saying the word "dead." Didn't see the body? It may help to hear the words.
2. Give voice to rage, praise, and sorrow with high drama we may shrink from in our own words.
3. Frame a future relationship with the lost beloved, present in nature and in our hearts.
4. Remind us that the dead are no longer suffering.

A funeral poem can rage for you, so you can rage without seeming deranged, and praise for you, so you can praise without restraint. You can dare to visit your most tender sadness, the poem's version of that sadness, knowing there's an exit at the final line. A poem chosen as an elegy is a movable memorial; wherever you reread it, you can visit.

Religion has gestures that help us know that a stupefying change is real. In premodern Europe a death in the village was announced with the knelling of a church bell. Think of how the sound reached into people down to the marrow in their bones tolling the knowledge that death had come. Where are our bells of knowledge? You can choose one for yourself.

* * *

I find myself thinking of that kid at the memorial wondering about the lamb meatballs and the honest and true location of his dead father. The *Moonlight* Sonata playing in the starlight, the air tinged with gardenia. Where was that young man's father? As I told him that evening, "I suppose where your father is now is in you." But that's not enough.

We need a way to enact that, in poetic ritual, and with the rereading of a poem.

Remember my student who skipped his friend's funeral? His final project gave me a gasp. It was an artful booklet with pictures of his friend and drawings about the death, and the possibility that it wasn't accidental, and the missed funeral, and about our talk, and taming nightmares. How is it fair that his teenaged self was required to navigate such a swarm of cultural smashups when he was only a boy who had just lost his best friend?

We are living in a time of change in deathways, and many of us will not have the benefits of ritual and meditation unless we make some choices. Traditional rules, with their scheduled demands for the period after a death, can illuminate a path forward. They teach us that people need a lot of time and support, whatever the details, which are today so much in flux. With ashes, there can be multiple locations, more than one ensorcelled place in the world (rare with burial, but arms and hearts do sometimes go astray).

As things stand today, what words are associated with a memorial? No one would be surprised if a daughter read a poem aloud at a memorial, but no one would be surprised if she didn't. At a funeral there is an expectation that if a father was not despised, and a son not prevented by grief, he will go to the front and give praise. That expectation presses him to prepare, to perhaps find a poem. Thus the mourners who have the experience of a funeral also get the portable essence of it, the poem. Mourners who don't have the funeral often don't have the poem either. They easily could, if we find a few that suit—preferably in advance of need.

EMERGENCIES AND
WISDOM QUESTIONS

16

On Depression

At Play with the Sacraments of Misery

"God never helps when I am depressed. But I have my idols."

A student waits everyone out and comes to tell me she misses religion when she is depressed. She tilts her head and adds that when she had religion, she wanted a different one. Rosewater fragrance hovers around her, and she's wearing only a denim jacket despite the cold.

"I had the wrong kind," she says, pursing her lips and pulling them to one side.

"Yours was the *unkind* kind?" I ask, knowingly.

She shakes her head *no*. I wonder why I guess so much and vow to quit doing it.

"Saints," she says. "I was jealous for saints."

Introducing herself, Zeda says she was raised Baptist and until college it had all felt true enough.

"Philosophy class got to you? Or comparative religion?" I guess brightly.

"No," she says.

"No," I echo, mocking myself.

"I took theater classes," she says, and laughs. "Either all my new friends were going to hell or what-all I knew about sin was wrong."

She says she doesn't believe in religion anymore, but still has God, usually.

"You have him when you are sad?" I ask.

"No," she says, "I have him except when I'm depressed. Then he won't come."

I am surprised. I'd accepted the idea of religion as a crutch enough that I can hardly imagine a believer who lost the help when it was most needed and yet continued believing. It's a lesson. People are interesting.

I ask her if she still thinks about saints, and she says, "I have statues." She had a windowsill featuring three figures, a brass Ganesh whom she momentarily mimed, sitting like a fat elephant god would, and a ceramic Virgin Mary in blue-and-white robes, who Zeda impersonated with head cocked up like she'd seen a hawk. "Also, an anime ninja," she blushes to admit, flashing fist and shoulder. We talk about the pleasures of little things, especially when you are too depressed to move much. Many of us create a pocket-size retreat in a fixed fixation, stay there a while, and let the great world spin. Zeda says she was apartment hunting, and one requirement was a nice windowsill for her icons.

She adds, "Sometimes I knock them over." Knife hand, sweeping gesture. Smiles, says, "Down, down, down."

I nod with recognition and manage to echo, "Down, down, down," with hand-sweep gesture.

A lot of us get depressed. Nearly all of us, at times, feel sadness, disappointment, and longing. We also find ourselves uncertain counselors to people in our lives who are feeling blue, navy or darker. For those of us who have depression, at times there's not much to do but wait—for the help to start working, for the glacier of strain to subside.

How Religion Helps

Religious ritual for bad thoughts and sad feelings may have exacting detail that makes no sense outside the religious story, but they also often contain activities that are naturally therapeutic. It is both good for you and part of many religious rituals to take healthy food, fluids, light exercise, a soak in a bath, or a good long rest. Some mandate time alone, some entail the human contact of a temple visit or visiting clergy. Some give you something to do with your hands and voice that feel soothing and are said to help.

Even if we can see they would be good for us, even if they are attractive, especially when we are down, it matters that these gestures are also reported to be important to a power outside the self. They can feel too pointless if they are worth only the small good you predict they can do for you. You show up if you are obeying an ethereal companion or ticking off acts that will restore life's supernatural balance.

In many religions there are spiritual objects people can own and interact with, casually or with a lot of rules. They have been honed for their capacity to keep company, to keep one's hands busy. Some are considered to be inspirited, some a religious tool, some a mere commemorative item.

Religious objects can be capable of being holy without being considered holy all the time. The *minikisi* in Central Africa are fabulously carved gourds or other container statues that can hold a spirit, but the spirit isn't always there. In Brahmanic India the last act in making a sculpture, which makes it come alive, is the painting of the eyes, or adding gold to them, often done by a priest, on-site. Any religious supply store shows the comedy of the sacred-in-abundance. Power flows through these objects only after they are chosen, singled out. Like all of us, come to think about it.

How do sacred objects work? One famous version of them are the icons of the Eastern Orthodox Church. These icons are paintings on wood depicting Jesus, Mary, saints, angels, and some Biblical scenes, at times embellished with metalwork, or a candleholder. In the medieval period, they might be pictures carved flat, bas-relief, in ivory. Also popular was the small triptych, a three-panel painting that closed in on itself, frequently worn as a necklace.

Icons are a weird fit for Christianity because it began as part of Judaism, which has issues with imagery. That's because Judaism started out as one temple people among many, and its first big invention was the invisible God. Originally, "Don't worship idols" meant, *Only do Judaism.* Later the commandment seemed to say, *No pictures, ever,* to some. It's never been universally defined across Judaism, but it is broadly true that Jews have a tension around imagery. Jews have been called "the people of the book"; and let's not forget that the Jewish God's *words* made light.

Time passes and the Roman Empire's collapse darkened European reading skills for ages, and so pictures were needed. Religious art was officially accepted when the Council of 860 avowed that "all that is uttered in words written in syllables is also proclaimed in the language of colors."

Still, because of all this, it is understood that the Eastern Orthodox icons stayed flat, over millennia, so they wouldn't look like the idols of ancient temple peoples. Think of them, long gone except for an absence, the shadow of their idols in the round. The Eastern Orthodox Church is forceful in its definition of icons as *only reminders* of the holy, deserving of respect, but not worship. Other than this definitional insistence, even the official take is that icons are helpful in reaching the depicted holy figure who might then be able to get things done for you.

Here is how Hindu idol worship is explained by the psychiatrist and author Nalini V. Juthani:

> Worship an idol of a deity of one's choice and learn to concentrate one's mind on the deity's virtues and absorb its values and philosophy of living. Idol worship leading to meditation is used to purify one's mind and become free of evil forces created by materialistic desires.

For curing depression, Ganesh is recommended, among other gods. Part elephant, he holds a mango and the broken-off tusk he used to write the beloved Hindu epic, the Mahabharata. Worshippers bring Ganesh treats and drape him in garlands of flowers. I'm glad Zeda happened to have him for her depression, for the poetry of it. Some Hindus keep small god statues and get them dressed for the day each morning and back into pajamas at night. The god Radha-Krishna is two gods in one, female and male, and has special clothes; one shops at markets or online for an array of wee outfits.

The ancient Greeks had a goddess of depression and anxiety, Oizys, whom the Romans called Miseria. You'll recognize that she is the origin of the word "misery" in the Romance languages. Miseria is depression herself—rarely its cause—and thus personified she visits to moan around with you. Within religion we have things we are supposed to do when depressed, and a good story to hang on to, an idea for bearing up. A good story can carry you where you need to be. You deserve a good story.

How Art and Science Help

In the secular world, modern psychology is a little warped from having been created in specific opposition to religion. It was established by doctors rejecting supernatural theories of mental illness, such as possession by the Christian Devil or witchcraft, in favor of science. With its back against that battle with the medieval, the discipline then had to defend itself as sufficiently scientific to even be called a science. Because of this need for clean science lines, they don't tend to send you home with a toy statue friend.

It seems there's another side to it though, as not for nothing was Sigmund Freud's office festooned with icons, totems, and talismans from around the world. True, the specimen-cataloging project of anthropology at the time gave this more of a science vibe than it would have in an office of psychology or psychiatry today. But Freud saw himself as dealing with fearsome human impulses that were externalized, in many cultures, into these statues or who they represented. Freud believed these impulses were still dealt with in symbols and stand-ins. He was conquering little meanies but surrounded himself with them. Also, people with troubles just like small items of poignancy, and Freud was a person with troubles, just like the rest of us.

Today we often address depression with medicine, which does work, but—and here I rattle my pill bottle—it has deficits as a friend. It's amazing that a lot of us feel better, but *better* and *rattle-rattle* are no place to stand when the sands of change fall through, or all the king's *no* stampede like cattle. Therapy is a variety of relationship that is rigged in such a way as to let you get a good look at how you behave in the rest of life. If you are in emotional distress or want to see the world from a wider perspective, you have to try it. Also helpful are more normal friendships. Seek occasions where you get to be the one in the reassuring role, leading cheer. It is easier to find encouragement when giving it away.

When we can take neither porch conversation, nor couch distraction, we head to our beds. On our nightstands there may be small companions to our nerves and notions. Perhaps a fidgety-type spinner where once there may have been a rosary? Maybe we can do better.

Your Ritual Draws on Both

If you were raised in a religion that has things to do for depression, I'd say don't let disbelief stop you from any such gestures that appeal to you. If you miss prayer, but you don't like talking to nobody, you might try talking to your future self. Tell that bastard what you are going through for them. Thank your past self for riding the becalmed or raucous sea of time it took to get you to today.

Why not establish some sacraments of misery? What if you collected some tiny objects and kept them in a good box or bag and took them out when you're sad? They can be reminders that you are precious and that it's not always up to you to understand why. It might also be nice to put them back in the box as you feel better.

The objects do not have to be symbolic. They should please you in some moody way. You don't have to see a little antique brass bell as a reminder of the bell chime associated with a moment of enlightenment, or the town church bell tolling news of a birth or a death, but the bell might strike you as pretty, with its tinny *jingle jingle*. In choosing items, I'd say at least one should have a face. It's nice to look into eyes, it seems to me, and many icons have them. So far, I haven't purchased any sacraments of misery for the purpose, but I bet I will.

A "sacred object" is the second dictionary definition of "sacrament." Its primary usage is in Catholicism, where it refers to seven lifetime rituals, most with archetypical objects and images, such as rings for the sacrament of marriage. Our sacraments of misery are determined by their items. Because they arrive with associations and inherent uses, merely unpacking them can be your starter ritual.

I've clustered mine in a card-catalog drawer next to my desk: old kaleidoscope disk of multicolor glass, turtle of glued crystals, tile from therapist's hallway, hand-tall reproduction of thin man statue by Alberto Giacometti, thumb-tall Lakshmi statue, pocket compass, tiny chair, Catwoman shot glass, millions-of-years-old clamshell fossil, brass bell, cereal-prize ring, polished labradorite stone in the shape of a heart, antique teal enamel beetle brooch, and dead bee that was in the card-catalog box when I opened it.

They all meant something to me before I put them in the sacraments of misery box, but some not much. Almost all were on my desk or in reach when I had the idea to do this, so a bit random, but not entirely. That was over a year ago at this writing. I have taken them out when sad. I ring the bell. I hold the compass and figure out what's north of me. I only get so far remembering Brooklyn is south of the East Village and that I'd go west to get to East L.A. It helps. It leads me into poetry when I've got time and trouble on my hands. It makes me smile and eases my mind.

Writing the above list, I had to decide on words for my items and, oddly, it changed my relationship to them. I'd suggest you name yours. Greet your sacrament and see what name comes to your mouth for it. Imagine that these items have a secret to teach you. Find out what comes to your attention.

Sacraments of Misery

1. Take out your sacraments of misery.
2. Have a special cup and a beverage in it. We create human value for one another so trying to take care of yourself is sacred. For the sake of humanity, endeavor to hydrate.
3. Preset some music that lifts you. Listen to it like a medical dose.
4. Greet your items.
5. If you are up to it, set them up in a pleasing new tableau.

6. Say something to an icon with a face. Aloud? You tell me.
7. Write something down, and the date, and put it with your items.
8. Take a picture of your tableau.
9. Read your misery poem.

Repeat when you want. The items are yours to play with until you are again interested in voluptuous clouds and luminous skin.

Our Poem

The Urdu poet Ada Jafarey (1924–2015, pen name of Aziz Jahan) was one of the most important modern Pakistani writers and the region's most celebrated female poet. This is a ghazal, a poetic form with rules and expectations, to which we'll soon turn, but we need no instruction to feel its heartbeat like the surf beats. It is untitled and reads here in full.

Let your name touch her lips, let that happen
Let that be for a blame, let that happen

Blossoms wonder; they are sad and silent too
May the fragrance bring your word, let that happen

The moments of pleasure are shy of my thoughts
Let me recall pains and pangs, let that happen

Why grudge the fellow travelers the change of path?
The path I choose may reach you, let that happen

I'm tired; I sit forlorn by the lane of desire
Let the failed emotions matter, let that happen

This wilderness, Ada, will surely prove worth its name
Let the fear of end crop in mind, let that happen

What does the first line mean to you? It feels like romantic jealousy to me, and a claim of acceptance, perhaps selfless, perhaps sarcastic. Or is this touch of lips what the poet wants, so that "let that happen" is a wish, an incantation? What if she is talking about herself? What if she is talking to herself, but not about love. What if she is in thrall to an idea of truth? How many meanings can flash out from "let that happen"? Lines by Rainer Maria Rilke from his *The Book of Hours* come to mind:

> *Let everything happen to you: beauty and terror.*
> *Just keep going. No feeling is final.*

You may also think of the Beatles song with that classic command to "let it be." In the song the meaning is at least double: *leave it alone* and *may it be true*.

What do you think blossoms would wonder? Why are they sad? They are silent by nature, so why mention it? Perhaps because when people are silent it is often *not* by nature, and they may be sad about it.

Flowers in poetry are often called in as evidence that splendor should be enjoyed immediately, because it doesn't last. Indoors, in vases, the extravagant color and complexity and the brevity of their freshness shake us. Outdoor poets say they are thrown into contemplation by the multitude of their uncultivated appearances; as hordes of daffodils. Poets on trains feel bad that they cannot stop and see them all, cannot do justice to them all. What then do the flowers themselves wonder? I bet they wouldn't say a thing about whether they'd been admired by apes; they seem almost abusively obsessed with the sun. What fragrance brings what word to mind? I'm reminded of rosewater.

The "let that happen" response is poignant when pointed at the human mind's steel-trap grip on bad recollections. I've only heard our tendency to retain bad memories spoken of as an atrocious glitch. It's nice to hear her say, *Let it happen that my good memories are shy, and the bad ones stalk me*. I think that's how it is for a lot of us. Let that happen.

The poem asks an incisive question, "Why grudge the fellow travelers the change of path?" Predictable though it may be for minds to change over time, it is a blow to hear that a fellow in your battle has dropped your flag and raised another. Why? If we know people change as they get older, meet new people, face new challenges, then why does it sting so much when it happens to us? Exactly what is the grudge?

The surface of the question has a political ring to it, since "fellow travelers" was the name for people who weren't Communists but had shared goals. Here though we see the question in terms of romance. The person broke our heart. Perhaps a good answer is that there is something in friendship and love that invented "forever" and wants it; it's part of what love is.

In the language of the poem, imagine how life would look if we valued whatever strikes us now as "failed emotion."

Finally, let's take in the confident chumminess of "This wilderness, Ada, will surely prove worth its name." What's the wilderness? Being in "the wilderness" classically means feeling lost, overwhelmed with the unfamiliar. A wilderness is something one emerges from improved. The actual wilderness we praise these days as majestic and restorative, but we don't forget that it can be perilous. So her line can mean on the one hand, *this wilderness will be the end of me, will never let me go*, and on the other, *this wilderness will remake me and set me free*.

Poetry Lesson: The Ghazal

The ghazal arose in seventh-century Arabic writing and flourished there alone until twelfth-century Sufi mystics moved into South Asia and brought the ghazal with them. There it took off, combining with Persian and Urdu literature. It is still a dominant poetic form in many languages of India, and in Turkey.

Ghazals are made of couplets that are independent statements, not paragraphs of a story or points in an argument. The couplets are called *sher*. What connects them is a phrase reoccurring in the second line of each *sher*. The repeated phrase is the *radif*. The *sher* are linked by theme or tone, and their number varies between five and fifteen. A good *radif* allows for multiple meanings. Jafarey's *radif* "let that happen" is a gem splendidly reset in *sher* after *sher*.

Longing is the normal voice of the ghazal. It began as a form of love poem, addressed to the beloved, describing lustrous hair, eyes, speech, and at times lamenting distance and loss. Out of that tradition a branch grew where the "you" addressed by the *sher* was also spiritual truth, a god, or God. Outside religion the "you" has been contemplation of philosophical and poetic truth. Jafarey identified as a humanist.

My favorite ghazal rule is that in the final *sher* poets address themselves by name. The turn to self-chat at the end often feels like a whisper, with the world overhearing. If ever a ghazal feels distant or preachy those faults are likely undone with the final *sher* when it is all revealed as self-addressed. All that said, in this form as others, rules are both fun and fun to break.

* * *

I took my sacraments of misery from my desk and put them into the card-catalog drawer. As grass grows, new items fill in their places on the desk. How does this thing work? Are they filling from below, like a well? I joke. But seriously, it is a new crop and not intentional.

A favorite is a wee vintage plastic fellow who seems to have lost his snowmobile. His face was not well-etched to start and is now dinged up, but if I look fast, I detect a smile. I don't think he knows the snowmobile is gone. His jacket collar is up around his ears, his hat has a peak like an acorn cap. Because he falls a lot, he is inattentively set down in new places and then I get to find him as if he were imping around the office on his own. He is presently seated on a pill bottle, arms expectant of a sudden bundle, or perhaps pleading.

Time keeps passing as I think this through and when I get back each time, lo and behold, things accrue. I'm in a family of magpies and also when we empty boxes in order to clean up or use things, intriguing items abound. Another fossil, another semiprecious heart. It's hard not to think of Carl Jung's idea of archetypes as I begin to see the same basic symbology repeated in what arrives on my desk: hearts, human figurines, symbols of meditation, toys that move a little, and any bitty fella made for elsewhere. Are you a magpie too?

Are there themes to your collecting? Items can hold memories. Why do we keep items that hold bad memories? Jafarey's poem speaks of shy good memories and tenacious bad ones. We might at least try to shift the balance by off-loading the ballast.

I sometimes think that if it weren't for embarrassment, I wouldn't remember anything. I'm joking, but you know what I mean.

Maybe we create ourselves nested with items because we lose ourselves otherwise.

Your Poem

The poem builds and layers a self-portrait by letting it happen. While I value Rilke's advice to let everything happen to you, Jafarey's poem shows what we are allowing when we say that. The pain of it. The repetition in her ghazal strokes us and gently tells us to *let go*, but we don't feel she is speaking to us from above the fray. She's inside it.

If it suits you better, find a gladder poem about conquering depression. What tends to feel right for me is an *I've been down there, and it bites* poem, or an *I'm down there now* poem, because I seem to want company, and because when sad I lose all ear for cheer. Still, I love to find poems suggesting that things will get better.

After all, the sacraments of misery come out of the box and then they go back in. The fact of the box won't let me forget that sturdy fact.

* * *

My mind goes back to Zeda, the student with depression and an idol collection. I hope she has come to know more about Ganesh, as I have, since then, and learned that depression is one of his specialties.

I hope she has North Stars that stay fixed and bright above the pit of despair. Sometimes the best we can do is try to stay put until it passes, and if we want, we can Godzilla-knock-down a town no larger than a map, as Zeda taught me all those years ago. By now she's probably older than me, happy, or at least somewhere with a lovely windowsill for the dear little items that roll through our years, some whimsical ephemera, some plangent and lasting, and all, unlike so much of this weird life, personal, and small enough to hold.

There are behaviors we see as religious that can make people feel better, and these include interacting with icons. In Freud's office, the icons and statues were far from their field of religious power, but symbolically they were still the subject under investigation—archetypical issues of being human. The secular ways of dealing with depression are therapy and pills, often effective but thin on big-picture meaning through community and art.

Poetry and ritual can be a deep comfort, deeper still when we remember the fellowship of the Interfaithless in struggle. Over time there is a good chance you will feel better, maybe even much better. If you don't, maybe you are the witness to the nightside of life, and precious. If you do at some point feel better, perhaps assess how ritual and poetry have worked for you. Tweak the setup to fit your ease and need. It's a brave new world because you are in it, and we're eager to know what you will say and be.

17

On the Social Contract Blues

Returning from Political Loss

"I feel like collapsing on the altar. Where's my altar?"

I'm chatting with Margo and David, and their punkish daughter Bee, after a poetry reading in Washington, DC. It's January and bitterly cold outside. It's cold inside too because two walls and the ceiling of the room we are in are entirely glass. The DC climate usually allows for this even in winter but an icy wind has come in for the weekend from farther north than I. The reading is over and we are just now loosening our coats. The venue is the atrium at the Mount Vernon Place United Methodist Church. It is a dramatic space, a tall-ceilinged glass room constructed between two old brick and stone church buildings.

The event planners, two tall, good-looking young men, are sorry about the temperature. They've been heating up apple cider and offering it free all night. One assures us that no one had counted on the band of deep freeze dipping so far south.

"It's not usually this cold," says the other, having made his way around again to our clutch of chairs.

"We kept warm," says Margo, raising her cup in thanks and lying.

"It's been worth it for the stars," I say, tipping my head back another degree. A clear view of a crisp night sky had been arresting but was now getting hazy, from the inside; it's an odd hothouse sweetness, a cloud of apple cider.

Margo mentions how nice it is that we're talking poetry, "Not," she shudders, "politics." The family is in from Seattle for a long weekend, and saw a notice for this poetry reading steps from their hotel. I am in town for this poetry reading and to give a talk on poetry and unbelief, so our shared nonbelief has come up in conversation.

David mimes collapse at his wife's mention of the word "politics." Popping up he adds, "I feel like collapsing on the altar." He gestures toward the two old church buildings on either side of us, two arms up, and says, "Where's my altar?"

Margo says, "Well, there's the pulpit," and she gestures toward the portable wooden pulpit borrowed to serve as as dais for the reading. She thinks about it and says, "Maybe this actually is the altar you keep talking about. You know? We come to book readings usually knowing we'll find our people there. Here. I'd say that pulpit is our altar, or wailing wall, or whatever."

Teenaged Bee was buzzing her attention around the room but is now intently tuned in. She says, "I liked the reading, but I don't think it helps when they talk about politics. You only get madder." That last "you" was directed at her parents but then she looked around at all of us and says, with feeling, "You are all so smart and kind, and right. I don't understand why we don't win."

All the grown-ups feel stung. It's her mom, Margo, who speaks, saying, "Oh, Bee, I'm sorry."

David looks at me and says, "Things fall apart."

I answer with the second half of that Yeats line, "the centre cannot hold."

I am sorry I don't have more to give. Or get, for that matter.

After goodbyes, I barrel out into the whip-cold night and find I'm still nodding in agreement with the dad's outburst about not knowing where to go with our political despair. Bee's indictment and scorching question burning like a wound. Flags on a pole that I hadn't noticed going in now snap in the frantic wind.

I felt as blue as my toes on the metro ride back to my friend Yvany's, where I was staying, but on the journey out of the metro I couldn't believe how far underground we were. It seemed like miles of escalator, and as it went on, and on, and on, a poem we hadn't mentioned that night came to my mind and made me smile. "Still I Rise" is the name of the poem, by Maya Angelou, and I smiled to rise and rise and rise. I felt oddly reborn when I hit the polar air again and hoped that little family found its way to hope as well. It certainly helped me that I already had the poem in my head and knew at least a bit of it by heart.

* * *

Any lasting religion amasses stories of loss and resolute survival. They are formidable stories, often in beautiful language. That's what withstands the glacial scrape of time. Religions have models for how to behave when beaten. What do you do when concussed by an unthinkable loss, on a national scale? What face do you make? What songs do you sing, or are you silent? What do you tell the young people? What do you tell yourself?

Religion's sad stories often give members input on what to say, what to do first, and how to show the world they're grieving. I think of the biblical Job howling in grief, rending his garment, sitting on an ash heap, unable to speak, and how still today the Jewish way of bereavement includes tearing one's shirt—an action now ritualized.

How Religion Helps

Long-standing religions have tales of times when they were forced underground, living close to the hearth and planning for redemption. Consider the biblical Psalm 137, "By the waters of Babylon we sat down and wept." It is a lament about an all-encompassing state loss. When the ancient Babylonians conquered Judea and destroyed the Temple, they rounded up skilled and educated Jews and forced them to come back to Babylonia, not to be enslaved, but to enrich the homeland. The first such mass deportation was in 597 BCE. The captives were far from the world they had known, and living with people who had butchered their families, and razed their Temple.

It's when the captives are asked to sing their beautiful songs that they crack open in pain. Some poet caught this pain in words, and the sublime lament has passed the lips of many breaking voices, over millennia. Last century, the Rastafarian band the Melodians pressed on the paradox—a beguiling song against singing—using the psalm's famous phrases. Here's the psalm in full:

Psalm 23

> *By the rivers of Babylon, there we sat down, yea, we wept, when*
>   *we remembered Zion.*
> *We hanged our harps upon the willows in the midst thereof.*
> *For there they that carried us away captive required of us a song;*
>   *and they that wasted us required of us mirth, saying, Sing us*
>   *one of the songs of Zion.*
> *How shall we sing the Lord's song in a strange land?*
> *If I forget thee, O Jerusalem, let my right hand forget her cunning.*
> *If I do not remember thee, let my tongue cleave to the roof of my*
>   *mouth; if I prefer not Jerusalem above my chief joy.*
> *Remember, O Lord, the children of Edom in the day of Jerusalem;*
>   *who said, Raze it, raze it, even to the foundation thereof.*
> *O daughter of Babylon, who art to be destroyed; happy shall he*
>   *be, that rewardeth thee as thou hast served us.*
> *Happy shall he be, that taketh and dasheth thy little ones against*
>   *the stones.*

Notice the unspeakable fury of the final lines. The psalm is a regular part of Jewish, Eastern Orthodox, Roman Catholic, Anglican, and an array of Protestant liturgies. The words of this psalm and song have themselves served as a grand altar, upon which a multitude have thrown themselves.

How Art and Science Help

The secular world harbors ideas for coping with large-scale losses, in election or war. One is to retreat into private life, as Voltaire advised at the end of *Candide*. The titular character's encounters with the world make mincemeat of his principles and shave pieces off his loved ones. So in the book's final words Candide vows to "cultivate my own garden," that is, to turn away from the world, to be morally decent but not actively helpful.

It's seductive, but it's not good. Humans are a communal species; our value and values exist in relation to one another. Also, even loners have to admit that if we ignore oppression too long, the jackbooted troops will come for our gardens, too.

Note that people are willing to live and die for ideals when inspiring words support the mission. When England faced invading fascism, in 1940, Winston Churchill rallied his nation against the immediately safer choice of working with Hitler's Germany, saying, "We shall fight on the beaches, we shall fight on the landing grounds, we shall fight in the fields and in the streets, we shall fight in the hills; we shall never surrender." Words have power. Stories change the world. What story leads us forward?

The Interfaithless do not at present have a coherent model for responding to disastrous political setbacks. There is the consolation of watching the other side crash and burn, at least in some instances. Think of it. After years of seeing a good leader plagued by obstructionists, it is a silver sliver of redemption to watch the erstwhile obstructionists battered by the same tactics.

Some of your enemies will rise obnoxiously, and soon be disgraced, and after you stomach the rise you'll enjoy the fall. Admittedly, that is not much to steel you in the instant of loss. While the religious can join religious rites when feeling destroyed, the Interfaithless are often on their own and feel nothing but frozen.

Your Ritual Draws on Both

We have a responsibility to revive, to fix what went wrong, to reassess. Pick a poem for political heartache and read it as you engage with action. Go to demonstrations when you can. If it helps, keep a political journal, take steno on your outrage, your times of apathy, and patterns of renewal. Change the world, but also survive and thrive.

When there is a seismic upheaval of many people's shared world, it helps to be together. Gatherings can have political influence, but they don't require specific justification. Rallies, meetups, and memorial shrines are a normal way people can be reassured when their sense of reality takes a hit. Go find out how you feel there. Join up with others and hit the streets in protest. It takes courage and steals time from our other pursuits, but sometimes we don't have a choice. It can be a relief, and it may give you an ineffable experience you will draw on in the future.

If you want, you can rue the vinegar of human ugliness by eating some. The Jewish Passover seder includes eating "bitter herbs" dipped in salt water to recall the bitterness of the slavery we've known and in solidarity with slavery that many human beings endure today. The Interfaithless too can learn from taking a moment to face and taste that bitterness. Eat some pickles. Any pickled vegetable will do; briny and spicy or garlic and dill. Let go of your hunger for protein and fat and let the vinegar of life be vinegar.

Another ritual for a time of shocking loss is to climb. Climb a hill, climb a tree, climb stairs to a view, rugged enough to feel it. There are poems that could accompany your steps, keeping time, and poems to read aloud when you reach the top. No nearby hills or skyscrapers? Clamber up a boulder. Look at that view; that's your view. Religions include rituals of climbing, too, leading members to ascend hills to worship.

Another religious way to ascend is by lowering and raising one's body, repeatedly, as in many religious services. Or think of qigong, a movement meditation of Taoism and Buddhism that began in ancient China. The qigong spinal stretch is another way to rise. You stand with feet slightly spread and slowly bend over, one vertebra at a time. From your neck down, you ease your backbone forward until you are hanging down from the waist. Then, sloth slow, you rise back up, again unfurling one vertebra at a time. Take a Taoist meditation class and you can fall and rise in community.

Our Poem

The poet and author Maya Angelou (1928–2014) had a profound effect on American culture. Her poem "Still I Rise" has the power to heal.

Still I Rise

You may write me down in history
With your bitter, twisted lies,
You may trod me in the very dirt
But still, like dust, I'll rise.

Does my sassiness upset you?
Why are you beset with gloom?
'Cause I walk like I've got oil wells
Pumping in my living room.

Just like moons and like suns,
With the certainty of tides,
Just like hopes springing high,
Still I'll rise.

Did you want to see me broken?
Bowed head and lowered eyes?
Shoulders falling down like teardrops,
Weakened by my soulful cries?

Does my haughtiness offend you?
Don't you take it awful hard
'Cause I laugh like I've got gold mines
Diggin' in my own backyard.

You may shoot me with your words,
You may cut me with your eyes,

You may kill me with your hatefulness,
But still, like air, I'll rise.

Does my sexiness upset you?
Does it come as a surprise
That I dance like I've got diamonds
At the meeting of my thighs?

Out of the huts of history's shame
I rise
Up from a past that's rooted in pain
I rise
I'm a black ocean, leaping and wide,
Welling and swelling I bear in the tide.

Leaving behind nights of terror and fear
I rise
Into a daybreak that's wondrously clear
I rise
Bringing the gifts that my ancestors gave,
I am the dream and the hope of the slave.
I rise
I rise
I rise.

The poet speaks from a place that is already wise to what the powerful can do and she's still standing. It hurts to be subject to "bitter, twisted lies," or to be stepped on "in the very dirt"—and what helps is knowing that people like her keep showing up. The opening neat quatrains revel in the revelation that underling "sassiness" truly irritates the ruling elite. The rich-in-money gaze at those wealthy in self-worth and know that in this crucial economy it is the rich who clutch checks too blank to brandish.

When the third stanza cites three things that rise, Angelou chooses examples that also wane, set, and ebb—the moon, sun, and tide—

reminding us of the back and forth of fortunes. The poem contains much violence, "you may shoot me," "cut me," "kill me." The poet's faith in this hateful world is that, despite all, the human spirit will rise. Like air held down underwater, you can hold it down as long as you want, it will still rise. It's science.

With the slightest chance, up it goes again. These buoyant, sexy stanzas build excitement and then Angelou lights the poem's fuse. Naming herself "a black ocean," huge, leaping, swelling, she goes on repeating, "I rise," ending the poem in a crescendo of three. I heard the actor Rosie Perez read this poem, coming off "I am the dream and the hope of the slave" rhyme, and issuing a fierce "I rise," a defiant second, "I rise," and then the floor dropped out, as if she at that moment understood that the tiny declaration is not a threat, but a calm truth, an odd but proven fact: "I rise."

The poem has regularity, a walking beat, a climbing rhythm, "You may kill me with your hatefulness," cuing up the satisfying final drumbeat, "But still, like air, I'll rise." That's the ultimate revival. The poem is a master class in losing but still winning—because you're right, and you have come true, and are a wonder. I know it as I know air will never decide to stay underwater. Bright stars like you will never stop rising.

I wish I'd had all this to give Margo and David, and especially teenaged Bee.

Poetry Lesson: The Conversation of Poems

Do you hear a conversation between Psalm 137 and "Still I Rise"? The psalm is familiar to the churchgoing, in several songs and other forms, some shortened or revised. Psalm 137 is known well, too, because it was set to music by Bach, Dvořák, and Verdi.

The singer Paul Robeson performed the Dvorak version of the psalm, intensifying the connection between images of the Judean captives and Black people in America. The song "Rivers of Babylon" has been performed by many artists as a song of liberation.

It's a sad psalm for all this, isn't it? All it says is: *There was a time when our captors asked us to sing one of our exquisite songs about our homeland as they were dragging us away from what they'd left of it. We couldn't do it. We hung our harps in the willow tree branches in protest.* Then it says, *I swear never to forget my homeland.* Then it pivots to trauma and fantasies of horrific revenge.

Where is the *We will survive* moment in Psalm 137? It goes unsaid. The poetic memory of hanging harps and heads with weeping willow trees is dejection. But also, less obviously, it's protest. They won't sing.

Angelou's "Still I Rise" feels its promised sun and lets us feel it. With a shift of inflection, *How can we sing in a strange land?* becomes the sassier question: *I suppose you are wondering how it is we sing in a strange land?* It is the teasing rhetorical riddle in "Still I Rise." The poem is both the report of deliverance and the promise of deliverance.

Verse converses (it's right in the name). As any acting teacher can tell you better, people don't speak, they answer. In Psalm 137, the oppressed people won't sing, but it is such a lovely poem that we sing it, around the world. Angelou's poem is vividly aware of nights of terror, and fear, and she keeps rising, sings. Like the Temple, she's supposed to be broken, but somehow survives.

This talk of singing may remind us of Maya Angelou's classic memoir of growing up in the South, called *I Know Why the Caged Bird Sings*. The title is a line from Paul Laurence Dunbar's poem "Sympathy." Dunbar lived from 1872 to 1906. His poem's three seven-line stanzas are all about this caged bird and its heartbreaking condition. The bird wants out, violently. For Angelou, in the memoir, there is redemption. There is freedom. There is so much pain, but in this story there is also joyous song.

* * *

Time has passed since I began this essay, which I started because of a political loss that was nearly unbearable. At the time I was in wreckage over the loss, so it was all I could manage to write about. Now it is years later and the problem of political division itself seems violent and sadly persistent. As much as this essay is about absorbing a loss, grieving, and reviving to fight for your rights another day, I want to be a voice against revenge and the mentality of feuds to the death. The last line of the Babylon psalm is bad news, I must insist on no baby dashing. Babies are innocent, in fact the sight of them should remind us that individuals get caught up in history and can be innocent of its atrocities. Anyway, I've learned over and over that you can't go around guessing what people are thinking and what they have done.

I went to Paris with a vibrant German woman I didn't know; I was nineteen, I think she was twenty-one. We'd both recently arrived at Caen, a town mesmerized by the sweet butter of its many cows, knowing no one. The dorm had a breakfast room that engrossed us every day in the aroma of coffee, the fresh cream, baguettes, and sumptuous crocks of that butter. She spoke English. One of us said, "Want to go to Paris for the weekend?"

It was me, now that I get down to it. I was socially brave. Maria was generally brave, such that she wouldn't have thought she needed a buddy for such an adventure. She often had a little smirk for me; she had traveled a lot, me none at all. Maria was tall and large framed, very pretty, with pale skin, delicate features, bright green eyes, and a majesty of long, full, black hair, this one feature out of control. Her dorm door faced mine and we foreigners had moved in two weeks early for French-language intensives.

We went to Paris, stayed at a cheap hotel, went to museums, and headed back to Caen. We're too broke for sleeping cars, but all the seats on the trains are in enclosed compartments, with two benches facing each other, and we have one such compartment to ourselves. It's evening and there is a luminous blue sky. The trees are mostly these weird French things cut into cubes, and as we leave Paris and its environs these squared trees grow less manicured and more wild.

We are lying on the benches, heads propped up on balled coats, watching dark France go by. Having sung together in orientation, we start now with our mutual Beatles songbook, and what we can put together of Paul Simon's "The Boxer" used by all guitar sing-alongs in multilingual Europe because of the easy-for-everyone "Li, la, li" chorus. The train chug-chugs along with us, the blue sky blackens, and the searingly beautiful countryside rolls by.

Then Maria asks me if I know any Jewish songs. Did I mention that this trip to France was the first time I ever met a German? This trip to France was the first time I'd ever met a German. So again, I'm a Jewish girl from far away. My people left Europe—those who stayed were murdered. In the streets. In their homes. In the camps.

My first German wants to hear a Jewish song. Would it be sacrilege or sacred? I went with poetic sacred. I sing "Hine Ma Tov," which was part of my otherwise secular repertoire with my sister, back home, mostly because we could find the harmony. It felt now like sublime world-healing was going on in our transcendent train car, singing my Hebrew song to a German, as France sped by and the sky turned from twilight into night.

Now Maria asks to learn the song. I have to take a breath, for a moment, to know it is alright. It hurts but feels magical to teach her the words. The song is only two lines of text, repeated, with lovely tune changes.

I felt like the forgiving spirit of grace, a Jew singing like this, light chugging by, in and out, to see her lovely face intoning the vowels of my people, my family, those who stayed in Europe, shot and killed, kicked and dead. I felt brave and frightened. And then Maria stops singing. Maria says, "I have to tell you. Something I never told in my life."

I say, "Okay." Expecting another stone in the psychic backpack I'm trying to carry, a sense of being a child wronged, a remnant alone with a child of the hating hate, the mystery of history.

She says, "No one in my family talks about this."

The light comes and goes on her face, her hands rise to cover her eyes. She's quiet so long, I say again, gently, "Okay," and then, getting concerned, "Ça va?"

She says, "We're not German, we're Hungarian Jewish." The train chug-chugs. Light crosses Maria's face. I feel my face flush, listening, with held breath. She says, "My whole family, we are still all pretending. The ones that wouldn't pretend—all are dead." I look over and tall, strong, not-German Maria has tears running down and curving onto her small ear, catching the strobing light. She's on a backdrop of her magnificent hair.

I'd been lying there so sure of my victim role in this one act, where so much was taking place in that little compartment. Come to realize all of that was taking place inside Maria.

For me it was the exact start of a lifelong process of realizing that there is always more going on than I guess, whether my guess uses scholarship or common sense. Those two may help you sort categories after the fact, but you can't begin to know what is going on inside a person until that moment of trust and quiescence in which they choose to reveal their story to you.

We need only listen to others for our own burdens to shift in heft and feel lighter. So go listen. In troubled times people gather in public places, parks and squares, to place flowers, poems, candles, and pictures, and stand around together. At times we end up singing. At times we end up talking. Even confessing to a stranger why this particular public loss has such a private sting and hearing their version of the same thing.

Your Poem

A well-made poem can be an altar to weep on. We go and gather together even if in the moment we do not know why. Political loss is such a twisted version of heartbreak. In many nations, certainly the United States, national elections are often won by so small a margin that it is ridiculous to feel that the country is suddenly revealed—with an election—to be either deeply progressive or conservative. Yet that's how it feels.

What can we do, for ourselves and for others, when the election viewing party goes from boppy to blighted, and what we'd hoped for is dashed against the rocks? You can cry. You can sing the psalm that asks, *How can we sing in a strange land?* You can "Candide" yourself into private life, lavishing focus on your trellis roses. But we can't hide for long and expect democracy to stand over us, allowing it. We have to shore up our institutions.

So where are its threatened ramparts? Where is democracy? I'm asking for the normal citizens for me and likely for you. When all the pop-up polling stations have folded and gone home? Aren't you the first unit of democracy? Or rather, isn't your political will the first unit of democracy? That's why it is sacred, and necessary, to find yourself some inspiration.

Seek a poem that has a beat you can climb to, as the metronome of "I rise" so deftly delivers. The act of putting the poem in your poetry collection, under this topic heading, can hook any number of poems to the work needed. One way to choose a poem is to focus your search in the community that you feel part of in this loss. It doesn't have to be a perfect fit in every way, but to either overlap with the kind of struggle you are in, or with the location or population of the struggle, can be galvanizing.

The poem may have a significance you don't know about yet that will make it fit perfectly. I, for instance, just looked up "Hine Ma Tov" for the spelling, and then it occurred to me to click further and find out what it means. I must have been told the meaning as a child, but it seems unlikely I remembered long—surely not on the train that night. Now looking it up, I was half-certain it would be about God and therefore of less help to me. Nope. "Behold how good and how pleasing / for people to sit together in unity." Isn't that something?

* * *

For today, take your seat on the broken-chances bench and marvel at the stellar company you're in, singing the team song. "By the rivers of Babylon, there we sat down, yea, we wept." We cry too and may hide awhile in solitary gardens.

We find the altar in our verses and in one another's hearts and courage. We find the altar in one another's outrageous imagination, in the immunity of the already beaten. We take a deep weep, and a deep sleep, and try not to get too deep pressed. We hold. We behold how good and how pleasing it is for people to sit together in unity. Then we rise.

18

On Choosing a Code to Live By

A Midnight Snack with the Flower of Toledo

"I have a code poem."

A friend asks if his cousin Katerina can stay the night on my couch. He praises Cousin Katerina, but not for attributes usually recommended in a lodger. "She's a drummer. She's a radical anti-colonialist and unbeatable at checkers. Everyone used to be scared of her but then they called her the Flower of Toledo."

"Okay, probably," I say, "but I have to meet her first."

We all meet for dinner. "Jen the Historian, I present Cousin Katerina, the Flower of Toledo." Then he drinks and talks about nihilism nonstop, so even after getting him into a taxi, she and I haven't exchanged many words. We are tired but hungry, so I invite Katerina to Veselka, open all night, to feast on potato pierogi. We walk into a rich fog of chicken soup, frying onions, the whiff of a late-night mop.

"You're brave," I tell Katerina. "Traveling around at loose ends like this." I say it because I was thinking, *I'm brave—letting this stranger stay on my couch*, but that isn't the sort of thing one says.

"Not really," says Katerina. "I can keep staying with my cousin, only it's crowded over there and I'm sick of him."

"What did it? The nihilism?" I ask.

Katerina's mouth is full, but she laughs, stunning face gone momentarily to clown. I see the platter is nearly empty and signal for another large order. It is occurring to me that the first restaurant we'd met at was basically burgers. Katerina can't answer the first question, because she's bitten off the important part of a pieróg, so I add, "You don't eat meat, do you?"

Katerina shakes her head *no* and blushes. When she swallows, she says, "The nihilism and the belching."

Now I laugh. "Well, but things like that. And all the things you do. I just . . ." I make a pained face and look up from the table to see Katerina making the same face and decide not to finish the sentence.

"My problem isn't nihilism, exactly, it's anxiety with rage? I don't know what it is, but you just go like you have a secret handbook."

Katerina laughs and puts up her hands. "I have a code, a code *poem* actually," she says. Then to my surprise, she recites her code from memory. She says, "It's a changed version of Kipling's poem 'If—.' My aunty changed it." The change is that it is only two stanzas of the poem, and that Katerina drops the "If" beginning any line, so that all six such lines begin with "You." Here are the two stanzas without Katerina's aunt's adorable dropping of the "Ifs," but read it that way in your head, too.

If—

If you can keep your head when all about you
　　Are losing theirs and blaming it on you,
If you can trust yourself when all men doubt you,
　　But make allowance for their doubting too;
If you can wait and not be tired by waiting,
　　Or being lied about, don't deal in lies,
Or being hated, don't give way to hating,
　　And yet don't look too good, nor talk too wise:

If you can dream—and not make dreams your master;
　　If you can think—and not make thoughts your aim;
If you can meet with Triumph and Disaster
　　And treat those two impostors just the same;
If you can bear to hear the truth you've spoken
　　Twisted by knaves to make a trap for fools,

Or watch the things you gave your life to, broken,
    And stoop and build 'em up with worn-out tools[.]

The new, hot, platter of delicious shows up and we thank the Ukrainian waitress, who seems oddly young and fresh for the hour. Katerina starts for the serving spoon, and I applaud her recital of the poem. I mention that there are more stanzas to the poem and ask Katerina if she'd stopped there because of the arrival of the pierogi. Katerina says no; her aunt gave the poem to her like this; two stanzas, no "Ifs." Here's the rest of the poem:

If you can make one heap of all your winnings
    And risk it on one turn of pitch-and-toss,
And lose, and start again at your beginnings
    And never breathe a word about your loss;
If you can force your heart and nerve and sinew
    To serve your turn long after they are gone,
And so hold on when there is nothing in you
    Except the Will which says to them: "Hold on!"

If you can talk with crowds and keep your virtue,
    Or walk with Kings—nor lose the common touch,
If neither foes nor loving friends can hurt you,
    If all men count with you, but none too much;
If you can fill the unforgiving minute
    With sixty seconds' worth of distance run,
Yours is the Earth and everything that's in it,
    And—which is more—you'll be a Man, my son!

If the ending irks, I made this one up as a stand in:

If you can fill the unforgiving minute
with sixty seconds like a hand in glove
Yours is the earth and everything in it,
what's more you'll be a mensch my love.

Speaking only of those first two stanzas, Katerina adds, "Only this makes everything possible for me. It makes me strong. The code makes it interesting to 'wait and not be tired by waiting' for its own sake. It's, um, a call to really live, and also the armor you need to do it. The armor is that I already know if I'm myself, doing what I want, I know I'm going to meet hate, and lies, and that these sad things will happen. I used to feel terribly about failing, but now it's just part of the business of my code."

I say, "You know you're a weird defender of Kipling, right? I heard you're a radical anti-colonialist. He was a big colonialist."

Katerina smiles slow and it's like sunrise on a dark night. She swallows and says, "That's funny, but yes, I am, I am. Of course, I am."

"So?" I prompt again.

Then Katerina, the Flower of Toledo, says, "I don't defend my poetry, my poetry defends me."

* * *

A lot of people have a code poem or something like it. They often haven't read it over in a while, but people collect ideas over time that make living better seem possible, and they hang on to them over a lifetime.

It can feel bad to live without a code. Sometimes you know that you miss having a code, because you aren't sure what to do, perhaps when you have to choose a course of action in a muddy situation.

More often, likely, the nature of the impoverishment isn't even clear. You are internally spinning like a top and unawake to the fact that most people in history and today have at least some adopted rules so they can reach out and stop. Taking "If—," the poem above, as the source, a man could say, "I 'don't deal in lies,'" not only to help him make decisions but also to look back on his life and know that of course there were choices between prizes-with-lies, or honest-and-prizeless, and he gets to say, "My goal was always to be a man who did not deal in lies. Everyone squeezes truth when needed, and a healthy human has a few secrets, but I did not allow myself to become someone who deals in lies, or not too badly, or not for long. I win."

A code poem says, *Do this, don't do that*, while a "morality poem" inspires inner searching on universal themes. A credo poem is chosen. Or for the chosen. Or may be an unusual challenge in itself, so that to do the rules is to become chosen. They have a few practical themes:

Why it's good to build despite loss and death.
How to explain injustice and cope with it.
What makes a good life.
How to be; how to carry oneself in the world.

If you have such a poetic credo, you can likely get more out of it with a fresh read, or a fuller read with additional context. If you don't have anything like a code poem, let's get you one and see how it feels.

How Religion Helps

Religious ethical codes morph over time. Often, they change because people made a conscious choice to change the rules. I'm telling you this next story because I think it will empower you to examine your rules.

The Ten Commandments is one of humanity's best-known ethical codes. It didn't exist, as such, until the sixteenth century. Prior to that, the "commandments" (not yet so named) were in two places in the Bible, stated differently, in a different order, and mixed with other laws, claims, and cautions. Scholars identify about fifteen distinct injunctions.

The Jews had them as "Ten Sayings," and in the Christian Tyndale Bible they were "Ten Verses." Not until the Geneva Bible of 1560 do we find the name "tenne commandments" [sic], and it caught on.

They have continuously been altered by theologians, translators, and editors. Christians changed the prohibition on "graven images" to "idols" because people like pictures; the Jewish prohibition against visual art was never doable when the Jesus sect spread across multiple cultures, each with its own historical relationships to images. Lutherans dropped the "make no graven images" law completely and got to Ten by doubling-up the rules against neighbor envy, one for house, one for spouse.

What do the Ten Commandments say? Three are accepted rules today. I've put them on top of this list, and they speak for themselves. I'd venture to say they help us function; they help us to feel we know something true about right and wrong. I'm not saying we always walk north, but we can't function without the sign. The rest are more problematic, and they follow with commentary.

Don't murder.

Don't steal.

Don't bear false witness.

No pictures please. The law prohibiting graven images was originally meant to stop the habit of ancient Hebrews dabbling in the other religions of the region, which were idol based. Much later the no-images rule was used to show Roman Emperors that Christianity was philosophical and not merely a dangerous cult feeding poor people impossible promises. Whatever past reasons, forbidding any art today seems horrible to me. Unsubscribe.

Go sit down and hush. The mandate for rest one day a week can be happiness oriented, but the question is, what should "rest" look like? Your ancestors may have enjoyed happiness-oriented laws that have become a chore. If you are so bored that it is a chore, isn't that labor? It's a social conundrum that compulsory rest is a joy for some and a prison for others.

Listen to your mother and father. In the ancient world "honor your father and mother" had a legal reality past childhood; in places, even full-grown men were legally under their father's command until his death. It is still good guidance to honor your elders, but modern culture also supports finding your own footing and your own voice.

Marriage is sacred. The rule against adultery is odd; it's not obvious that people would so enthrone a rule against any married man or woman having sex with anyone else. If we recall that marriage here defined is meant to encompass all of one's younger adulthood, this rule is not going to be everyone's cup of sex.

Don't envy. The only "thought crime" on the list is envy. A rule can't stop a thought but can dissuade us from indulging in rumination.

"I am your God you shall have no other gods above me" comes from the age of Hebrew "monolatry" (which means believing that other gods exist but worshipping only one), which predates monotheism. It reminds us that there are more possibilities out there.

Don't take God's name in vain. I mean, wow. This one seems the easiest to keep and is comically disregarded, omg.

So as a credo the Ten Commandments has content problems, but I suppose it makes up for that with style. A guy comes down a mountain with rules cut in stone. They have their own shape! Right? Believer or not the silhouette of a Bactrian-camel tablet is a symbol for the rule of law. When a person's cultural liturgy about good laws matches up to our truest beliefs, it feels supportive. When you've long accepted that as a glitch, it is possible that makes you feel glitchy.

How Art and Science Help

There are many secular codes of purpose and honor: the doctors' Hippocratic oath, the Bushidō code of the Japanese samurai, the Italian Mafia's omertà, the Bill of Rights, the rules of *Fight Club*. In fiction and nonfiction we can see these at work. For instance, if a person goes to a medical office and requests to be maimed, a doctor can refuse without having to puzzle out the moral question for herself. The oath she took reads, "First, do no harm."

The Bushidō code was unwritten for many centuries before it found its poetic form in Nitobe Inazō's *Bushidō: The Soul of Japan* (1899). His "Eight Virtues" are based in neo-Confucianism. They still read as nuanced and inspiring; for instance, one is *Righteousness*:

Be acutely honest throughout your dealings with all people. Believe in justice, not from other people, but from yourself. To the true warrior, all points of view are deeply considered regarding honesty, justice and integrity. Warriors make a full commitment to their decisions.

Credos may be similar to one another in their advice, but the small differences matter. For instance, many codes suggest that you avoid trouble unless it comes to your door. The Bushidō code says if a "true warrior" sees no trouble with which to assist, "they go out of their way to find one."

Your Ritual Draws on Both

People who don't read poetry may have found a code poem in song lyrics. Here is an ancient code poem that is likely part of your private wisdom already, because it was made into a song. It was loved for centuries before that, as Ecclesiastes 3:1–15, in both religious and popular culture.

> To every thing there is a season, and a time to every purpose under the heavens:
> A time to be born, and a time to die; a time to plant, and a time to [glean];
> A time to kill, and a time to heal; a time to break down, and a time to build up;
> A time to weep, and a time to laugh; a time to mourn, and a time to dance;
> A time to cast away stones, and a time to gather stones together; a time to embrace, and a time to refrain from embracing;
> A time to get, and a time to lose; a time to keep, and a time to cast away;
> A time to rend, and a time to sew; a time to keep silence, and a time to speak;
> A time to love, and a time to hate; a time of war, and a time of peace.

The song, "Turn! Turn! Turn!" by the Byrds, quotes these phrases to superb effect and has been played at life events since 1965, often enough to call it cultural liturgy.

Ecclesiastes was written by a man called Koheleth ("preacher") between 450 and 200 BCE in the ancient Mideast. Koheleth is here saying that we're not supposed to always be laughing, always be harvesting, always dancing, nor always alive. One day you sew a shirt, another day you tear it ("rend it") in ritual response to a death. While some religions claim that good people thrive and sinners meet with illness and failure, Koheleth avows that life's extremes come for all. The construction of "There Is a Season" is sublime, and its balance of realities rock the reader like a cradle.

Use this for your ritual. Rock on your feet, or seated, while you read or recite your poem. Go someplace where you can throw stones, and then gather them, as in the passage above. Or if you prefer, sew and rend. Light some incense for the aroma and to make visible the invisible air all around us.

Our Poem

George Eliot (1819–1880, pen name of Mary Ann Evans) wrote *Middlemarch*, and seven other novels beloved by Victorians through Gen Z, and much poetry. Here is her terrific life code:

O May I Join the Choir Invisible

O May I join the choir invisible
Of those immortal dead who live again
In minds made better by their presence: live
In pulses stirred to generosity,
In deeds of daring rectitude, in scorn
For miserable aims that end with self,
In thoughts sublime that pierce the night like stars,
And with their mild persistence urge man's search

To vaster issues.

   So to live is heaven:
To make undying music in the world,
Breathing as beauteous order that controls
With growing sway the growing life of man.
So we inherit that sweet purity
For which we struggled, failed, and agonized
With widening retrospect that bred despair.
Rebellious flesh that would not be subdued,
A vicious parent shaming still its child,
Poor anxious penitence, is quick dissolved;
Its discords, quenched by meeting harmonies,
Die in the large and charitable air.
And all our rarer, better, truer self,
That sobbed religiously in yearning song,
That watched to ease the burthen of the world,
Laboriously tracing what must be,
And what may yet be better,—saw within
A worthier image for the sanctuary,
And shaped it forth before the multitude,
Divinely human, raising worship so
To higher reverence more mixed with love,—
That better self shall live till human Time
Shall fold its eyelids, and the human sky
Be gathered like a scroll within the tomb Unread forever.
   This is life to come,
Which martyred men have made more glorious
For us who strive to follow. May I reach
That purest heaven, be to other souls
The cup of strength in some great agony,
Enkindle generous ardor, feed pure love,
Beget the smiles that have no cruelty,
Be the sweet presence of a good diffused,
And in diffusion ever more intense!

So shall I join the choir invisible
Whose music is the gladness of the world

I don't think I was charmed by all that the first time I read it. It seemed flowery and hard to decipher. I love it now, as many have before me. Let's look at it as a list of instructions:

1. Aim to join "the choir invisible" whose good influence is felt in life and death.
2. Inspire people to generosity.
3. Take risks in standing up for what is right.
4. Avoid goals that help only you.
5. Keep pointing to the stars, persistently, to help people focus on the vast realities.
6. Cherish music.
7. Recognize the "order that controls" our lives.
8. Don't mourn for a purer age; "Rebellious flesh" never was subdued.
9. Don't shame children.
10. Don't be a self-hating penitent; tell your "sins," and the air will kill the shame.
11. Once we "sobbed religiously," now we fix the world, with more love than in religion.
12. Help the future, as people of the past lived and died to give us what *they* wanted.
13. Be someone's "cup of strength" in a "great agony."
14. Model passion.
15. Induce true smiles.
16. Be a "sweet presence"; spread the love and it will grow.
17. Learn to sense the choir, all those who fought hard to create what you love.

Poetry Lesson: George Eliot

Eliot was raised in provincial England but read expansively in several languages and was a critical thinker early on. At age twenty-one she became friends with Charles and Cara Bray, whose home served for her as a freethinking salon. At parties there she met many doubters of received religion, including the utopian socialist Robert Owen, the social theorist and atheist Harriet Martineau, the political theorist Herbert Spencer, and the American Ralph Waldo Emerson, who called himself a "transcendentalist."

Eliot translated Ludwig Feuerbach's *Essence of Christianity*, an atheistic humanist book that had electrified the German-speaking world. She also translated portions of Baruch Spinoza's *Ethics*, also an atheist masterpiece of morality and meaning.

Though hailed as a national treasure at the time of her death, Eliot was too famous an unbeliever to be buried in Westminster Abbey, where the other treasured English bones are stored. She was interred instead at a nearby plot with such godless British luminaries as Karl Marx and Herbert Spencer. It's sweet to report that recently a memorial stone for her was set in Westminster Abbey's Poets' Corner.

I don't know what I believe about progress, but I like to hang out with a Victorian-era girl with a boy's name, who believes in the future and sings in its choir. The poem can feel archly starchy before you understand it, and starry-eyed after you're used to it, but a lot of good work gets done. There is a reason to live spelled out here.

* * *

Eliot's poem reminds us of a comedy skit where many of us first heard her mellifluent phrase, "the choir invisible." It was in a John Cleese moment, in his role as shopper, when he explodes in a cry for truth in an absurd world. This comic digression will loop us back to the poem, with more understanding, so stay with me.

In case you are unfamiliar with it, the British TV show *Monty Python's Flying Circus* was arguably the funniest thing in the twentieth century. In one of its most iconic sketches, a proper gentleman, played by Cleese, arrives at a pet-shop counter carrying a birdcage, and reports he's been sold a dead parrot. The store's owner, sweet-faced Michael Palin, denies the death.

Cleese points to the obvious signs of death and Palin delivers inane counterclaims, including that "'E's resting," and that (as the bird is a Norwegian Blue) he's simply "pining for the fjords," and this sadness mimics death. Cleese, his role is "Mr. Praline" in the script, insists the bird is dead, repeatedly, and Palin cheerfully lies to his face, despite the rigor-hard evidence. Mr. Praline flips his lid.

Owner: No, no! 'E's pining!

Mr. Praline: 'E's not pinin'! 'E's passed on! This parrot is no more! He has ceased to be! 'E's expired and gone to meet 'is maker! 'E's a stiff! Bereft of life, 'e rests in peace! If you hadn't nailed 'im to the perch 'e'd be pushing up the daisies! 'Is metabolic processes are now 'istory! 'E's off the twig! 'E's kicked the bucket, 'e's shuffled off 'is mortal coil, run down the curtain and joined the bleedin' choir invisible!! THIS IS AN EX-PARROT!!

I bet you always thought "the choir invisible" was a religious term—I did—from the Bible or maybe the Anglican Book of Common Prayer? Instead, George Eliot made a phrase of such noble sonic grace that it sounds ancient and serves as Mr. Praline's ecstatic crescendo.

The rant of riffing death metaphors is a revolt in the name of reality, against the claims of capitalism, that the relentless cheer will save you, and against the claims of Christianity, that the dead are not dead. What is funny is all that passion is expended for redress of a ridiculous problem.

Monty Python's skit killed; every time we watched, we could barely breathe. It seemed madcap zany at the time, but there we all were, faces to the big box of TV, as a man of common sense attempts a fruitful conversation with a believer who won't budge. When Mr. Praline lost patience with the civil rule to go along with lies, we shrieked with laughter at death words bellowed by a reasonable gentleman who could take no more. It's deeper than your average pet-store gag.

We are all sold life and may find ourselves angry that it comes with death. We may find ourselves angry that we are so often given credos that stand us up by nailing our feet to the perch. Eliot's poem is a nice choice for a credo poem because it begins with an acceptance of the reality of death and moves heroically on from there.

Your Poem

It's okay to pick a credo poem that has parts where you don't agree; let its mistakes remind you of the humanity of the author. Even God had some duds—you'll remember that law against pictures. But seriously, what's important is that you feel inspired and guided by some of them. Also don't worry if you dislike the actor that spoke the code you love. Or if the director is in disgrace. Up to a point, it doesn't matter where a rose grew. Remember the words of Katerina, the Flower of Toledo—you don't defend your poetry, your poetry defends you.

In your poetry collection the credo poem section can include a few choices, but I'd say keep one on top and see how it feels to make it your rule.

One of the best poetic credos is not a poem, but Walt Whitman's prose soars too. I've taken it from a preface to *Leaves of Grass*. There is precious advice here. I'm endlessly revived by his mood of glory and light.

> This is what you shall do: Love the earth and sun and the animals, despise riches, give alms to everyone that asks, stand up for the stupid and crazy, devote your income and labor to others, hate tyrants, argue not concerning God, have patience and indulgence toward the people, take off your hat to nothing known or unknown, or to any man or number of men—go freely with powerful uneducated persons, and with the young, and with the mothers of families—re-examine all you have been told in school or church or in any book, and dismiss whatever insults your own soul; and your very flesh shall be a great poem, and

have the richest fluency, not only in its words, but in the silent lines of its lips and face, and between the lashes of your eyes, and in every motion and joint of your body.

Did you catch the reward for such good living? It is that "your very flesh shall be a great poem." Care broadly, risk discomfort, comfort the suffering, question everything they tell you to believe, and protect your inner compass, and you will grow into wonder, truth, and beauty.

We've tried life without a code; it's an ex-parrot.

* * *

All thanks due to the Flower of Toledo, wherever she may be today, and everyone who has told me they love Kipling's "If—" poem, or another credo, poem, or quotation.

I hear, "What's the point of anything? Life is just an accident," a lot. Listening to nonreligious people discuss a postreligious lack of meaning, I find most are troubled by it and many tortured by it. Some light up and recite the world-fixing words they live by. The ones with the world-mending credo may have only one line memorized, and a sense memory of words that reset the world for them, at some point in their lives.

Few seem to reread the work—even if they've tacked it to a wall. Likewise few of the memorizers seem to read more work by the author. The sense memory alone can stabilize the dreadful punch-drunk spin of nihilism; but think what more you can do with the rest of the text. If that is you, go back and read it. With no answer to *What is all this about?* how could we not suffer nervousness and lethargy and failure to launch? In one way or another. There's a really good chance that rereading or researching your code will bring insights and surprises.

George Eliot found a phrase for us so exquisite in its echo of religious grandeur that we the Interfaithless forgot it was ours. But it is, and it is grand. It reminds us that much of who we are and how we live was sweated for by those now dead. The choir can't be seen, but without them, no music. In "O May I Join the Choir Invisible" Eliot hopes to excite in others a yen to be generous; she'll live on "In pulses stirred to generosity." We once "sobbed religiously in yearning song," but now that we know it's in our hands, we'll fix it.

Whitman's instructions are easier, in a way, but also manage to encompass everything. Go freely with persons of powerful mind who walked away from standard education, and listen to young people, and hang out with mothers. Also, reexamine all you have been told in school or church or in any book, and dismiss whatever insults your own soul; and your very flesh shall be a great poem.

19

On Talking to Children About Heavenlessness

Trusting Our Future Selves

"I'll live, but I really wish I could let Ollie believe in heaven."

"I wish I could let Ollie believe in heaven," says Alex, a dad at our kids' school. We are in the playground chatting, watching our children. He has three boys, two accosting a tree with my little girl right now, one in the sandpit, visibly moping. I had asked why he seemed so withdrawn and found that he was losing his grandmother and his belief in the heaven that grandma had briefly convinced him existed.

I groan and say, "I've been through that myself—explaining death to a child you love—it's tempting to just say heaven. If I had 1 percent of belief in an afterlife, I'd have given it to Max when we were facing this, but I couldn't find a lie I was willing to tell him." We stare over at Ollie. A sharp smell of autumn comes up as wind rustles a nearby leaf pile. Alex is quiet, so I ask him how he is doing.

"My mother's dying," he answers fast, nodding. The wind picks up and the few still-lush trees around us wave a loud hush. Alex sighs and reminds me that his mom had raised him mostly alone. He explains with insight and wit about his own nonbelief, and his mother's untroubled conviction that she's going to heaven. Then his subject returns to Ollie and his whole manner changes.

"I hate this," Alex confesses and slumps; tears up. He's angry, red-faced as he describes the situation. The eldest of his young sons is gloomy but coping. The smallest son jolts them all with wisdom about "always having Grandma Nat with us." But not so much the middle kid, Ollie.

"Ollie isn't having it," says Alex, with shining eyes. "My mother told him she'd be in heaven and they'd be together again someday." When Ollie had reported this back to his parents, Alex and his wife, Jules, they gently gave him a more realistic take on death.

They were all in their nightclothes, their dog asleep on the bed. Alex said, "The cycle of life all around us continues and babies are born and new things grow . . ."

Jules added, "Grandma Nat has had a long, full life, right?" Trying to lighten things up she smiles and says, "Really, Ollie, it's amazing all your grandmother got to do!"

Ollie listened thoughtfully, says, "Yes," and seems okay, but the next day is inconsolable about the idea that life ends. Alex shakes his head at the memory of it and tells me that a few days have passed since that conversation and things aren't getting better.

"Now what?" asks Alex.

"I don't know what to say," I say, with the wisdom of Socrates.

The wind blows up so I tilt the brim of my ball cap against the playground silt. A juice box some careless mom left on a nearby bench is suddenly airborne, bouncing toward us with speed. I'm annoyed until I clock that the careless mom was me. Alex extends a foot to stop it and heroically crashes his heel to collapse it, at which time I exhale as do Alex and the box. Crush. Then I remember what worked for me and Max.

In my experience, in books and conversation, many adults say they've grown used to the loss of heaven. Some speak with poetic grace on the idea that the fact of death is part of what makes life precious. That said, there's often a bit of bullet-biting bravado, too, a belief that real adults should be able to chew the hollow-point truth. So it's a dramatic change to witness when they ache to feed their children that fairy-tale-frosted angel cake of heaven.

A child's sorrow can bring the parent's buried pain to the surface. There you are, your heart on fire because your beloved dog has died or your head is a howling void because your father fell and they can't wake him; and the light of your life, the beamish boy for whom you do it all, he loves the dog or grandpa too, and is crying all day and won't eat and started a baby brawl at school. He's put himself to bed in full daylight and is weeping there. He never liked endings, never wants to leave a party, and it has just come into his consciousness that death ends everyone, that he will lose everyone, and that someday, with shrieking inevitability, he dies too.

You're sitting on the side of his bed, rubbing his back with one hand and holding your forehead with the other, a parental version of Auguste Rodin's *The Thinker*. You're droning, "It's okay," and then you hear yourself announce, with a bit of pep, "It's okay!" and he at last turns to look at you, with eye contact and expectation. You're going to tell him why it's okay.

But before I give you my special-for-children answer, let me suggest you take Alex's lead and start with whatever keeps you going, whatever you think might resonate with the child. It might work. If it doesn't, here's my suggestion: You look him in the eye and tell him he'll understand when he grows up. Tell him it feels different when you are older. That's it. "You'll understand that it's okay when you grow up." Children classify sex and employment as adult concerns; they understand that they don't have to worry about them yet. We tell them to put off worrying about it until they are biologically equipped, and they believe us.

They can do this about death too. Very likely, they will dry their eyes and move on. The child is able to return to play, and you to your thinking, because *living with the question*, to paraphrase Rilke, has become an option. Along with imagining the future as a place for answers, I suggest a poem. It worked for Alex with Ollie, as it had worked for me with Max. Then, after a while, it worked on me—in a way I hadn't foreseen.

How Religion Helps

Religions around the world put death remembrances on the calendar, and children are often included. Ash Wednesday, celebrated by Catholics and Anglicans, includes children when they reach the "age of reason," by age seven, when most children gain a sense of how the world works and start working it. Other churches start the ashen death rite with babies—citing the New Testament, where Joel 2 says to include even "infants at the breast" (2:16).

Note that Joel 2 does not describe the ash cross or sprinkle of blessed water, but across Christian communities the passage has long been part of the celebration of Ash Wednesday. Religions are human projects, always in motion, and they know a lot about the otherworld of childhood and how it responds to death. Ritual is attractive to children, with its oversize symbols, pageantry, and hints of secret power. In a world largely incomprehensible to them, some children love to be taught a sequence of events and then invited to express that knowledge through repetition.

Many religions have a first ritual at the time of burial or cremation, and a second ritual at a designated future date. Jews return to the cemetery a year after a funeral to "unveil" the headstone; in my part of the world this means that a cloth has been minimally masking-taped to its face and is then removed. In the years after, on the anniversary of a death, Jews light a yahrzeit candle at home in memorial.

Millions of the Malagasy people of Madagascar practice the funeral rite of Famadihana, "Turning of the Bones," every seven years. They take the bodies out of the crypts and refresh their wrapping cloth; this includes bodies so fresh they're still wet and bones so crumbling-old they must be reshaped into human form. The tightly wrapped forms are then passed around to family and friends. A girl puts out her arms for her grandmother's body and starts talking, catching her up on school, crying and hugging her in reunion. She passes grandma to an aunt and leaves to join her friends in cheery play. Then a brass band starts and the living dance holding the dead, and then it's back to the crypt. Some participants report believing only that the ritual is worth celebrating because it gathers the family from afar to remember the lost and enjoy the living.

What Ollie's Grandma Nat was trying to give him, a promise that death is not real, may be a beautiful solution for as long as they can believe it. But consider that religious promises of an afterlife must be reinterpreted at successive points in childhood and maturation. At some points, for some children, parts of the afterlife-promise might smack up against common sense. Children at times know they are being told something that is a curtain over a more difficult truth; sometimes they're okay with it and let it be, sometimes they push for more.

Some children, whether or not they had suspicions, feel furious and betrayed when they work out they were not told the truth. Anything you can say that isn't actively untrue is going to be a better choice for that reason. Better to shine a gentle light on a cruel truth then to insist it isn't what it is.

How Art and Science Help

When someone close to a child has died, caregivers can find consistent good advice from experts and institutions. Begin with honesty about what has happened. Tell them without delay, directly, that the person has died. Death means the person is gone. We won't see them again. Generally speaking, the experts say it beats all false comfort to know that you can trust the people who care for you and translate the world for you. It sounds like good advice to me.

Experts also advise we say something like, "This death wasn't your fault in any way." We all fall into magical thinking when grieving—for good and for ill, but children seem especially prone to imagining themselves at fault.

Psychology also tells us that when stressed with grief, children tend to regress, which means they go back a step in behavioral development—returning to wetting the bed or refusing grown-up foods. The way to help children deal with a death is to support them when their behavior is speaking for them, answering with behavior, kind and gentle. A child who has grown out of wetting the bed doesn't recommence as a conscious message of distress, but when his bedclothes are tidied up without critique and he is treated with no reduction in tenderness, it is a message back of support and grace.

Children should be involved in general rituals in whatever ways feel okay for them and seem right to you. The work they need to do, like anyone else, is to take in the fact that the death is real, to celebrate the lost beloved's life, and to say a solid goodbye. Invite young people to be involved, by drawing a picture, reading a poem, or singing a song.

More broadly speaking, secular culture has invented poetic ideas for dealing with death.

> *Rational Ghosts.* In response to an immediate loss it can help to talk about the way that people live forever in our hearts. This might be called the *rational ghost*: it is common for the bereaved to feel the lost one's presence. We find that we live for and with them in a new way. It's as if we are recording one another in discrete fields in our minds, and when a loved one dies we can activate their field to hear them.
>
> *Good Life Stories.* If a death came at the end of a long life, we can focus on the idea of a completed story arc and the incredible era witnessed. When the death is premature, it can often be accurately noted that the person packed a lot of living into their shorter time here. If not, maybe there was a rich inner life? You can say the person had a lifetime's worth of love.
>
> *Refreshing Nature Cures.* It helps many people to think about how our atoms return to plants and animals and eventually back into stars. Some like the idea that we are all a piece of greater humanity, like cells in a body, and we all do our bit and then move on, making room for fresh incarnations of life. My Great Aunt Edie used to explain, "We have to make room for the babies."
>
> *The Deathlessness of Discovery.* Our angst over death is in part a crisis about the meaning of life. Why do we struggle to get through each day's pain or boredom when our lives are only headed into

nothingness? Many answer with the idea of living for discovery, for the sublime: enjoying music and books and science, and adding to the story of those arts and disciplines, finding out how the universe works over generations of scientists, and expanding the story of humankind.

Happy Helpers. Death can be less of a looming doom to those who live for ongoing causes, trying to comfort the afflicted and mend the broken world. The philosopher Bertrand Russell spent the later years of his life in a campaign against nuclear war and wrote that this activism made the fact of his own inevitable death less problematic for him, because through it he could feel himself connected to the future. Working for any ideal that transcends a single life can change your whole perspective. The stories of lives devoted to heroic helping can sometimes spark a child back to the business of life.

Your Ritual Draws on Both

If you like the sound of your people's mourner's prayer, even one in another language, consider teaching it to your child, or learning it together. If you remember your grandfather saying it, that's going to come out in your voice, but also tell your child the story of how you learned it. If your mother lit candles to mourn and memorialize, as mine did, it might be a gift to your child to join that family history, when coping with grief. If you draw from the past, it will often come with filigree that's hard to invent and instill when starting from scratch, on your own. There's nothing wrong with keeping inherited gestures and explaining that you do them in memory of your loved one. You can simply leave out any supernaturalism.

Or start fresh. If you are creating a ritual outside religious tradition, consider going to a place of relative wilderness. The cycle of life and death can feel more natural there. When you are in a place of relative wilderness you are likely surrounded by processes of decay and rebirth. In the forest you can smell the rebirth and even in the less fertile world of a sand dune a handful shows the gem-polished fractions of a million mollusk lives. Where have all those bivalves gone? Here. They're here, dust to dust. While in the manufactured world, death can seem like a frustrating design flaw, nature can help us leave that headspace. We're part of a big roiling thing of birth and death and you have to go with it; likely, when nature shows this to you, everywhere in action, you take it in and are consoled.

Following the examples of the Jewish and the Malagasy peoples, try making it a two-part ritual. I've made one up called Letting Go and Letting Grow. Especially for children, it's nice to have an idea of what happens next. It's a forest visit as an immediate response, and a planting ritual a short time in the future. For the first part, you take them into nature and spend some time, read a poem, pick up leaves and let the wind take them—or whatever such makes sense for a "letting go" gesture in your setting. Then plan "letting grow" by deciding what kind of plant you'd like to start and nurture. Set a date for it. When it's time for planting, you read the poem again and plant a seedling.

Check to see what your children think of a poem before you finalize your choice, and help children acclimate to the ritual by making sure they know some lines of the poem. Invite them to bring their own poems to read that are their own contribution.

The goal is to connect death to new life and to return to the poem as you tend to that new life. It models dealing with pain by spending time with loved ones, taking solace in art, poetry, and nature. They get a plan right away, and later, they get a plant. Children can show what they can't say when they care for a plant. Just as importantly, the Earth and the plant return their affection. It's a small but true relationship of nurturing and being nurtured.

Our Poem

The poem I gave Max, and then Alex and Ollie, is by the Bengali writer Rabindranath Tagore (1861–1941). It's untitled, but known as "O Beautiful End," after one of its final phrases.

Peace, my heart, let the time for the parting be sweet.
Let it not be a death but completeness.
Let love melt into memory and pain into songs.
Let the flight through the sky end in the folding of the wings over
the nest.
Let the last touch of your hands be gentle like the flower of the
night.
Stand still, O Beautiful End, for a moment, and say your last
words in silence.
I bow to you and hold up my lamp to light you on your way.

Well, poem, I bow back. The tension of the poem is quivering in that first line, where the poet invites us to a formidable task, to let "parting be sweet." But if we double back we see he is talking to his own heart, which is not being peaceful at all—otherwise why mention it? That's the poem's taut bow, now we are handed four arrows, four lines that begin with "Let." Each can be a command to his own heart to *calm down*.

Each line that begins "Let" propels us into the next. Each changes the meaning of endings, of partings, of death. In the first one, the poet asks his heart to remember how much it enjoys completing jobs. Life isn't a chore, sure. A lot of life is chores, though.

The second is a flip trap into happiness. Here I am on my glum random Tuesday, July 27 at 4:40 p.m., willing to dejectedly "Let love melt into memory." But there the sentence does not end, it picks up without punctuation to alert me to a change in mood and speaks of melting pain into songs. That is not unfamiliar as a description of how one writes a song. In order to write this sentence I put on Erik Satie, *Trois gymnopédies*, and while this choice of song does not have my pain "melting away" in the meteorologist's or dietician's sense of the phrase, I feel my glumness rising to the surface of me and merging with the song. I "let love melt into memory and pain into songs."

The third "Let" is a strike of poetic beauty. The bird is folding up as one folds up one's tents and tables when the adventure is done—but also folding up over what I have protected, what I am still protecting, for having lived protecting it. Imagine yourself a grand gray bird soaring. Imagine the blue sky, the brisk wind smoothing down your feathers, and far below you the tips of pine trees and tops of houses. Imagine you're headed home, happy and weary, with love in your nest, waiting for you. Now slow and lower and find a landing. Imagine your wings folding over your nest. Imagine a bloom of light within you. Stay with this line and it can arouse inside you a knowledge to sustain you even if you don't have a hold of it in words.

What I mean is that some knowledge really can bypass the mind; or being in the mind, some knowledge still takes a long time to get into the body, such that the body can finally, for instance, calm the hell down. Nature and stories give us models and rhythms that have always made life feel like it makes enough sense. For many of us our own death and the deaths of whomever we love are just fundamentally tragic, but at least the models and rhythms that we find in nature and in poetry give us a context, a connected field of feeling and meaning and movement and stillness. For this kind of knowledge to get into your body requires spending time with it.

Okay, last "Let." This one has the diction of *benediction*; and it is the kind of *saying good words* (that's what "benediction" means) that has instruction in it. *Let the last touch of your hands be gentle like the flower of the night.* The poet seems to be asking himself to use his hands gently with people, all the way to the end. The finale of the poem is drenched in the sensual touch of night flowers.

"O beautiful end." Tagore asks the end to stand still, but only for a moment; he asks for last words, but allows for them to be silent. Finally, with the poet, you strive to hold up your lamp to light the way. For whom or what? You hold up the lamp for whatever lives from light to light, for whoever needs your help with the darkness.

Poetry Lesson: Elegy and Anti-Elegy

Tagore's poetry took inspiration from the Hindu Upanishads and brought together world styles in poetry and ideas, including Persian literature, Buddhist philosophy, and European and American literature.

He translated his own poems into English and won the Nobel Prize in Literature in 1913. Tagore was invited to speak around the world. When Albert Einstein interviewed Tagore, he asked if he believed in a divinity separate from the human experience, and Tagore said that he did not. Scholars call him a humanist, atheist, and agnostic; and yet many of his poems have become Hindu devotional songs. I've seen "O Beautiful End" with the subtitle "A Nonreligious Funeral Reading." I make this point so that this exquisite poem is not dismissed as religious and therefore unconflicted. It *is* conflicted; that is why it is so sublime.

In this poem Tagore avoids two common extremes by neither howling about the torment of death nor praising brevity as inherent to true beauty. The poem balances on a deep fault line of inner experience. It *is* bleak that people die, and it's also okay to keep living. I get scared of sickness, suffering, dying. I don't mind the idea of oblivion, but I'm not keen on missing out. I have been liberated from some fear through this poem and the experience of sculpting this response to a child in anguish. Trusting that you will know more when you live more can be a potent weapon against despair, and fear, for adults, too.

You are going to know more in the future because you are going to do some work, but also because our bodies often lead the way. Not everyone feels sexual in their adolescence, or right on cue broody for babies, but we know that a six-year-old's disdain for those activities is not predictive. Our physical feelings can bring us to a new phase of life that once seemed alien. My mom helped me find a job as a camp counselor one summer in high school at Camp HES, the Hebrew Educational Society, and on the last day I sprained my ankle. In Grand Central Station coming home I was first realizing how bad it was. Hobbling, I became aware of the other people in the crowd walking with a hobble or otherwise traveling at a crawl. I hadn't quite known they were there. I went back to rushing as soon as I could, but I knew something new. We all come to know how much the body determines.

Also people throughout life may say that they are done with romance and their body will surprise everyone by leading them in another direction. We all have to leave room for the possibility that things will feel different when we get there.

Only lucky parents have the opportunity to worry over when and how their children will learn about death. Saddled with that opportunity, some adopt a pet with Spot's demise in mind. Other parents don't have the luxury of delaying their children's awareness because deaths come and everyone—young and old—has to find a way to cope with it. Whatever the level of anxiety or grief, parents can help their children through ritual, whether it means a backyard burial for a betta fish or revisiting the favorite things of a loved one gone and much remembered.

* * *

The truth is, I wrote the above sentence a year ago and reading it now I see that it conceals in lyricism a hard and stupid moment in the author's real existence. It's summer and we take the kids, very little, to Coney Island, to splash in the waves, ride kiddie rides, and play boardwalk games, whereat we win a goldfish. We inform the kids that such fish are infamous for barely surviving the trip home, but this one does. To our regularly expressed surprise, pop-eyed Igor enlivens his bowl for two weeks.

Not surprisingly, Igor is mostly ignored by the small children. Goldfish are boring. When the tykes see the empty bowl, they understand on their own that the presaged end has come. They give solemn nods and are done. Terrific. But later in the day it comes out among us that I still *have* Igor.

"Really?" they ask, eyes like Igor's.

"Yes," I say. "In a paper cup." I hadn't been sure what to do and John was out, so I'd scooped him up and paper cupped him for the time being.

Then they ask, "Could we see him?"

I say, "Yes, I guess." They are cheerful and I'm thinking this will be a mellow teaching moment, a scholastic look at the nether-side of life's rich pageant.

I open the squeezed-shut, folded-down top of the cup and there it is. The fish body is dried now to my surprise. Igor is now something like an orange cracker with eyes and fins, hard as a credit card, and pressure-suspended by tail and nose against the inside of the cup. When

I tilt the cup to look, the fins make a loud click-clack in the silent room. Click-clack. My eyes take in this comedy macabre in a Dixie, and just as the thought, *This is a little awful*, flows into my consciousness, my ears catch a hushed twin gasp. I look up and see two little faces who just met death. They'd heard of it and had their separate reactions, but this is the first thing they knew alive and then got a look at lifeless.

Crying and consolation. We go out for a walk, treats, and come home to find that John, ignorant of the drama, saw the cracker-creature that Igor had become, and flushed the ex-fish unceremoniously back into the Earth's wine-dark sea. Crying, apologies, and recriminations.

The defense: Igor had been ours for only two weeks and made no impression, so John and I didn't treat it as a death.

The prosecution: A little grace is required, even in small things, especially with small people.

They forgave and moved on in the moment, but, for years after, the children would randomly recall the story as an operatic screwup by their parents, to friends, family, acquaintances. There are probably strangers out there who heard about the Igor-in-a-cup debacle, and that further indignity of the toilet flush. Rookie mistake.

When my parents later give Jessie a betta fish for her birthday, she names him Aqua Jack and I keep that bright blue guy alive for years, both of us stuck at the kitchen sink. When he died we had a proper ceremony. I've racked my memory, and asked the family, and we don't remember the details. Still, I know it helped that we went out back and dug a hole and said careful words. I know it helped to give the imagination all the respect that worshippers give their gods. How do I know? Because the hard and washed-up demise of Igor, the fish we didn't ease out of existence with a humane gesture, was discussed for years—while sweet blue Aqua Jack is remembered for his life.

Your Poem

Find a poem that recasts an ending. A poem is a look at things outside the prosaic, an enchantment of the ordinary through attention. A death in one's close circle can feel dizzying. When the world whips at a spin it is often reported to feel like hell. Alone in such grief, one can feel alone indeed. A poem can be company, can hold a place for you. Of course, check to see what your children think of a poem before you make a habit of reading it with them.

If you find a poem you all love, you can conjure the otherworldly for a child in need of time off from the real. In poems you will often see the Newtonian laws of nature broken, just as we fly in dreams. In poems the weather may have a flavor, maybe chocolate, and time can go backward; animals might say what they are thinking. In Tagore's poem above, animals do what we are thinking. Children do too.

Choose a poem that moves you. It doesn't have to be about death, or even endings. Any famously splendid little poem may give a child a lift, a lifeline.

* * *

If you are a person born into some religion and culture, or several, don't you deserve the gift? Don't you deserve a link to the solace therein cultivated? Don't the kids? When you incorporate the poem it makes the ritual your own. For a child, the magic of a gifted poem can last a lifetime. Children need to be told these big transitions are being taken care of, by the upper brass (above their pay grade), but they often want—and need—to take part in the doings.

The idea that we can trust our future selves to do what's appropriate to their season works in a lot of ways. It helped Alex to help his son Ollie, because Ollie needed a way to stop thinking about annihilation for a while. It helps us all to listen when a child speaks without speaking.

You can tell children to trust a later version of themselves to handle death. We can partake in that remedy, too. Why not have some faith in the version of yourself who may have to do what you are so scared of? Time may be after us, but it is also before us. I try to remember that time makes a lot of it funny. Think of the majesty of death delivered in a paper cup. By the rigid likes of rigor Igor. Click-clack.

Anyway, for now, we can take a rest from time, in nature. In art we encounter this time-stopping aspect of natural beauty remade in the smithy of a human. Solo nature is exquisitely wordless, but add a poem and you gain company, too; a friend in secret comedy and tragedy. Thinking of this should secure your oxygen mask well enough so you can assist your children with theirs.

20

On Morality

The Big Question and the Poetic Realist Answer

"No God, no morality, right?"

I'm attending a talk on religion and morality at a college, and it's question-and-answer time. A line has formed at a standing mic in the aisle. A big man in a sweatshirt shares something wise, the response is warm. I'm sitting near the front, where I mostly see what the speaker on stage sees. The big sweatshirt man leans down to the mic to say, "Thanks," and there's an odd moment when he bends down where we in the front can see an also-tall man behind him, looking too distracted for a guy who's up next. Just as I think, "He looks relaxed for a person on deck to speak in public," the first man steps away and reveals a heretofore hidden woman. Small. She's got the *Here I go* face I'd expected.

She looks to be midtwenties, wears her hair scalp-short, has on a suit jacket with jeans, and a frown. She steps up, flashes a striking grin, then back to the brow-bunched scowl. Then comes the airy soprano voice that clashes, like the fleeting smile, with the rest of her look, and she says, "If there is no God, that means there's no morality."

The room had been engaged with lighter stuff, so it was like a gruff angel has crashed our party bearing rotten news.

She says, "Hello everybody," and we in the front see the fast smile again. "I'm Leaf, people know me here. People here know I'm in a sobriety program." She swivels right and left to deliver neat salutes to the audience behind her, and me, on either side.

The speaker says, "Hi, Leaf," and Leaf turns her attention, with force, to the stage.

She says, "I was raised with no religion. I didn't believe in God until the program. Now I'm telling you, I'm glad to have a reason to be good. As a kid I wondered why anyone would be. I couldn't figure it out!" she says with a trill of laughter. "If no one sees, whatever you do is nothing." She shakes her head and says, "Face it," and sums up with punchy modern emphasis: "There can be no morality. If. No. One. Is. Watching."

Her genuine urgency about morality without a witness freezes the memory for me and I've been shivering a bit since. It still rankles that this lovely being was stuck in a world where virtue needs a superhuman monitor. Her culture, our culture, failed her. There are beautiful reasons to be good and they ought to be as well-known to us as the chorus to a favorite song.

How Religion Helps

I recall my mother at the kitchen window, looking at our tomato patch in late summer, too tired to harvest but sweating the sin of wasted food—God's anger at seeing plump red fruit rotting on the vine. The rule against wasting food makes sense, but scolding yourself for failing to consume a tomato you grew is exhausting and helps no one. Religion often does worse by asking for obedience to rules that make no good sense in the first place. We might think that at least in religion's basic stories of morality all the laws would be reasonable, but no.

Judging by usage in culture, people love morality stories like Prince Arjuna stopping the battle in the Bhagavad Gita, and Adam and Eve in the Garden of Eden in the Bible. These two religious stories in particular are so vital and poetic that they cross over as classics of world literature. Weirdly, they don't support the specific morality of their respective religions; in fact, as straightforward morality tales they have real problems. I'll lay them out for our perusal.

In the Bhagavad Gita—a key part of an important text in the Hindu world, the Mahabharata—we are on a battlefield with our hero, the warrior Prince Arjuna, and he is freaking out.

Surveying the opposing army, Arjuna's eyes alight upon friends, family, and heroes. Horror flips to epiphany and Arjuna calls out to his bosom friend, the god Krishna, saying this battle is wrong; true our foes are guilty of greed and betrayal, but our side should be wise and refuse to fight. Spotting venerable teachers armed against him, Arjuna cries, "It would be better to live on alms in this world than to slay these noble gurus, because, by killing them I would win wealth and pleasures stained with their blood." (2:5)

He adds that he will forgive all faults and debts to escape the bad karma of killing friends and family. Krishna's answer is a shocker. He says *no*, you have to fight. Chuckling at Arjuna's pretense of wisdom, Krishna says killing friends and family is fine, since only their bodies die; the true self, the atman, survives. "Just as a person puts on new garments . . . Atma acquires new bodies . . . Weapons do not cut this Atma, fire does not burn it, water does not make it wet, and the wind does not make it dry." (2:23) I love this way of saying the atman is real but inexpressible, water does not make it wet. But you have to believe in the most boldly drawn idea of rebirth to see avoidable murder as a matter of no importance.

If not life, not even these notable lives, what *does* matter to Krishna? The value he vaunts is role fulfillment. The warrior should be a good warrior and jump up to engage in a "righteous" war. He counsels humble submission to the historical plans of the gods. Stunned, Arjuna argues energetically, even describing to Krishna all the widows this battle will create, how they'll have to work, seek outsider mates, and the community will collapse.

Krishna responds abrasively that "the great warriors will think that you have retreated from the battle out of fear"—and keeps extolling the fulfillment of one's role. Krishna wins Arjuna over.

I'd agree that one part of our moral lives is learning to embrace our roles, whether we feel randomly born into them or borne to them by chance. Let Krishna's laughter remind us that much of life is determined by forces beyond our ken. It's frustrating but realistic, and takes off some of the pressure of personal responsibility, marooned as we are by errant winds. But Hinduism is a religion of inner and outer peace, when it can manage it, and this story acknowledges profound suffering to be brought on by an avoidable war and the cascading traumas to follow, and encourages the killing.

The Genesis story also has strange values, establishing right and wrong without a mention of not doing harm to others. And this story is truly central to Judaism and Christianity.

God tells Adam and Eve to tend Eden's garden, and to eat anything except the apple, fruit from the Tree of Knowledge. A serpent of badness pushes an apple on Eve, who resists awhile but listens, bites, and brings the crunchy orb of innocence-defeated to her man. He figures they're done here anyway, might as well apple-up to the dame's level. Both now notice their own nakedness with anxiety and find fig-leaf cover. God roars into the dad rage for which he's later famed. He curses Adam and all descendant men to backbreaking farmwork, and curses Eve and all women to agony in childbirth. The chastened pair head out east of Eden, surely upset, even full of regret, but I have to think also super happy to have discovered sex, and to get a chance to see the world, maybe eat some meat. Get some distance from God's attention.

There is much wrong with this lovely story. It rejects discovery. We have to marvel at the chutzpah of believers admitting that the scariest plant in the world to them is "the Tree of Knowledge." With strain we can read "knowledge" as awareness of death, sex, or another innocence-wrecking revelation, but in plain speech it's a rejection of knowledge—that's the word. To the ears of a science-loving poetic realist, that is a rejection of a sacred value. To anyone who trusts knowledge over ignorance, the apple is what you work for, not what you shun.

The Eden story shames the body. The hatred of nakedness here justified millennia of relating to the body with distress and shame. Often that distress has been about shaming sexual desire as necessarily beastlike and beneath our more angelic inner spirits. There is another way of seeing this, which first came to my mind as a joke about sticking to a healthy diet—*Fabulous, so the origin of evil in human life is that our heroine ate what she swore she wouldn't eat.* In whatever form, the body in this story is a location for uncontrollable wrongness, desires not to be harmonized, but shackled.

Its law is arbitrary. A rule without explanation or evident logic is a morality of obedience, rather than one that follows good sense and good feeling. It is true that we often in life have to obey rules before we understand them, but it isn't ideal. The human urge to be good can be used against peace and honorable behavior when a leader tells us that what is *good for us* is all the good we need to consider. Freedom and respect are high values that I do not casually trade for the sake of anyone's idea of order. When others exert arbitrary control over one's life, for the glorification of their own power, I'd say with the philosopher Henry David Thoreau that the right thing to do is rebel.

So this story is morally heinous, too. Both remind us that the natural moral inclination can be co-opted for purposes other than kindness and reciprocity. They encourage the idea that the content of right and wrong is not the business of humans, so our struggle is merely to follow as closely as we can the tenets we are given and the situation in which we find ourselves. How awful. It abdicates the best thing about us.

How Art and Science Help

Morality exists. I make this weird claim only because it has been boldly and variously denied. What I mean by "morality" is the human inclination to do good, whatever its limitations, and our attention to sorting right from wrong. I mean that morality exists within the human experience, just as most of us would answer the claim, "Love doesn't exist," with "Yes, it does," and we would mean it within the human experience.

Love and morality are real facets of humanity because you could time machine together a crowd from whenever and hear, "I love my family," and "I should share this food," and "Murder is wrong." Doctrines can fade out and cultures can be suppressed but there are aspects of humanity that hang on and reappear with the relentless tenacity of nature.

For me, the woman at the mic was a perfect revelation of morality, because she cared so much; because she was so glad to have a reason to be good.

In one dominant religious story, morality is dependent on God, a being said to have originated goodness and formalized it into rules; a being who watches everyone for infractions and punishes accordingly. Seeing things this way, if we lose God, morality goes with him. In the old picture, morality was carried to life's picnic by a mystery strongman. A truer image may be that morality is carried to life's picnic in small pieces, by the ants, as it were, and that these pieces link up larger when we are together.

Some who say morality doesn't exist do so because they have been trained by religion to think of morality as stable and singular. After all, the Mosaic religions have moral law literally written in stone. So it might help to clearly state that, in moral choices, muddiness of data and competing scales of value are normal. Often we must weigh up allegiances and make good-enough choices. Keep family peace or expose a disturbing truth? Finish work or show up for a friend? This messiness can be troubling, but step back and see that it functions—we live, have relationships, raise children, build careers that serve the public good. Take account of our failures with our triumphs, always, but remember, too, the poetic sacred tenderness of how we try and try.

There are robust nonsupernatural moral arrangements. They all need to be flexible or they can become oppressive, but there are some excellent designs for good lives and communities that are not based on God or his ilk. Confucianism is a morality based on serving those above you in social status and looking after those of lower status in relation to you, with no god or gods involved. From the European Enlightenment we get a "social contract" idea where we all trade away some of our natural liberty in exchange for a measure of safety; opinions vary on the ideal balance, since freedom is a frolic to some, and a fright to others.

Utilitarianism is the idea that morality could be derived by working out what would bring the most people the most happiness. Capitalism says the strong survive and that leaves the body politic strong, and too bad for the losers. Meritocracies level the playing field for the young so as to discover all valuable talent. Communism holds, in the words of Karl Marx, "From each according to their ability, to each according to their need" (1875). Socialism has meant many similar things, but today says we can care for everyone's basic needs, and we should.

Your Ritual Draws on Both

Ritual and poetry can help us spend time with these ideas so we can absorb them. Religions have holidays and rituals to support the virtues they admire, perhaps in some way common to human groups, but often with some strange mix of history, accident, and taste that few from the outside see without raising an eyebrow. In some cases, the celebrated virtue isn't unusual but the intensity is; for reasons real or imagined, groups can become convinced that protecting particular virtues are fundamental to their survival. Which virtues are prone to be overvalued in cultures, to extreme degrees and to the suppression of the others? My list would include chastity, fierceness, youth, innocence, age, sobriety, knowledge, meekness, piety, sensualism, recklessness, revenge, safety, cowboyism, Lord Byron-osity, bucket-list completism, thinness, fatness, and working your life away.

One way cultures reinforce a particular virtue is by the veneration of a hero who is said to exemplify it. Consider a hero of your target virtue, and vice versa (who do you admire? now ask their symbolic virtue). If you want to stay away from the whiff of saint worship, why not pick a random day to think about this. I'm going to say Friday the Thirteenth for those of us who want to all do it on the same day. The date is famously unlucky, so a nice occasion for celebrating our capacity to change one another's luck. Some years have three such dates, most have one or two. We could give the day to kindness, transcendence, and knowledge—three great goods.

How would you conjure the mood? Eat and drink a medley of world fruits, say apple, dates, mango, lychees, and grapes? It would be festive and healthy, and remind us that the tree of knowledge is not the problem, nor its fruit.

Find something in your home you don't need and give it away. Try to be cheerful with people. Go out of your way to be selfless every Friday the Thirteenth. Read a poem that lights up your moral message center and smokes your motherboard. Think about the hidden ways we know things, all the subliminal messages we get from the world. I think of the riddles I've solved while purposefully observing myself for the moment of understanding, and not being able to tell anything about how the light turned on. I think of the way Leaf appeared from between two big people in line. The way we could almost read her existence from the relaxed face of the man behind her. I think of the way we know the invisible man is there because he's covered up.

Our Poem

The poem "A Mother in a Refugee Camp" is a poem of witness by Chinua Achebe, the Nigerian author of the classic novel *Things Fall Apart* (1958). The poem is a deep report of one moment of suffering, so rendered that the image is carved into the cave wall of readers' skulls.

A Mother in a Refugee Camp

No Madonna and Child could touch
Her tenderness for a son
She soon would have to forget. . . .
The air was heavy with odors of diarrhea,
Of unwashed children with washed-out ribs
And dried-up bottoms waddling in labored steps
Behind blown-empty bellies. Other mothers there
Had long ceased to care, but not this one:
She held a ghost-smile between her teeth,
And in her eyes the memory
Of a mother's pride. . . . She had bathed him
And rubbed him down with bare palms.
She took from their bundle of possessions

A broken comb and combed
The rust-colored hair left on his skull
And then—humming in her eyes—began carefully to part it.
In their former life this was perhaps
A little daily act of no consequence
Before his breakfast and school; now she did it
Like putting flowers on a tiny grave.

All the mothers of dead and dying children have gone stupefied to the world, except one, who combs the hair on what is left of a head, and we don't know if she's gone mad or we have. The scariest thing in the world is that girl who didn't go numb.

We're going to look closely at the poem. Before reentering its hell, we're going to ask ourselves some questions. How would you write a poem about the hardship of the lives of refugees? Tasked to poet this situation, it would feel right to give witness to the stories of many people, or at the least, a representative few. Or telling of this one woman, the poet might feel compelled to share more of her story. Let's say you have to get it down on paper. How do you start? Let's say instead I give you one page to voice the suffering of planet Earth. It would be challenging. It would be hard not to sound, well, wrong. I just wanted to remind us of the blank space between witnessing suffering and offering it as art.

The title feels plain, a simple description, but makes a powerful couplet when read with the poem's first line: "A Mother in a Refugee Camp / No Madonna and Child could touch." It is a stunning idea packed in tight. Note that the words "Madonna and Child" are capitalized. It implies that along with any sense of the historical Mary and Jesus, we are talking about the archetype, and the many paintings and sculptures with that title. In those artworks Jesus is an infant or tiny kid. He and his mom are serene.

Often in art both Mary and baby Jesus are enchanting, beautifully healthy, and serenely self-contained. The history of his divine chubbiness may be said to culminate in Fernando Botero's portrait wherein both figures are so fat their faces are almost square. Yes, that's what

Botero does with all his subjects, but it's still interesting. In Botero's *Madonna and Child* their blank features are islands at the center of large, empty faces.

In various artworks the pair interact in that lovely way mothers and babies can, some ordinary touch between them, surprising because of who they are. To see this image, mother and child in ordinary touch, conflated with the idea of the Pietà, that other famous image of Mary and Jesus, where she's cradling his dead body, is ghastly. She's looking younger than him. He's all bones now. The third line lands hard; her son is going to be dead, her life is such that she "soon would have to forget."

When the poet starts to catalog the horrors, we are nevertheless relieved because it brings us into the past tense; we are hearing a drama that is over. In one sentence, but through poetic device, the poet says much.

To say "heavy with odors" gives the smell weight, it is stifling, it is also heavy emotionally, the facts gravitational. The sentence is missing the punctuation it would need to be proper prose grammar, so the reading fractures: it is diarrhea of children who are unwashed, but it is also the two smells. Unwashed is echoed by the ribs being "washed-out," which we take as blown out, emptied.

The next sentence trails off and the one that follows is the end of the poem; so the rest is all one, in a sense. We are in a world where most mothers had long ago ceased to care. What could be more wretched? Then we find out what. The repetition of the word "mother," the ghost-smile, the singing in her eyes, the pride. Then the poet yanks us into another life, where the mother's small act is free to mean nothing—and then pow, we're back in the terrible now. But this true "now" is a short one, "now she did it" and then we are in a metaphor, "Like putting flowers on a tiny grave."

Poetry Lesson: Poetry of Witness

The poet and memoirist Carolyn Forché has written about *poetry of witness* as a necessary third term between political poetry and personal poetry. It doesn't have designs on your vote but shows what it saw and how it felt to see it.

Does it matter that we witness and give witness in art? There are simple moral reasons it matters, as empathy can lead to actions. But think back to how much it can mean to people to feel their lives are witnessed by God. The artist sees too.

The artist is moved by the world to make a record of what is real but unreachable by ordinary means. I don't mean to overdo the analogy from God's eye to the billion eyes of us and all our lenses. I'm just reminding us that it matters that we see one another and that artists and poets capture what they can see. The seeing can matter, more than ever.

* * *

There is a public conversation between James Baldwin and Chinua Achebe, filmed, where the subject turns strikingly to morality. Achebe says that in his Ibo culture, there is no separation between art and morality. "Our art is based on morality. Perhaps this sounds old-fashioned to you, but it is not to us." Indeed, he says, "An abomination is called an abomination against the arts. So you see in our aesthetic you cannot run away from morality. Morality is basic to the nature of art."

I'm reminded of similar words by the philosopher and novelist Iris Murdoch: "Art and morality are, with certain provisos . . . one. Their essence is the same. The essence of both of them is love. Love is the perception of individuals. Love is the extremely difficult realization that something other than oneself is real. Love, and so art and morals, is the discovery of reality."

Achebe's word "abomination" is commonly understood as monster, atrocity, ugliness, filth, an act or object of disgust, and by contrast lights up the natural sacred quality of truth. Then suddenly, as Baldwin is responding, the camera captures a man in the audience yelling at the speakers, trying to shout them off the stage. As the disruptor is removed Baldwin says firmly but with obvious emotion that "White Power is over," and the audience applauds. That eruption helps us feel the heat of the room in which these words were spoken.

When the conversation resumes, Achebe offers the Ibo proverb,

"Where something stands, something else will stand beside it." The proverb doesn't say why, and scientists can't say why either, but they have noticed the same thing. You have to show up and stand up to find out what would happen if someone showed up and stood up.

Achebe goes on to say that great art comes from more than one perspective. "Single-mindedness . . . leads to totalitarianism of all kinds, to fanaticism of all kinds." We only see at all when we see more than one side.

> Wherever something is, something else also is. And I think it is important that whatever the regimes are saying—that the artist keeps himself ready to enter the other plea. Perhaps it's not tidy—perhaps we are contradicting ourselves. But one of your poets has said, "Do I contradict myself? Very well."

That's Whitman who wrote, "Do I contradict myself? / Very well then I contradict myself, / (I am large, I contain multitudes.)" This straining to know more, even as it is painful to see outside the self, is the key link between poetry and morality. We use what we've got. I grew up with an ancient religion and a modern science. I grew up into a world of great unfairness and also abundance and I try to keep finding hope and surprise.

Your Poem

Choosing a single poem for your poetry collection's morality section might seem especially tough because multiple perspectives—listening to other people's experiences—is part of the message. But we need close listening, too.

Determining what is right or wrong is partly based on reason and also judged in an inner world of rollicking certainties and roiling retractions. Meanwhile real life also goes on changing, demanding and allowing for real-time adjustments.

It's *so* not the kind of thing you can write in stone. The fluidity of the moral search is crucial.

The crucial thing is to have a poem you return to on this theme, as it will be more meaningful to you over time. You will understand it better, by living with it, but also, you will change over time and see it in your shifting relationship to the piece.

* * *

We should stop saying that without God morality doesn't exist or isn't real. It's evident that wanting to be good is a facet of the human experience. If God didn't make morality—and he didn't—then we did, and I for one am very impressed. We do not need a full-on theory of the good, but we ought to have a preset way to meditate on the good, and a way to be nudged to action—with at least enough strength so the bastards can't shout us down. People thrive when they have an image of a struggle toward the good, even if it is fragmented or uncertain. Virtue is an astounding thing to have developed in this rock-studded expanse of dark matter. To choose to engage with it is to join a lively tradition.

I wonder if these ideas would sway Leaf, so certain that no God means no morality. She was so pleased to have a reason to be good, now that she thought God was watching, and I'm inspired by her joy at the prospect. I trust that human heart. There are vile hearts too, I know, but in bulk, over time, I don't see anything better to rely on, so let's keep trying with the hearts.

Look at what is achieved by the Achebe poem, which argues nothing. Achebe's poem just makes us want to help, to do better, to face the truth of privilege of everyone whose baby is more like a Botero. And do something about it. Or try, anyway, as you really never know. Any help can help change things. Where one stands, two stand.

I'm not saying I manage even as well as anybody to do what I ought to at times. But I'm not here for nothing and *to further the good* holds up to the most scrutiny. Some of us live seeking poetic truth—in music, for example—and some prize scientific discovery; many live for romantic and family love, too. But what the hell is it all about if we aren't also in pursuit of goodness? How about if all I mean by "good" is *Knew what good was and preferred it*? I think I have it: *Knew the feeling of good and adored it and tried at least to find out more about it, and could be, at many times, driven like a windy leaf around it*." You know, "Good."

The trying is the sacred. In whatever broken way, we're trying together. You are a miracle for trying. Your trying might be the miracle that matters.

Notes

Introduction

4 *"After one has abandoned"*: Wallace Stevens, *Opus Posthumous*, Samuel F. Morse, ed. (New York: Alfred A. Knopf, 1958), 158.

7 *"Be patient toward all"*: Rainer Maria Rilke, *Letters to a Young Poet* (New York: W. W. Norton, 1954), 27. The quote is in Letter Four, July 16, 1903.

8 *"That you are here"*: Walt Whitman, "Oh me! Oh life!," in *Leaves of Grass* (1867). Whitman first published *Leaves of Grass* in 1855, and rather than write a second book, he just kept adding to it and editing it. This poem first appeared in the 1867 edition. Whitman's shocking experience visiting wounded soldiers and then working as a nurse in the Civil War (he famously insisted on tending to soldiers on both sides) gave him a case of the blues that led to the writing of this poem. Here it is in full:

Oh me! Oh life!

Oh me! Oh life! of the questions of these recurring,
Of the endless trains of the faithless, of cities fill'd with the foolish,
Of myself forever reproaching myself, (for who more foolish than I, and who
*   more faithless?)*
Of eyes that vainly crave the light, of the objects mean, of the struggle ever
*   renew'd,*
Of the poor results of all, of the plodding and sordid crowds I see around me,
Of the empty and useless years of the rest, with the rest me intertwined,
The question, O me! so sad, recurring—What good amid these, O me, O life?

Answer.
That you are here—that life exists and identity,
That the powerful play goes on, and you may contribute a verse.

10 *"O for God's sake"*: Muriel Rukeyser, "Islands," in *The Collected Poems of Muriel Rukeyser* (Pittsburgh: University of Pittsburgh Press, 2006), 528. "Islands" was first published in Rukeyser's last book, *The Gates* (1976). Rukeyser (1913–1980) was a prolific, politically engaged, and brilliant writer.

10 *We may think of rituals as*: Studies have supported the value of ritual along many measurements of health and flourishing. For example, researchers have found a reduction in performance anxiety through ritual. It isn't only the repeated behaviors but also the specialness of them, the fact that they are marked off as ritual. "Belief that a specific series of behaviors constitute a ritual is a critical ingredient to reduce anxiety and improve performance: engaging in behaviors described as a 'ritual' improved performance more than engaging in the same behaviors described as 'random behaviors.'" Alison Wood Brooks, Juliana Schroeder, Jane L. Risen, Francesca Gino, Adam D. Galinsky, Michael I. Norton, and Maurice E. Schweitzer, "Don't Stop Believing: Rituals Improve Performance by Decreasing Anxiety," *Organizational Behavior and Human Decision Processes* 137 (November 2016): 71–85.

13 *Cultural liturgy*: As a phrase "cultural liturgy" exists in the Romance languages today but none of its several definitions have caught on or kept a stable singular meaning. In anthropology the phrase can be used to refer to all social custom; in Christian social theory it is often a derogatory term for popular culture.

1. On Decisions

20 *"Traveler, There Is No Road"*: Antonio Machado, *"Caminante, no hay camino."* This is my translation of the excerpt most often associated with the poem's title. It is sometimes presented as a section of a longer poem of the same name. The original can be found as part of "Proverbs and Songs," in *Border of a Dream: Selected Poems of Antonio Machado*, Spanish and English ed. (section 30), Willis Barnstone, trans. and ed. (Port Townsend, WA: Copper Canyon, 2003).

22 *For instance, in 2005 German*: Mario Fernando, "Religion's Influence on Decision-Making: Evidence of Influence on the Judgment, Emotional and Motivational Qualities of Sri Lankan Leaders' Decision-Making" (Berlin: 21st European Group of Organization Studies Colloquium, 2005), 1–17.

23 *The Vietnamese Buddhist monk Thich Nhat Hanh*: Nguyen Anh-Huong and Thich Nhat Hanh, *Walking Meditation: Easy Steps to Mindfulness* (Boulder, CO: Sounds True, 2019); and Thich Nhat Hanh, *How to Walk* (Berkeley, CA: Parallax Press, 2015).

25 *Machado was also influenced by*: Regarding his own irreligion, Machado's poem "LIX," known as "Last Night When I Was Sleeping," reads to many critics as on the experience of his unbelief, culminating in the lines, "Last night as I slept, / I dreamt—marvelous error!— / that it was God I had / here inside my heart." The Machado scholar Antonio Sánchez Barbudo, for example, notes, "But do not forget what he never forgets, that all of this was only an 'illusion': that it was only a dream . . . It was a revelation, but in dreams; a revelation from which he woke up and, regretting it, did not believe." Antonio Sánchez Barbudo, *Los poemas de Antonio Machado* (Barcelona: Lumen, 1969), 115–17.

2. On Eating

30 *"I take my wine jug out"*: The poet Li Bai, once better known as Li Po, has been translated many times, in many ways. I included the first four lines of the fourteen-line poem "Drinking Alone Under the Moon." The translation here is mine, informed by published versions by Shigeyoshi Obata, Arthur Cooper, Sam Hamill, David Hinton, Ezra Pound, and others, as well as the translation by Paul Rouzer at Asian Topics: An Online Resource for Asian History and Culture at Columbia University, http://afe.easia.columbia.edu/at/libo/lb04.html (last consulted May 12, 2022). Along with his translation, Rouzer discusses that drinking was understood as necessarily social in Li Bai's time and so the poet's speaker feels he has to invite the moon and his shadow in order to not behave scandalously. Where Pound says "party of three," the translator David Hinton ends the line saying the moon and his shadow "makes friends three." Both are a bit stylized for my taste. Li Po, *The Selected Poems of Li Po*, David Hinton, trans. (New York: New Directions, 1996), 43.

30 *"If I've left the mosque"*: Hafiz (or Hafez) was a profoundly important figure in Persian literature and culture. The three lines here are from the center of the poem "Song of Spring." There are many translations; I've followed *Hafez: Dance of Life*, Michael Boylan, trans. (Washington, DC: Mage, 1988), 12.

32 *"Tea began as a medicine"*: Okakura Kakuzō, *The Book of Tea: A Japanese Harmony of Art, Culture, and the Simple Life* (New York: Duffield, 1906), 3–4, 20–21. *The Book of Tea* significantly influenced many various artists, including Frank Lloyd Wright in architecture and Georgia O'Keeffe in painting.

33 *The Epicurean ideal friendship*: Epicurus (341–270 BCE) broke away from the Platonism of his day and started his own philosophical school in Athens, "the Garden." He welcomed women, enslaved people, and anyone else who wanted to talk about happiness and meaning, while walking in nature and enjoying simple meals. Only centuries later did his name become associated with the meals rather than the philosophy and friendship, as in "epicurean."

35 *"From blossoms"*: Li-Young Lee, "From Blossoms," in *Rose* (Rochester, NY: BOA Editions, 1986), 21.

36 *"Two roads diverged"*: Robert Frost, "The Road Not Taken," in *Selected Poems* (New York: Henry Holt, 1923), 103.

38 *"Do I dare to eat a peach?"*: T. S. Eliot, "The Love Song of J. Alfred Prufrock," in *Collected Poems, 1909–1962* (New York: Harcourt, Brace & World, 1991), 7. "Shall I part my hair behind? Do I dare to eat a peach? / I shall wear white flannel trousers, and walk upon the beach / I have heard the mermaids singing, each to each. // I do not think that they will sing to me."

38 *"I believe that aesthetic presence"*: Li-Young Lee reading and interview, with Michael Silverblatt, March 29, 2000, Sante Fe, NM, Lannan Podcasts, https://podcast.lannan.org/2010/06/01/li-young-lee-with-michael-silverblatt-conversation-29-march-2000-video/.

40 *"A Bird, came down the Walk"*: Emily Dickinson, "328," or "A Bird, came down the Walk," or "In the Garden," in *The Complete Poems of Emily Dickinson*, Thomas H. Johnson, ed. (Boston: Little, Brown, 1960), 156. These are the first two stanzas of five.

41   *"Wild Geese"*: Mary Oliver, "Wild Geese," in *Dream Work* (New York: Grove/
      Atlantic, 1986), 8.

3. On Gratitude

46   *Consider too the title*: Anne Lamott, *Help, Thanks, Wow: The Three Essential
      Prayers* (New York: Penguin, 2012).

46   *Gratitude itself is praiseworthy*: "And whoever desires the reward of this
      world—We will give him thereof, and whoever desires the reward of the Here-
      after—We will give him thereof. And We will reward the grateful." Quran 3:145.

46   *The Quran suggests the same*: "And . . . your Lord proclaimed, 'If you are grate-
      ful, I will surely increase you in favor; but if you deny, indeed, My punishment
      is severe." Quran 14:7.

47   *There is also a Muslim teaching*: Azra Pervez, "The Concept of Thankfulness
      in Islam," WhyIslam.org, https://www.whyislam.org/on-faith/the-concept-of
      -gratitude-in-islam/ (last consulted May 19, 2022).

48   *But art and science have their own*: On the study of gratitude, see: Robert A.
      Emmons and Michael E. McCullough, eds., *The Psychology of Gratitude* (Ox-
      ford: Oxford University Press, 2004).

48   *Even just trying to think*: B. H. O'Connell, S. Gallagher, and D. O'Shea, "Feel-
      ing Thanks and Saying Thanks: A Randomized Controlled Trial Examining
      If and How Socially Oriented Gratitude Journals Work," *Journal of Clinical
      Psychology* 73, no. 10 (October 2017): 1280–1300; L. S. Redwine, B. L. Henry,
      K. Chinh, et al., "Pilot Randomized Study of a Gratitude Journaling Inter-
      vention on Heart Rate Variability and Inflammatory Biomarkers in Patients
      with Stage B Heart Failure," *Psychosomatic Medicine* 78, no. 6 (2016): 667–76;
      and Agnieszka Lasota, Katarzyna Tomaszek, and Sandra Bosacki, "How to
      Become More Grateful? The Mediating Role of Resilience Between Empathy
      and Gratitude," *Current Psychology* (November 2020), https://link.springer
      .com/article/10.1007/s12144-020-01178-1. This study involved 214 participants
      and found a strong positive correlation between gratitude and resilience.

48   *"Life and the world, or whatever"*: Percy Bysshe Shelley, *The Necessity of
      Atheism and Other Essays* (Buffalo, NY: Prometheus, 1993), 45. Shelley was
      inspired by Thomas Paine's radical pamphlets and by Mary Wollstonecraft's *A
      Vindication of the Rights of Woman*. He was later married to Wollstonecraft's
      daughter Mary, the author of *Frankenstein*.

49   *"A thankful heart is not only"*: Marcus Tullius Cicero, *The Orations of Marcus
      Tullius Cicero*, C. D. Yonge, trans., vol. 3 (London: George Bell, 1851), 139.

50   *"alphabet"*: Inger Christensen, *alphabet*, Susanna Nied, trans. (New York:
      New Directions, 2001), 1–6.

53   *The sublime diary*: With a few simplifications of language (as in some literal
      translations, I used "vest" instead of "waistcoat" and "string" instead of "ro-
      sary") this is the version in Sei Shōnagon, *The Pillow Book*, Meredith McKinney,
      trans. (London: Penguin, 2006), "Refined and Elegant Things," 46, 148.

55   *Griots have their own instrument*: Both Sibo Bangoura and Sona Jobarteh were
      born into griot families. Bangoura, originally from Conakry, Guinea, lives in
      Sydney, Australia. One of his songs, "Nan Fulie," is about the importance of

the griot people. The name of his band, Keyim Ba, means "very beautiful." Jobarteh has Gambian roots and is the first female professional kora player to come from a griot family. Her musical style blends European and West African traditions. Youssou N'Dour has been nominated for a Grammy six times and won Best Contemporary World Music Album in 2005 for *Egypt*.

55 *Large swaths*: James Joyce, *Ulysses* (New York: Dover, 2012), 282. The vegetable known as a "swede" in Ireland is known as a rutabaga in the United States and France, and turnips or "neeps" in Scotland.

55–56 *"of many things: / Of shoes—and ships"*: Lewis Carroll, from "The Walrus and the Carpenter," in *Alice's Adventures in Wonderland and Through the Looking-Glass* (New York: Rand McNally, 1916), 160.

56 *"For whatever reason, people are waking"*: Mark Strand, from "Night Pieces," in *Collected Poems* (New York: Knopf, 1990), 141.

56 *"So much world all at once"*: Wisława Szymborska, from "Birthday," in *View with a Grain of Sand*, Stanisław Barańczak and Clare Cavanagh, trans. (New York: Harcourt Brace, 1995), 79.

58 *"for not making the earth"*: Billy Collins, from "As If to Demonstrate an Eclipse," in *Nine Horses* (New York: Random House, 2002), 45.

4. On Sleep

62 *We are facing Dolly Parton and Fran Lebowitz*: Just for the record: "Interviewer: How did you meet Dolly? Fran Lebowitz: I probably met her through Sandy because Sandy was her manager. I used to see her very often." Mickey Boardman, "Fran Lebowitz Has All the Answers," *Paper*, March 15, 2021, https://www.papermag.com/fran-lebowitz-netflix-2651091035.html.

62 *"I love sleep"*: Fran Lebowitz, "Why I Love Sleep," in *The Fran Lebowitz Reader* (New York: Random House, 1974), 97.

63 *"There I go again"*: Stevie Smith, "Thoughts About the Person from Porlock," in *Collected Poems* (New York: New Directions, 1983), 87–88.

64 *"Now I lay me down"*: The bedtime prayer first appears in its well-known form in Thomas Fleet, *New England Primer* (1737).

65 *"May all be happy"*: *Jain Prayers*, Sima Sheth, trans. (Ontario: Prakash Mody, 2005); and Yogendra Jain, *Jain Way of Life* (Federation of Jain Associations of North America, 2007).

66 *"Man is a genius"*: Carl Pletsch, "Akira Kurosawa's Reflection on Becoming a Genius," *Journal of Popular Film and Television* 32, no. 4 (2005): 192–99.

68 *"The sleep"*: Fernando Pessoa, "The Sleep That Comes Over Me," in *Poems of Fernando Pessoa*, Edwin Honig and Susan M. Brown, trans. (San Francisco: City Lights, 1998), 115.

71 *His best known work is*: Fernando Pessoa, *The Book of Disquiet* (New York: Penguin, 2015).

73 *"Sleep that knits up"*: William Shakespeare, *Macbeth* (1606), act 2, scene 2, lines 36–39. Macbeth tells Lady Macbeth, "Methought I heard a voice cry, 'Sleep no more! Macbeth does murder sleep,'" which leads into the lines I've cited.

5. On Meditation

76   *I later learned more*: Meditation's origins are in poetry. Earliest mentions of dhyana are in the Vedas, at the origins of Hinduism; the *Rig-Veda* is the oldest religious text on Earth, dating at least as far back as 1100 BCE, possibly 1700. The goddess of wisdom and poetry is Saraswati. The Buddha lived in India around 500 BCE (we can't pin it down), and Buddhism developed, spinning off subsets for centuries, and then changing radically in its encounters with Confucianism in China, and, later, Shinto in Japan, and Bon in Tibet (a lively shamanic animism).

76   *"Meditation practices"*: See: Stephen Batchelor, *Buddhism Without Beliefs: A Contemporary Guide to Awakening* (New York: Riverhead, 1997).

78   *"One hour and then another"*: This version of "One hour and then another" begins with the one rendered by Hsu Yun's student Charles Luk, but his "Inexorably march, step by step" felt awkward and I replaced it with "Inevitable trek, step by step," as in many literal translations.

78   *The term "mindfulness"*: For a brief history of mindfulness in mental health and medical studies and a roundup of results, see: "The Science of Mindfulness," Mindful.org, September 7, 2020, https://www.mindful.org/the-science -of-mindfulness/.

81   *"I have learned to be still"*: Thylias Moss, "Wannabe Hoochie Mama Gallery of Realities' Red Dress Code," in *Wannabe Hoochie Mama Gallery of Realities' Red Dress Code: New and Selected Poems* (New York: Persea, 2016), 236–39.

6. On Happier Holidays

97   *Secular holidays can fill*: For a storyteller's history of American holidays, try the Great Courses recorded book by Hannah Harvey, *The Hidden History of Holidays* (2019). Fascinating and fun. For more on holidays around the world, see: Stephen Prothero, *Religion Matters: An Introduction to the World's Religions* (New York: W. W. Norton, 2020).

100   *"New Year's Day"*: Kobayashi Issa, "New Year's Day," in *The Essential Haiku: Versions of Bashō, Buson, and Issa*, Robert Hass, trans. (New York: Ecco, 1994), 151.

100   *"April is the cruellest month"*: T. S. Eliot, "The Waste Land" (1922). First in Eliot's magazine *Criterion*, a few days later in the magazine *The Dial*, then later that year as a book by Boni & Liveright (New York).

7. On Scary Holidays

105   *the novel's own crash*: F. Scott Fitzgerald, *The Great Gatsby* (New York: Scribner, 1925).

109   *the elements that make up human beings*: Carl Sagan, *Cosmos* (New York: Ballantine, 1985), 190. Still a great read, poetic and philosophical.

111   *"It could have happened"*: Wisława Szymborska, "Could Have," in *Poems New and Collected*, Stransław Barańczak and Clare Cavanagh, trans. (New York: Harcourt, 1998), 111.

8. On a Day for Shame and Grace

124   *People's happiness shifts*: Kieran Setiya, *Midlife: A Philosophical Guide* (Princeton, NJ: Princeton University Press, 2018).

126   *"When in disgrace"*: William Shakespeare, Sonnet 29, or "When in Disgrace with Fortune and Men's Eyes," in *Shakespeare's Sonnets*, Katherine Duncan-Jones, ed. (London: Arden Shakespeare, Methuen Drama, 1997), 169.

9. On Sabbaths and Fools' Days

139   *"it's 1962 March 28th"*: Nâzım Hikmet, "Things I Didn't Know I Loved," in *Things I Didn't Know I Loved: Selected Poems*, Randy Blasing and Mutlu Konuk, trans. (New York: Persea, 1975).

144   *Rivers, for example*: He describes rivers delicately, "they curl skirting the hills," but also hints at politics when he shows two rivers, one monarchically curving around "European hills crowned with chateaus," the other flat equality reaching out into the future "stretched out flat as far as the eye can see."

145   *The date at the end*: The poem begins in the intimacy of lowercase letters, noting the date. Date-noting, as a way of opening a poem, reminds American poetry readers, at least, of Frank O'Hara and the New York School poets of the mid-twentieth century. It's funny that in O'Hara's beloved book *Lunch Poems*, written on his lunch break, only one poem starts with a date. It is one of his best known, "The Day Lady Died," for Billie Holiday. It says "it is 1959 and I go get a shoeshine"; the book came out in 1964. So Hikmet's opening "it's 1962 March 28th" is too early to be accused of copying a trend started by O'Hara; it has its own originality. This moment in time is noted both as ordinary, and perhaps noted down because days were not feeling ordinary.

10. On Earth Day and Rebirth

150   *To paraphrase her*: Suzanne Simard, *Finding the Mother Tree: Discovering the Wisdom of the Forest* (New York: Knopf Doubleday, 2021), 5, 6.

150   *We don't have to feel in charge*: Robin Wall Kimmerer, *Braiding Sweetgrass: Indigenous Wisdom, Scientific Knowledge, and the Teachings of Plants* (Minneapolis, MN: Milkweed Editions, 2013). "Remember to remember," 5. This book is a gift; insightful and inspiring.

152   *the Great Law of Peace of the Iroquois Confederacy*: This was created sometime between 1142 and 1500 CE. Expert estimates vary.

155   *"We were dreaming"*: Joy Harjo, "When the World as We Knew It Ended," in *How We Became Human: New and Selected Poems 1975–2001* (New York: W. W. Norton, 2004), 198–200.

160   *"for you, if there were any left"*: Sherman Alexie, "I Would Steal Horses," in *I Would Steal Horses* (Niagara Falls, NY: Slipstream, 1992).

161   *"In Xanadu did Kubla Khan"*: Samuel Taylor Coleridge, "Kubla Kahn," was completed in 1797 and published in 1816.

163   *"I met a traveller"*: Percy Bysshe Shelley, "Ozymandias" (1818). First published in the London magazine *The Examiner*, the following year in his collection *Ro-*

salind and Helen, a Modern Eclogue; with Other Poems, and in a posthumous compilation in 1826.

11. On Weddings

172 *"We have taken the Seven Steps"*: K. V. Singh, *Hindu Rites and Rituals: Origins and Meanings* (New Delhi: Penguin India, 2015).

173 *Rites of Passage*: Arnold van Gennep, *The Rites of Passage* (New York: Routledge, 1977).

176 *"Married Love"*: Guan Daosheng is also known as Kuan Tao-Sheng. Guan Daosheng, "You and I Song." My version owes much to the version by Kenneth Rexroth and Ling Chung, "Married Love," *Women Poets of China*, Kenneth Rexroth, Ling Chung, and Ling Zhong, trans. (New York: New Directions, 1982), 53. Rexroth and Chung create "a figure of you / And a figure of me," whereas I follow literal versions that make only "a you" and "a me." Their version also starts five of the fifteen lines with the word "And," which I chose to do without. Rexroth once wrote that "poetry has ceased to be a public art and has become, as [the philosopher Alfred North] Whitehead said of religion, 'What man does with his aloneness.'" Kenneth Rexroth, "Tu Fu" in *The New Directions Anthology of Classical Chinese Poetry*, Eliot Weinberger, ed. (New York: New Direction, 2004), 198.

179 *"Thou [and] I"*: Jennifer Purtle, "The Icon of the Woman Artist: Guan Daosheng (1262–1319) and the Power of Painting at the Ming Court *c.* 1500," in *A Companion to Asian Art and Architecture*, Rebecca Brown and Deborah Hutton, eds. (Hoboken, NJ: Blackwell, 2011), 290–311.

180 *The poem "i carry your heart"*: e. e. cummings, "i carry your heart with me(i carry it in," in *Complete Poems 1904–1962* (New York: Liveright), 766.

12. On Welcoming Babies

192 *"You were born with potential"*: Jalāl ad-Dīn Rumi; translations of Rumi's poetry began to appear in French and German in the late eighteenth century, and in the late nineteenth century, in English as well. In the 1920s Cambridge University linguist and Persian scholar Reynold A. Nicholson was the first to publish a complete translation of Rumi's poetry into English.

193 *"Your task is not to seek"*: Rumi, *Rending the Veil: Literal and Poetic Translations of Rumi*, Shahram Shiva, trans. (Chino Valley, AZ: Hohm Press, 1995).

13. On Coming-of-Age

199 *Japan's Seijin no Hi*: There are many ways to see photos of Coming-of-Age Day online. Have a look at: Julia Glum, "Japan Coming of Age Day 2015: Facts About Japanese Holiday Celebrating Young People," *International Business Times*, January 11, 2015, https://www.ibtimes.com/japan-coming-age-day-2015-facts-about-japanese-holiday-celebrating-young-people-1775200.

201 *Margaret Mead thought it unfair*: Margaret Mead, *Coming of Age in Samoa* (New York: William Morrow, 1928).

202   *The Hindu* Sanskara *rituals*: Swami Achuthananda, *Many Many Many Gods of Hinduism: Turning Believers into Non-believers and Non-believers into Believers* (CreateSpace Independent, 2013). A lively treatment of Hindu rituals and beliefs.

205   *"'Twas brillig"*: Lewis Carroll, "Jabberwocky," in *Alice's Adventures in Wonderland and Through the Looking-Glass* (New York: Rand McNally, 1916), 130–31, 187–88.

207   *Carroll wrote and published*: Lewis Carroll, *The Rectory Umbrella and Mischmasch* (New York: Dover, 1971). This collection includes Carroll's early single-stanza version of "Jabberwocky," with his annotations.

210   *"Why should we be"*: Henry David Thoreau, *Walden and Civil Disobedience* (New York: Warbler Classics, 2021), 196.

14. On Love Poetry

215   *"'I carried a watermelon'"*: In the classic romantic comedy *Dirty Dancing*, of 1987, the first time Jennifer Grey's Frances "Baby" Houseman meets smoldering Patrick Swayze's Johnny Castle, she stammers out her excuse for coming to a staff-only dance. She'd helped out: "I carried a watermelon." She then tilts her head down and repeats the line with iconic self-deprecation.

218   *"tell him I'm sick"*: "I charge you, O daughters of Jerusalem, if ye find my beloved, that ye tell him that I am sick of love." Other translations have "lovesick," "sick with love," "sick from love."

221   *Eugene Onegin*: Alexander Pushkin (1833). Pushkin chose a complex rhyme scheme, AbAbCCddEffEgg, where capital letters are "feminine rhymes" and the lowercase are "masculine." Those odd terms correspond to lines ending on a stressed syllable, masculine, and lines that end on a syllable that is not stressed, feminine. This is known as the Onegin stanza or the Pushkin sonnet. Now get this, *Eugene Onegin* is a story told in 389 of these stanzas. They are in iambic tetrameter, which is just like Shakespeare's iambic pentameter, but with only four feet per line. Christopher Marlowe's "The Passionate Shepherd to His Love" provides a nice example: "Come live with me and be my love." The technical mastery of *Onegin*, and the beauty Pushkin produced within its bounds, is staggering. On top of that, the poem's story is as rich as you could want from a novel. Some translations privilege delicacies of inner experience and forget about rhyme altogether, while others get into it with all those gendered ays, bees, cees, dees, ees, effs, and gees.

222   *Yes, watch rom-coms, but*: Henry James, *Washington Square* (New York: Harper and Brothers, 1880). I think also of his *The Aspern Papers* (1888), for disappointment. James isn't a modernist in the obvious ways, but he wants to know what happens if he disrupts the payoff. There can be a sense of conclusion in the not-marriage, the not-discovery of the truth.

223   *"I'm glad you've lost your mind"*: Marina Tsvetaeva, "I'm Glad You've Lost Your Mind Over Someone and It's Not Me." This is my translation based on study of many versions. I followed literal translations, seeking to preserve meaning before all else. I was aided by the website Russian Poetry in Translations, which offers versions by Elaine Feinstein, Lydia Razran Stone, Dina

Belyayeva, Maya Jouravel, Ilya Shambat, Andrey Kneller, Daria Karaulova, Evgenia Sarkisyants, Alexander Shaumyan, and more. RuVerses, https://ruverses .com (last consulted May 15, 2022).

226 *"Bright star! would I were"*: John Keats, "Bright Star," in *The Poems of John Keats* (New York: Dodd, Mead, 1905), 288. The poem was begun in 1818 and completed in 1820.

227 *"if she's escaping"*: Sappho, from "So I Called to Aphrodite," in *The Love Songs of Sappho*, Paul Roche, trans., Page duBois, intro. (Amherst, NY: Prometheus, 1998), 59. The poem happens to be the only complete poem of hers that has survived down to us; the rest are fragments. I love duBois's insightful and learned introduction here. It's where I got the battle comparison to Homer; 16–17.

15. On Funerals and Memorials

235 *"A surge in the number"*: Quotation from the National Funeral Directors Association. Simon Davis, "How the Nonreligious Are Reshaping American Funeral Rituals," *Washington Post*, December 17, 2015, https://www.washingtonpost .com/national/religion/how-the-nonreligious-are-reshaping-american-funeral -rituals/2015/12/17/7344eb52-a4fb-11e5-8318-bd8caed8c588_story.html.

240 *"When I die I want your hands on my eyes"*: This is my translation, close to the precedent of other translations. Pablo Neruda, "LXXXIX," or "Cuando yo muera quiero tus manos en mis ojos," or "When I die, I wish your hands upon my eyes," in *100 Love Sonnets* (bilingual ed.), Gustavo Escobedo, trans. (Mount Forest, ON: Exile Editions, 2007), 184–85. My translation owes most to Escobedo's, but is also influenced by other translators. A key difference from Escobedo's is that I have "and for you to go on walking the sand where we walked" instead of "and for you to go on treading on the sand we trod on." Neruda won the International Peace Prize with Paul Robeson and Pablo Picasso in 1950 and the Nobel Prize in Literature for his poetry in 1971.

244 *"'Hallelujah,'"* he said: Alan Light, *The Holy or the Broken: Leonard Cohen, Jeff Buckley, and the Unlikely Ascent of "Hallelujah"* (New York: Atria, 2012), 30–31.

16. On Depression

252 *Religious art was officially accepted*: The church councils are listed in Giovanni Domenico Mansi, *Sacrorum Conciliorum Nova et Amplissima Collectio* (1758–98), xvi, 40D. See also Paul Evdokimov, *L'Orthodoxie* (Neuchatel, Paris: Delachaus et Niestle, 1965), 222.

252 *"Worship an idol of a deity"*: Nalini V. Juthani, "Hindus and Buddhists," in *Handbook of Spirituality and Worldview in Clinical Practice*, Allan M. Josephson and John R. Peteet, eds. (Washington, DC: American Psychiatric Publishing, 2004), 125–38.

256 *"Let your name touch her lips"*: Ada Jafarey, "Let your name touch her lips, let that happen," Rekhta, https://www.rekhta.org/poets/ada-jafarey/all (last consulted May 16, 2022).

257   *"Let everything happen to you"*: Rainer Maria Rilke, from the poem "Going on the Limits of Our Longing," in *The Book of Hours*, Joanna Macy and Anita Barrows, trans. (New York: Riverhead, 2005), 159.

17. On the Social Contract Blues

264   *"the centre cannot hold"*: William Butler Yeats, "The Second Coming" (1920). First published in the magazine *The Dial*, then in his 1921 poetry collection *Michael Robartes and the Dancer*.

265   *"Still I Rise"*: Maya Angelou, "Still I Rise," in *And Still I Rise: A Book of Poems* (New York: Penguin, 1978), 41–42.

267   *"cultivate my own garden"*: Voltaire, *Candide* (1759). He published it himself simultaneously in five countries.

272   *This talk of singing*: Maya Angelou, *I Know Why the Caged Bird Sings* (New York: Random House, 1969).

272   *The title is a line from*: Claudia Tate, "Maya Angelou: An Interview," in *Maya Angelou's I Know Why the Caged Bird Sings: A Casebook*, Joanne M. Braxton, ed. (New York: Oxford Press, 1999), 158. The title of Angelou's sixth autobiography, *A Song Flung Up to Heaven*, was also inspired by the poem.

272   *The bird wants out, violently*: Paul Dunbar, "Sympathy," in *Lyrics of the Hearthside* (New York: Dodd, Mead, 1899). Dunbar's parents were both formerly enslaved people from Kentucky. "I know why the caged bird beats his wing / till its blood is red on the cruel bars" is how the second stanza begins. The final stanza begins and ends with "I know why the caged bird sings," and tells us that the bird sings "When his wing is bruised and his bosom sore." The bird is singing a plea for freedom. That's it. "It is not a carol of joy or glee." It isn't about finding happiness in song despite the cage. His heart's deep core wants freedom and is howling for it in the only voice it has.

18. On Choosing a Code to Live By

278   *"If you can keep your head"*: "If—" appeared in Rudyard Kipling, *Rewards and Fairies* (Garden City, NY: Doubleday, 1910), 181. The book is a collection of poems and stories.

281   *"Ten Sayings"*: Jews recognize 613 commandments, 365 of which are positive, actions to be performed, and 248 of which are negative, actions to refrain from doing.

281   *Christians changed the prohibition*: Early Christians struggled with the prohibition on images. Consider that around 325 CE the Church Father Eusebius wrote, in a letter to Emperor Constantine's sister, "To depict purely the human form of Christ before its transformation . . . is to break the commandment of God and to fall into pagan error." Also revealing is that she did it anyway, decorating her tomb with paintings of the life of Jesus.

283   *"Eight Virtues"*: Nitobe Inazō, in *Bushidō: The Soul of Japan* (Philadelphia, 1899), 81. The preface describes his impetus for writing the book and it speaks to our theme: "About ten years ago, while spending a few days under the hospitable roof of the distinguished Belgian jurist, the lamented M. de Laveleye,

our conversation turned, during one of our rambles, to the subject of religion. 'Do you mean to say,' asked the venerable professor, 'that you have no religious instruction in your schools?' On my replying in the negative he suddenly halted in astonishment, and in a voice which I shall not easily forget, he repeated 'No religion! How do you impart moral education?' The question stunned me at the time. I could give no ready answer, for the moral precepts I learned in my childhood days, were not given in schools; and not until I began to analyze the different elements that formed my notions of right and wrong, did I find that it was Bushido that breathed them into my nostrils," i.

285 *"O May I Join the Choir Invisible"*: George Eliot, "O May I Join the Choir Invisible," in *"O May I Join the Choir Invisible" and Other Poems* (Boston: D. Lothrop, 1884), 1–3.

289 *"Owner: No no! 'E's pining!"*: Graham Chapman, John Cleese, Terry Gilliam, Eric Idle, Terry Jones, and Michael Palin, *The Complete Monty Python's Flying Circus: All the Words*, vol. 1, Roger Wilmut, ed. (New York: Pantheon, 1989), 320.

290 *"This is what you shall do"*: Walt Whitman, *Leaves of Grass* (1855), v, vi. The next lines of this famous quote are wonderful too. "The poet shall not spend his time in unneeded work. He shall know that the ground is always ready ploughed and manured . . . others may not know it but he shall. He shall go directly to the creation. His trust shall master the trust of everything he touches . . . and shall master all attachment. The known universe has one complete lover and that is the greatest poet."

19. On Talking to Children About Heavenlessness

296 *the funeral rite of Famadihana*: Jo Munni and Katy Scott, "In Famadihana, Madagascar, a Sacred Ritual Unearths the Dead," *CNN Travel*, March 27, 2017, https://www.cnn.com/2016/10/18/travel/madagascar-turning-bones/index.html.

300 *"O Beautiful End"*: Rabindranath Tagore, "O Beautiful End," or "61," its number in *The Delphi Collected* (Hastings, UK: Delphi Classics, 2017).

20. On Morality

316 *"A Mother in a Refugee Camp"*: Chinua Achebe, "A Mother in a Refugee Camp," in *Collected Poems* (New York: Penguin, 2009), 16. The poem is also published under the title "Refugee Mother and Child."

318 *poetry of witness*: Carolyn Forché, *Against Forgetting: Twentieth-Century Poetry of Witness* (New York: W. W. Norton, 1993).

319 *"Our art is based on morality"*: Dorothy Randall-Tsuruta, "In Dialogue to Define Aesthetics: James Baldwin and Chinua Achebe," April 9, 1980, in *Conversations with James Baldwin*, Fred R. Standley and Louis H. Pratt, eds. (Jackson: University of Mississippi Press, 1989), 210–21. The men were close contemporaries, Baldwin (1924–1987) and Achebe (1930–2013).

319 *"Their essence is the same"*: Iris Murdoch, *Existentialists and Mystics: Writ-

ings on Philosophy and Literature (New York: Penguin, 1997), 215. Murdoch (1919–1999) was an extraordinary novelist and philosopher.

320 *"Do I contradict myself?'"*: Walt Whitman, *Leaves of Grass* (1855), 55. Just prior to this well-known quote he speaks of the future and says, "Listener up there! Here you . . . what have you to confide to me? Look in my face while I snuff the sidle of evening, / Talk honestly, for no one else hears you, and I stay only a minute longer." This ability to imagine us and even try to listen is one of Whitman's cunning charms. On this same page he sees a hawk and feeling accused by it for all his "gab" he famously responds, "I too am not a bit tamed . . . I too am untranslatable, / I sound my barbaric yawp over the roofs of the world."

Acknowledgments

Thanks go to John, Max, and Jessie, for helping me through this colossal experience. You were all incredibly supportive and your visions of the world have influenced me at every step. Thanks to my early readers John Chaneski, Mary Keller, Amy Hecht, Carolyn Hecht, and Gene Hecht. I am grateful that Stephanie Steiker, my agent, told me it was time to write another book and gave her great understanding and enthusiasm to the idea and helped me shape the project. I am grateful too for the insight and vision of my editor, Jenna Johnson. Over the years of writing, she helped me to see the book clearly and pushed me to find a structure that could carry through all the many characters and ideas. Thanks to my legal reviewer, who was a terrific reader. Thanks to editorial assistant Lianna Culp, to designer Gretchen Achilles, and to the careful copyediting of Logan Hill.

Thanks, too, to all the people who ask me their questions and tell me their stories.

Index of First Lines

Index

Permissions Acknowledgments

Blasing and Mutlu Konuk. Reprinted by permission of Persea Books, Inc. (New York), www.perseabooks.com. All rights reserved.

"New Year's Day," from *The Essential Haiku: Versions of Bashō, Buson, and Issa*, by Issa, edited and with verse translations by Robert Hass, translation copyright © 1994 by Robert Hass. Used by permission of HarperCollins Publishers and Bloodaxe Books.

"From Blossoms," from *Rose*, by Li-Young Lee, copyright © 1986 by Li-Young Lee. Reprinted with the permission of The Permissions Company, LLC, on behalf of BOA Editions, Ltd., boaeditions.org.

"Wannabe Hoochie Mama Gallery of Realities Dress Code," from *Wannabe Hoochie Mama Gallery of Realities Dress Code: New and Selected Poems*, by Thylias Moss, copyright © 2016 by Thylias Moss. Reprinted with the permission of Persea Books, Inc. (New York), www.perseabooks.com. All rights reserved.

"Wild Geese," from *Dream Work*, by Mary Oliver, copyright © 1986 by Mary Oliver. Used by permission of Grove/Atlantic, Inc. Any third-party use of this material, outside of this publication, is prohibited.

"The Sleep That Comes Over Me," from *Poems of Fernando Pessoa*, by Fernando Pessoa, translated by Edwin Honig and Susan M. Brown, English translation copyright © 1986 by Edwin Honig and Susan M. Brown. Reprinted with the permission of The Permissions Company, LLC, on behalf of City Lights Books, citylights.com.

"Could Have," from *Poems New and Collected*, by Wisława Szymborska, copyright © by The Wisława Szymborska Foundation, English language copyright © 1998 by Harcourt, Inc. Used by permission of HarperCollins Publishers.

Printed in the USA
CPSIA information can be obtained
at www.ICGtesting.com
LVHW050155140324
774450LV00007B/151

9 781250 321855